# PUBLIC AND PRIVATE MAN IN SHAKESPEARE

# Public and Private Man in Shakespeare

J. M. Gregson

CROOM HELM
London & Canberra
BARNES & NOBLE BOOKS
Totowa, New Jersey

© 1983 J. M. Gregson
Croom Helm Ltd, Provident House, Burrell Row,
Beckenham, Kent BR3 1AT

British Library Cataloguing in Publication Data
Gregson, J.M.
  Public and private man in Shakespeare.
  1. Shakespeare, William – Characters
  I. Title
  822.3'3    PR2989
  ISBN 0-7099-1124-6


First published in the USA 1983 by Barnes & Noble Books
81 Adams Drive, Totowa, New Jersey, 07512

Library of Congress Cataloging in Publication Data
Gregson, J.M.
  Public and private man in Shakespeare.
  1. Shakespeare, William, 1564-1616 – Characters.
  2. Shakespeare, William, 1564-1616 – Political
  and social views. I. Title.
  PR2989.G73  1983     822.3'3        83-3750
  ISBN 0-389-20394-7

Printed and bound in Great Britain by
Biddles Ltd, Guildford and King's Lynn

# CONTENTS

# PREFACE

When I first read *Richard II* many years ago, I was struck not only by the very different personalities of Richard and Bolingbroke, but by the way in which Shakespeare built all the dramatic tension of the play's great scenes around this conflict. Richard, it seemed, indulged a whimsical individuality in a disastrous kingship, whereas Bolingbroke progressed by subduing individual, spontaneous reaction until it disappeared entirely beneath a calculated public conduct.

Continual contact with the whole canon over some thirty years has made me realise that it is not just in the history plays but in almost all of his work that Shakespeare is fascinated by the divergence between individual feeling and public office, and by the different qualities which characterise the admirable private man and the successful public man. Only in the early and middle comedies does he turn aside from the exploration of the theme, though even in plays like *The Merchant of Venice* and *Twelfth Night* the most radiant representatives of good and the eventual resolvers of conflict are those without conventional authority.

In the rest of Shakespeare's work, the public-private conflict is never far away, and in many plays it is the dominant theme. In an early work such as *Richard III,* it is a straightforward, even crude, dramatic device which is nevertheless highly effective: the play's construction depends throughout upon the contrast between Richard's private face and his public effects. At the other end of his work, Shakespeare builds *Antony and Cleopatra* entirely around the conflict between private feeling and public responsibility, but by this time the divergence is used not merely as a dramatic device but as a means of illuminating profound areas of human nature. In the interim, Shakespeare has explored to the full the possibilities of the public-private tension both in dramatic construction and in exploring the complexities of human conduct and feeling. Hamlet for instance, is a private man placed in a public situation for which he feels his contemplative, reflective nature profoundly unfitted. Othello is a man supremely confident of broad public effects who flounders in the unfamiliar framework of a domestic tragedy.

There is a sort of academic blinkering which always threatens a book like this one. The danger is that one becomes so insistent upon one's theme that one ignores all other considerations, except as they may be treated as lesser threads in one's own tapestry. I have tried to remain aware of the danger throughout: it would be ridiculous to imply that this theme in Shakespeare's work developed independently of others, even though I think it a most important strain. Around it, he developed his stagecraft and the greatest range of language effects of any writer, both of which are used to supplement his exploration of public and private man. Wherever space permitted, I have paid due homage to these other elements of genius; where it does not, I take refuge in the thought that there is no other writer whose quality is as self-evident as Shakespeare's.

# EARLY WORK

In the material from which Shakespeare constructed his early dramas, there is ample scope for investigation of those tensions between private thought and public behaviour which are to become such a prominent feature of his major work. However, he makes slight and intermittent use of the opportunities available: his stagecraft, like his other skills, is undeveloped, though we can see signs everywhere of the hammering out of a method in this busy forge. Had Shakespeare died after the completion of *Richard III* and *Romeo and Juliet*, he would have been accounted a major writer, and these perhaps the most interesting products of the teeming Elizabethan play-house. It is a measure of his later achievement that even these popular works are often studied, and sometimes indeed produced on stage, with an eye to the masterpieces which follow.

It is generally agreed the first tetralogy of history plays, comprising the three parts of *Henry VI* and *Richard III*, is Shakespeare's earliest work. Shakespeare entered a theatre dominated by Tarlton and the Queen's Men in the decade 1583 to 1592, in which the chronicle history play seems to have been the dominant and most popular strain of drama. The Spanish peril and the defeat of the Armada in 1588 encouraged the taste for stirring retrospects of England's past. Shakespeare, revealing from the outset that sure feel for the popular pulse, found material ready at hand in Holinshed and Hall's highly coloured accounts of 'York and Lancaster's long jars'.

The three parts of *Henry VI* show Shakespeare instinct with the spirit of his age and not yet full of those insights which will enable him also to transcend it. The traditional view is that Shakespeare worked over the chronicles scene by scene in compiling *Henry VI*, an unambitious and patient journeyman learning his craft. He then 'laid such models aside and followed the promptings of his own spirit upon the lurid theme of *Richard III*'.[1] More recent commentators have shown that the plays are more than a stringing together of episodes from the chronicles; they have stressed the author's consistent awareness of a central theme and his subordination of every episode to this.[2] Recent productions of the plays, influenced by Peter Brook's famous 'Wars of the Roses' Stratford production of 1964, have followed this interpretation. To emphasise the epic conception, a rather truncated version of the tetralogy is sometimes shown in three sessions of a one-day theatre marathon, with the crown as symbol passing from its highest, sacramental point on the coffin of Henry V to the degradation of its loss in a bush in the hurly-burly of Bosworth Field, as Richard reels hopelessly through the battle.

Chambers was right in noting a new quality in *Richard III*, but this stems rather from the author's realisation of the dramatic possibilities of his central figure than from a switch in conception from his original design. That design, as worked out in *Henry VI*, had great success; Thomas Nashe records the reaction in 1592:

> How it would have joyed brave Talbot (the terror of the French) to think that after he had lain two hundred years in his tomb, he should triumph again on the stage and have his bones new embalmed with the tears of ten thousand spectators at least (at several times).

In all ways, *Henry VI* is a starting-point. The verse-form is inflexible and generally end-stopped, the variety of both image and syntax is limited, with much repetitive vituperation, much rhetoric which threatens monotony and sometimes descends into it. The dramatic construction is also crude, with a welter of retributory violence, small range of character, and little comic relief: there is no Falstaff here to add breadth of ironic commentary and bring human reaction springing out of the dusty chronicles and down the centuries.

Despite the leap in quality of many speeches and certain stage effects in *Richard III*, there is ample evidence that the play was conceived as the culmination of this first tetralogy of history plays. Shakespeare interrupts even the rather lumbering impetus which *Henry VI* generates to introduce Richard and prepare us for the part he is to play in the later play. At the end of the second part of *Henry VI*, Richard's first statement proclaims his disposition:

> Priests pray for enemies, but princes kill.

By the time of his abrupt entry into the third part of *Henry VI*, he is translating this motto into action, as he flings the Duke of Somerset's head upon the stage with the words,

> Speak thou for me and tell them what I did.

In the middle of this play, he is permitted a soliloquy which shows him conscious of the skills necessary to prosper in this harsh world:

Why, I can smile, and murder while I smile,
And cry 'Content' to that which grieves my heart,
And wet my cheeks with artificial tears,
And frame my face to all occasions . . .
I can add colours to the chameleon,
Change shapes with Proteus with advantages,
And set the murderous Machiavel to school.
Can I do this and cannot get a crown?

This is the note on which he will open *Richard III*. After he murders saintly, ineffective Henry, he refers again to the physical deformity with which Shakespeare will make such play in the later work, and puts himself unequivocally before the audience as the Machiavellian figure:

Then since the heavens have shaped my body so,
Let hell make crook'd my mind to answer it.
I have no brother, I am like no brother;
And this word 'love', which greybeards call divine,
Be resident in men like one another,
And not in me. I am myself alone.

All this is evidence that *Richard III* is conceived as the culmination of an epic tetralogy, as the final piece of a grand design rather than as a self-contained unit. Yet we have centuries of evidence that this fourth play is immeasurably more effective than the first three in the scheme, especially on stage. Shakespeare's imagination, his excitement in the exploration of his own developing powers, take wing when he comes to the figure of Richard, the first of his creations which he builds around exploitations of the contrast between private thought and public bearing.

The contrast is crude and straightforward: the concept of the Machiavellian villain which Shakespeare found ready-made in his theatre depends for interest entirely upon this kind of deceit. Such villains do not need to show the conscience which would shade villainy. They are expected to hug themselves with delight in their own villainy and to encourage their audiences to share the amoral thrills, like Marlowe's Barabbas in *The Jew of Malta*:

Now tell me, worldlings, underneath the sun
If greater falsehood ever has been done?

For the Elizabethan dramatist the Machiavellian villain is as conveniently uncomplicated a figure as the hired gunman is for the maker of Hollywood westerns; the convention means that his amorality does not need explanation. He is a more flexible and individual development of the Vice of the old moralities, so that Shakespeare can make his Aaron in *Titus Andronicus* say:

> If one good deed in all my life I did,
> I do repent it from my very soul.

Marlowe will build his *Edward II* around such a villain in Mortimer; later Shakespeare will develop the concept with his full powers of language and psychological insight in Iago.

In theatrical terms, the most effective use made of the stage concept of the Machiavellian villain is *Richard III*. And, as usual when Shakespeare picks up something which lies conveniently to hand, he makes more of it than anyone before him. The most remarkable evidence comes in the first speech of the play, which is easily Shakespeare's greatest achievement to date. W. Clemen shows how Shakespeare constantly discovers new possibilities inherent in the soliloquy.[3] Before and even well after Shakespeare, the soliloquy is most commonly used for primitive self-explanations and movements of plot. Even in his great plays, Shakespeare sometimes finds it useful for such purposes: in the most intellectually sinuous of all of them, Hamlet will take eighteen lines to whet the appetite of his audience and explain to them why

> the play's the thing
> Wherein I'll catch the conscience of the King.

The opening of *Richard III* shows Shakespeare at once bringing his psychological insights to bear upon his Machiavellian villain and embodying those insights in a soliloquy which conveys them with incomparable verve: he takes two instruments ready to hand and familiar to the meanest of his audience, the soliloquy and the Machiavellian villain, and exploits them with a subtlety which heralds a new master.

The soliloquy begins conventionally enough with a chorus-like introduction to the point where the action is taken up from *Henry VI*:

> Now is the winter of our discontent
> Made glorious summer by this sun of York;

And all the clouds that lour'd upon our house
In the deep bosom of the ocean buried.
Now are our brows bound with victorious wreaths;
Our bruised arms hung up for monuments;
Our stern alarums changed to merry meetings;
Our dreadful marches to delightful measures.
Grim-visaged war hath smooth'd his wrinkled front;
And now, instead of mounting barbed steeds
To fright the souls of fearful adversaries,
He capers nimbly in a lady's chamber
To the lascivious pleasing of a lute.

So far the verse, like the material, is measured, incantatory: if the actor cares to suggest an irony in adjectives such as 'glorious', 'dreadful', 'delightful', or to suggest a flash of envious hate as he savours the hissing of the last phrase, that will be because of what he knows of the rest of the play.

It is in the lines which follow, couched in form and language as well as theme as a deliberate antithesis to the opening passage, that the speech turns abruptly away from the general and into the intensely personal, as Shakespeare sets about giving convincing life to his Machiavellian villain:

But I, that am not shaped for sportive tricks,
Nor made to court an amorous looking-glass;
I, that am rudely stamp'd and want love's majesty
To strut before a wanton ambling nymph;
I, that am curtail'd of this fair proportion,
Cheated of feature by dissembling nature,
Deform'd, unfinish'd, sent before my time
Into this breathing world, scarce half made up,
And that so lamely and unfashionable
That dogs bark at me as I halt by them.

After the elaborate formality of the speech's first section, the verse springs away as Richard comes forward to reveal to the audience the full venom of that private face that he will keep continually before them, even as he continually dissimulates to those on stage. The pace of the verse, the piling of adjective upon adjective in a convulsion of hate, shows a new grasp of the blank-verse medium. Richard collects himself, slows the pace again, and moves through the chilling image of the shadow of his deformity to an announcement of his intentions:

> Why, I, in this weak piping time of peace,
> Have no delight to pass away the time,
> Unless to spy my shadow in the sun
> And descant on mine own deformity:
> And therefore, since I cannot prove a lover,
> To entertain these fair well-spoken days,
> I am determined to prove a villain.

The conception of Richard here embodied is even more remarkable than it first appears. We are familiar in the twentieth century with the idea of a warped mind produced by a warped body. Yet psychology is a word which has entered our vocabulary only in the last hundred years. The most learned of Shakespeare's dramatic contemporaries, Ben Jonson, put dwarfs and other freaks on stage for little more than cheap laughter. Here is Shakespeare at the outset of his career using a quite modern psychological insight to motivate and make convincing a character his audience would have accepted without difficulty as a monstrous villain. Presented with the Tudor view of history, which determined that Richard must be a bogey-man, and the ready-made convention of the Machiavellian villain, Shakespeare accepts the gifts, than goes beyond them to make his villain believable. How on earth could the Richard he has to put on stage have arrived at his villainies? The Chronicles give some details of his deformities: Shakespeare seizes upon them, accentuates them, uses them as direct paths into the dark mind of his psychopathic man of power.

His stagecraft in this play is built around a single telling effect, his first exploitation of the dramatic possibilities of public face and private thought. Alongside this he is developing a psychological insight and a control of the effects of language which will enable him to point this contrast. The play is the first great example of the parallel development of different aspects of his mastery, with each making the others more effective. In his finest work, the strands will be interwoven to supreme effect. In *Richard III*, they work intermittently and almost entirely around the person of Richard himself, but they are at times thrillingly effective: the first instance is this opening soliloquy.

There is much in the play that is crude, much writing that is facile or careless by comparison with the opening soliloquy, much that Shakespeare himself would have dispensed with a decade later. The elaborate antitheses and piled up parallelisms in some scenes, emphasising the formal, ritualistic aspect of the degradation of the crown which is the theme of the tetralogy, sit uneasily beside the life and vigour of Richard's verse and conduct. Static speeches of recrimination and antiphonal laments are no match for Richard's energy and irony. Formal structure and formal language are not the best settings for his dynamism. Dream is used clumsily in the last section of the play, as a substitute for conscience in Richard, and as an instrument of plot earlier for Hastings, Clarence and the superstitious Edward IV.[4]

Richard himself owes much to the devices of a cruder theatre. He begins by acknowledging his debt to 'the murderous Machiavel'. There are obviously connections also with the Vice of the morality play; indeed Richard as he prepares his most outrageous crime, the murder of the princes, compares himself to 'the formal Vice, Iniquity'. Charles Lamb pointed out long ago that Richard should be regarded as a bogey-man or fairy-story villain.

Yet if the play draws much upon existing convention, it is the capacity Shakespeare has to take useful old devices and extend them which is the clue to its continuing effectiveness. He breathes life into his Machiavellian villain by his vivid and individual use of the man's physical deformities in the opening speech of the play. He uses the connection with the Vice of the morality plays to give Richard that vigorous simplicity of approach which will be his most telling stage quality. An Elizabethan audience knew that Vice must be defeated in the end; in the meantime they would suspend moral judgements and enjoy his outrageous energy and skill in the pursuit of evil. Richard's identification with Vice enables him to advance fearlessly and directly upon his outrageous path of crime. Shakespeare's contemporary creation King John[5] gropes uncertainly towards the murder of Prince Arthur; Richard contemplates the princes and says to Buckingham,

Shall I be plain? I wish the bastards dead.

There is no doubt which is the more effective stage creation.

There is another use also of the connection with the Vice of the moralities upon which Shakespeare seizes. Nicholas Brooke points out that:

Vice was commonly the star of a morality play, what the audience most wanted to see. He had, like other kinds of clown, a special relationship with the audience, a kind of sly ironic confidence insinuated between them and the other players.[6]

This is the device around which the whole play is designed, enabling Shakespeare to show us Richard's private face continually alongside his public posturings, until those posturings become an elaborate and extended play within the play. Richard alone is permitted direct contact with the audience; when Shakespeare is more confident of complex material, Lady Macbeth and Banquo will be permitted soliloquies alongside the agonised central figure, but Richard's bond with the audience here is uncomplicated and superbly effective for the more limited theme it accommodates.

Alongside this, Shakespeare gives to his Machiavellian villain all the qualities to secure that dynamism on stage which drives the play out of the chronicle-drama and into a more modern theatre. John Palmer catalogues these: 'He is brave, witty, resourceful, gay, swift, disarmingly candid with himself, engagingly sly with his enemies.'[7] He is also untroubled by conscience, until the later, less effective, stages of the play when his outrageous goals have been achieved. It is a recipe for dramatic success, and one can see the attraction for Elizabethan dramatists of the Machiavellian villain, growing out of, but less predictable than, the old Vice of the moralities. Shakespeare achieves a series of stunning theatrical effects by pointing up the two contrasting faces of the dissembler at every opportunity and making them the mainspring of his construction.

Richard's joy in the techniques of villainy, his delight in the intellectual challenges of Machiavellian monsterhood, are constantly set before us. He turns from his opening soliloquy to an elaborately paraded innocence before the Clarence he is sending to his doom. Looking after him as he is borne away to the Tower and his death, Richard comments to us with a whimsical, half-blasphemous wit:

> Simple, plain Clarence! I do love thee so,
> That I will shortly send thy soul to heaven,
> If heaven will take the present at our hands.

It is the design with which we become familiar as the play proceeds: Richard mouthing righteousness with 'goblin solemnity'[8] in public, then hugging himself in a private glee which he shares with us. The interest comes from the variety, daring, and increasingly sensational character of his villainy.

He turns to his wooing of Anne, and Shakespeare realises as clearly as any plotter of horror films the connections in the dark recesses of the psyche between sex and violence:

Nay, do not pause; for I did kill King Henry,
But 'twas thy beauty that provoked me.
Nay, now dispatch; 'twas I that stabb'd young Edward;
But 'twas thy heavenly face that set me on.

His delight in the success of his virtuoso performance is expressed with his usual vigorous irony:

I do mistake my person all this while:
Upon my life, she finds, although I cannot,
Myself to be a marvellous proper man.
I'll be at charges for a looking-glass,
And entertain some score or two of tailors,
To study fashions to adorn my body:
Since I am crept in favour with myself,
I will maintain it with some little cost.

Richard II will indulge his narcissism at great length as his fortunes decline. Richard of Gloucester pauses over it only in a scornful reversal of the shadow conceit of his first soliloquy, showing his excitement at his success and scorn for his victims.

Shine out, fair sun, till I have bought a glass,
That I may see my shadow as I pass.

Hazlitt dismissed the scene which prepares the murder of the princes (Act III Scene i) as altogether unworthy of Shakespeare. Yet it is wholly of a piece with the play's design, just as the murder is artistically logical as the culminating outrage in Richard's escalating series of crimes. The boy Prince of Wales is shown as innocent, winning and pathetically vulnerable in his last appearance. It is brief and without sublety — the doomed Duncan's gracious innocence will be more tellingly used in *Macbeth* — but it gives opportunity for some Iago-like asides from Richard's grim wit.

So wise so young, they say, do ne'er live long.

he says as the rest of the court murmurs approval over young Edward's brightness. When the boy evokes memories of Henry V with a determination 'to win our ancient right in France again' the wicked uncle is waiting with his sardonic verdict on such precocity,

Short summers likely have a forward spring.

By means of these flashes of his private face, Richard presents to the audience a menacing and ironic commentary on the public posturings: the scene is given a dramatic life which remains perennially effective. It provided one of the most memorable moments of Olivier's film of *Richard III*.

In the delicious scenes in which Richard contrives his crowning, there is a secondary irony which has not been remarked. Buckingham stage-manages the process as carefully as any modern dictator's henchman, but this prototype Himmler has already been earmarked for the axe by his Führer:

> The deep-revolving witty Buckingham
> No more shall be the neighbour to my counsel:
> Hath he so long held out with me untired,
> And stops he now for breath?

Richard, standing prayer-book in hand between two clergymen, now links Buckingham with the rest of his dupes, as he accepts his destiny:

> Cousin of Buckingham, and you sage, grave men,
> Since you will buckle fortune on my back,
> To bear her burden, whether I will or no,
> I must have patience to endure the load.

This, like other scenes, is highly effective because Richard has displayed his real feelings so openly and so pithily towards us that we are aware of his tongue in his cheek, his delighted contempt, even as he casts his eyes down and utters the doggerel phrases of political progress on stage. He is continually ahead of the game, and we are allowed to know all that he knows. He is, as John Masefield said, the one great intellect in the play, and it is his supple wit which makes him what Shaw called 'the ecstatic prince of mischief'. His condemnation is left to a ritual chorus of queens and apparitions who have no dramatic impact to compare with his.

If Richard is the strength of the play and the interplay between his two faces the source of all its best dramatic effects, his centrality is also the source of the play's limitations. Colley Cibber's 1700 version of *Richard III,* concentrating exclusively upon Richard himself, minimising Margaret's role and cutting several scenes, was so effective that it dominated stage presentations for two and a half centuries:[9] Olivier's film still followed this selective procedure. Although the play has since been staged in a more complete form, this has generally been as a culmination of the first tetralogy or a part of the full history cycle, where the static ritual scenes can be played as devices which have a part in an epically conceived design, which extends beyond a single play.

This emphasis upon the simplified and repetitive moral message of the first tetralogy certainly detracts from the dramatic impetus of this play as a self-contained performance. A single example will suffice. The chorus of weeping dowagers in Act IV brings together ritual and the individual villain who drives forward this play, but the elaborate parallels of the dirge merely slacken the action which surges so exultantly when Richard drives the play forward:

> I had an Edward, till a Richard kill'd him;
> I had a Henry, till a Richard kill'd him:
> Thou hadst an Edward, till a Richard kill'd him;
> Thou hadst a Richard, till a Richard kill'd him.

Formal, sacramental condemnations of this kind act out a ritual deriving from an older theatre: they are no match and no setting for Richard's energy and irony.

This is one reason for the falling off in energy and dramatic interest after Richard has completed his progress to the crown with the murder of the princes. Coleridge, commenting on Richard's delight in the cerebral challenges of his villainy, contrasted the two great opportunists of the history plays: 'In Richard III the pride of intellect makes use of ambition as its means; in Bolingbroke the ambition is the end and his talents are the means.' Palmer notes that, after the crown is secured for Richard, 'the dreadful inspiration which carried him to the achievement of his purpose now visibly flags . . . there will be something almost mechanical in his further performances'.[10]

An instance of this again shows the limitations of the play's construction around the two faces of its central character. The passage between Richard and Queen Elizabeth in Act IV Scene iv, in which he demands her daughter as a bride, is no more than a repeat of his earlier outrageous performance in wooing Anne. Because it is a repetition and because the wooing is conducted at second hand, the scene is much less effective than the earlier one. It has an elaborate, artificial quality, characterised by measured antitheses and elaborate verbal conceits. Only when the play's dominant animal imagery flashes out in a memorable phrase, such as Queen Margaret's earlier

From forth the kennel of thy womb has crept
A hell-hound that doth hunt us all to death

or Richard's half-lascivious, half-contemptuous description of young Elizabeth's womb as 'that nest of spicery' does this section of the play splutter into life.

Shakespeare has the problem that, having shown us Richard at his dazzling virtuoso peak, he can do little more than repeat the performance, with resulting anti-climax. We should remember that he cannot surprise his audience through plot as he can in, for instance, *Hamlet*, which for contemporary audiences had a continuous suspense as to the next twist of its story. Shakespeare's audience knew that Vice must be confounded; they also knew, more clearly than most modern spectators, the historical details of Richard's decline and fall. It is no wonder that Shakespeare takes refuge in the formal, ritualistic aspects of the fall everyone knew must come.

The truth is that neither the author's dramatic nor his other skills are yet equal to megalomania or remorse. Both are suggested; neither is developed with any subtlety. As even Buckingham pauses at the prospect of murdering the princes, Richard finds hesitation to be taken as opposition. He glares after his henchman, then turns to us in wide-eyed psychopathy:

None are for me
That look into me with considerate eyes:
High-reaching Buckingham grows circumspect.

It is the attitude of Lear as he plays the tyrant before his assembled court: but madness must await the author's maturity for fuller investigation.

And Richard's remorse sits in a dream-world outside the rest of the character, a convenient morality ending to a figure who loses dynamism and conviction once the crown has been achieved. Significantly, the creation with whom Richard is most often compared is Macbeth, that other high-reaching murderer who finds the forbidden fruit rotting in his mouth. Superficially, their careers as royal murderers and usurpers and their eventual downfalls have much in common. Yet while Macbeth is Shakespeare's deepest and most convincing study of ambition turned sour, Richard remains a bogey-man, a nightmarish caricature. By the time of *Macbeth*, Shakespeare is able to combine the issues of individual ambition and the responsibilities of state within the tortured condition of one man. At the beginning of his career he cannot do that. By the simple but forceful device of setting Richard's private face continually alongside his public behaviour, he gives his play for two-thirds of its length an ironic interest and a dramatic excitement which endure to this day. He has discovered a dramatic design which he will invoke with increasing subtlety and many variations in the next two decades.

In the rest of Shakespeare's 'prentice work, there is little use of the public-private contrast: having discoverd its most straightforward use in *Richard III*, Shakespeare does not employ it much until he comes to treat the promising material of the second tetralogy of history plays a few years later. The comedies, particularly the early ones, give him little opportunity for interplays of this kind, and the early plays are a series of experiments in form whilst the dramatist continues to forge his dramatic and linguistic techniques.

*The Comedy of Errors* preserves unity of action and attempts comedy in the manner of Plautus and Terence; *Two Gentlemen of Verona* shows clear links with the sonnets. *The Taming of the Shrew* revolves around the clash of temperaments, with choleric, peremptory Petruchio set against proud-minded Katherina: as his career proceeds Shakespeare will become preoccupied increasingly with warring elements within a single personality, with the different and sometimes contradictory demands which life will make upon that personality. Some men, like Henry V, will opt consciously for success in one of these at the expense of the other; others, like Othello, will be destroyed by a failure to recognise the different demands of public and private life. But all this lies well ahead.

Shakespeare tries his hand at the bloodletting then in theatrical vogue in *Titus Andronicus*.[11] Lavinia has her hands cut off and her tongue cut out after she is raped; Titus cuts off his own hand for her to pick off stage with her teeth; the Empress eats her sons after Titus has cooked them in a pie. This Grand Guignol *melange* had a success which lasted for twenty years after its composition, but has been seen to lack Shakespeare's subtlety of design and psychological insight ever since then. There is little interplay here between public and private conduct, and the continuous vituperative rhetoric loses its effect as it becomes monotonous, until the play depends for interest almost entirely upon the horrors of its action.

At the end of Shakespeare's 'prentice period there is a tragedy of much greater interest. There are no doubts as to the outcome of *Romeo and Juliet,* for the Prologue announces the eventual death of the lovers at the outset. Moreover, the lovers fall because they are 'star-cross'd', not because of defects in themselves or their love. This tragedy of lyric emotion stands clearly distinguished from the great group of plays written some ten years later, with their determined personal questionings into human aspirations. There is just a suggestion of material for such probings, which is instantly dismissed in comedy. Romeo at the outset of the play is a self-conscious amorist, revelling in his distress as heavily as Orsino at the outset of *Twelfth Night*. At the first sight of Juliet all this vanishes, falling away even as it is mocked by Mercutio. Where Othello is left with Iago to probe an insecure love, not only are Romeo's posturings suddenly transformed into a more genuine emotion, but Mercutio is banished from the play. As *Henry V*'s design will not accommodate Falstaff, so Mercutio is dismissed before he can tarnish this play's brilliant centre. At the other end of love's continuum, Shakespeare will eventually arrive at Antony and Cleopatra, and there he will leave Enobarbus to comment on the foolishness and the grandeur as he dare not leave Mercutio here.

There is another, more important, reason why Romeo remains a simple character. He is not a public figure with a position to maintain as a man of power whilst his private emotions rage. He harnesses a poet's temperament and a gift for lyrical statement to his individual fortune, and the equipage races ahead at headlong speed. Richard II, with much the same lyrical gifts but less taste for action, produces the greatest tension of the play by setting his indulgences of his private self against his public predicament in a world of blood and iron. Romeo has no such concern: poetry in him fuses unforced with his destiny as he speaks his first words to Juliet:

> If I profane with my unworthiest hand
> This holy shrine.

The dominant image of this most straightforward of tragedies is of light, the greatest and simplest of natural forces. Romeo, catching his first glimpse of Juliet, fixes it for ever in characteristic and exhilarating Elizabethan hyperbole:

> O, she does teach the torches to burn bright.

He banishes Mercutio's merry obscenities from the audience's mind as he moves out of the darkness and towards Juliet's balcony with the most famous of all his light images:

But soft! What light through yonder window breaks?
It is the east, and Juliet is the sun!
Arise, fair sun, and kill the envious moon,
Who is already sick and pale with grief,
That thou her maid art far more fair than she.

Juliet, waiting in Act III for doomed Romeo to come to her bed, is impatient for the night and its cover:

Gallop apace, you fiery-footed steeds
Towards Phoebus' Lodging.

The dominant image of the play, like the action and the characters, is swift, uncomplicated, remorseless: no jaded passions here, none of the clipped understatement of more complicated emotions in the later plays.

Yet because it is so uncomplicated, because the major characters have neither the self-doubts nor the dual roles of later tragic figures, there is a danger of a flagging of dramatic interest. When the dazzling fireworks of the exchanges between the central characters or the earthy commentary of the Nurse are available, there are no difficulties for the author. Elsewhere, the constant word-play is surely more than a developing writer's delight in the possibilities of language. M. H. Mahmood points out that '*Romeo and Juliet* is one of Shakespeare's most punning plays; even a really conservative count yields a hundred and seventy-five quibbles.'[12] As in some of the early comedies, Shakespeare is constantly on the look-out for the word-play beloved of Elizabethans to sustain interest.

The author's power over words is still developing, alongside his other skills. Benvolio stills a sword-fight as effectively as Othello in a similar situation. But he is not an important character and Shakespeare is still only learning the economy of language which will enable him to suggest character by the manner as well as the matter of speech. Benvolio's 'Put up your swords; you know not what you do' is effective enough for his purposes. But he cannot yet encapsulate character in a single line as he does when the poet-commander Othello steps out of the darkness with

Keep up your bright swords, for the dew will rust them.

Juliet's personification of night, 'Thou sober-suited matron all in black,' is a conceit plucked from outside the play, whereas Lady Macbeth pins herself in her nightmare world when she invokes night:

> Come thick night,
> And pall thee in the dunnest smoke of hell,
> That my keen knife see not the wound it makes,
> Nor heaven peep through the blanket of the dark,
> To cry, Hold, Hold!

The power of this derives not just from a Shakespeare in full and incomparable flow, but from the design of the drama: sixty seconds after this intensity, we shall see Lady Macbeth putting on her public, hostess's face to greet the gracious Duncan.

Partly because of the absence of inner tensions in the lovers, Mercutio's vigorous presence would be a threat to the dramatic balance of the central scenes of the play. That most famous of critic-directors, Granville-Barker, saw him 'Dominating the stage with his lusty presence, vomiting his jolly indecencies'.[13] There is a constrast in his death to the attitudes struck in the early histories, a contrast which looks forward to the achievements to come. As Mercutio looks at his death-wound, Shakespeare knows now the understatement, the simplicity which cuts through even a brave, nervous quibble to make a man's departure linger in our affections:

> 'Tis not so deep as a well, nor so wide as a church-door;
> but 'tis enough, 'twill serve: ask for me tomorrow, and
> you shall find me a grave man.

His death shows his creator's affection for him, but Mercutio has to go. The framework is too simple, the flow of lyricism too central to the tragedy, to accommodate him.

The two plays from Shakespeare's early period which have had the most continuing success are *Richard III* and *Romeo and Juliet.* Both are very simple in design. In the first, he makes straight-forward but copious use of the public-private faces of his eponymous villain to secure a series of comic and melodramatic effects. In the second, the absence of inner questionings in his hero and heroine gives Shakespeare some problems in sustaining dramatic interest, which he solves generally through the intensity of the verse and imagery of his lovers. In the years of his maturity, he will look increasingly to inner conflicts in his characters, and use constructions which will enable him to make the most effective dramatic use of such conflicts.

# Notes

1. E. K. Chambers, *Shakespeare: a Survey*, p. 13.
2. See preface to Arden edition of *Henry VI* for a summary of this view.
3. *Shakespeare's Dramatic Art*, Chapter 4, pp. 147–62.
4. See M. B. Garber, *Dream in Shakespeare*.
5. The Arden editor puts a convincing case for the completion of this play in 1590, earlier than the play used to be placed.
6. *Shakespeare's Early Tragedies*, p. 57.
7. *Political Characters of Shakespeare*, p. 65.
8. Palmer's memorable phrase, p. 79.
9. In the first of the series *Plays in Performance*, on *Richard III* (Junction, London, 1981), Julia Hankey shows the success of a series of great actors in this version, notably Garrick, who seized on Richard's 'dreadful energy'.
10. Palmer, p. 103.
11. Though the degree of his authorship is still disputed. See Brooke, *Early Tragedies*, p. 14, and introduction to Arden edition.
12. Mahmood's 'Wordplay in *Romeo and Juliet*' is included in L. Lerner (ed.), *Shakespeare's Tragedies*, pp. 17–35.
13. *Prefaces to Shakespeare* (Batsford, London, 1969), vol. IV, p. 50.

# 2 THE MAJOR HISTORIES: *RICHARD II*, *HENRY IV*, PARTS 1 AND 2 AND *HENRY V*

The second tetralogy of history plays which comprises *Richard II*, the two parts of *Henry IV*, and *Henry V*, is Shakespeare's greatest achievement thus far. It has been variously suggested that the tetralogy is an epic, a sustained allegory of English life, or a combination of the two. It is, in fact, Shakespeare's first successful fusion of his interest in the different faces of men with his developing powers over dramatic material and the language. These plays are his first intensive examination of man in high and important positions in the state, of how different personalities affect the way in which power is won and exercised, and of how power itself affects those personalities. The first play, *Richard II*, sets an ineffective king in his moments of crisis against a usurper whose responsiveness to the political realities about him makes him Richard's appropriate foil. The other plays examine the effects of power struggles and public roles upon various holders of high political office; through the plays there steadily emerges the most effective ruler and leader of men whom Shakespeare ever drew, Harry of Monmouth.

## Richard II

Shakespeare's modifications of his sources are always interesting and this is not least so in *Richard II*. Holinshed wrote of the two kings involved in the tale: 'In this dejecting of the one and advancing of the other, the providence of God is to be respected and his secret will to be wondered at.' Whilst he preserves this mystical element in the tragedy, Shakespeare is at pains to make Richard's fall and Bolingbroke's rise entirely believable. This he achieves by showing us a Richard whose decline and a Bolingbroke whose advance are entirely credible in psychological terms. Richard's public conduct is an increasingly desperate avowal of his private feelings. Bolingbroke's political success comes with his steady denial to himself of all individual emotions in public.

This concern of Shakespeare's with the private man and the exterior he chooses to show to those around him explain the unevenness of *Richard II* which has caused some critics to impose rather high-flown theories of symbolism and ritual upon the play. While the elements of ceremony and formality are important in a play whose central act is the deposition of a lawful king, they are not Shakespeare's main concern. Rather are they important as creating the appropriate setting in which private man in political crisis might be studied. Shakespeare's concern is with the effectiveness or otherwise of his two central figures as men of power and with their attractiveness or otherwise as private individuals. Yeats[1] was at the heart of the play when he said Shakespeare

> made his King fail, a little because he lacked some qualities that were doubtless common among his scullions, but more because he had certain qualities that are uncommon in all ages . . . He saw indeed, as I think, in *Richard II* the fate that awaits all, whether they be artist or saint, who find themselves where men ask of them a rough energy and have nothing to give but some contemplative virtue.

Once we accept that the major theme of the play is the examination of the tensions of individual man in the position of highest power, the unevenness of the play is easier to understand and there will be less temptation to explain away what is simply poor or careless writing by invoking larger theories of allegory. The high proportion of artificial rhyming or end-stopped verse in some sections of the play may represent unrevised snatches of an earlier play. Such passages of obviously ineffective writing are rare in the important sections of the play. The importance of the garden scene, for instance, has been too much stressed. Its elaborate symbolical representation of Richard's neglected realm in horticultural terms is obvious enough, but it is lifeless compared with Shakespeare's energy of thought and charged sensitive language when he is at his best. Macbeth's Scotland, Claudius' Denmark, the Rome to Octavius Caesar and the Egypt of Cleopatra will all be caught more tellingly and with greater subtlety. Within the history plays, we may contrast this scene with the terse 'Most subject is the fattest soil to weeds' with which the central symbol of this scene is dismissed in *2 Henry IV*. Again, there is much slack writing in the fifth act of the play. We need to look no further for explanation than the fact that with Richard's deposition Shakespeare's main interest is at an end; thus this section springs to life only with Richard's death scene and with Bolingbroke's ambivalent reception of the news of that death in the final speech.

The truth is that the scenes in which Shakespeare treats of his central interest — those in which Richard and Bolingbroke are concerned, especially where they are on stage together — are dramatically and linguistically superb. The rest is in a minor key and often carelessly put together.

Yet the major scenes are intensely effective, and effective as much by their dramatic power as by their piercing psychological insights and their memorable matching of language to personality. The drama is not of physical happenings, however, but of the tensions of men's minds. Richard, as power passes from him, forges his own private drama and draws Bolingbroke into it at every opportunity.

In the first scene, the tension between Richard's public performance as King and his private persona is soon evident. At first all is measured formality and ritual; as the scene proceeds only Richard, with comments whose intelligence is individual and discordant, disturbs this. The scene establishes the formal setting in which Richard has to act a formal role, but it also contains the first hint of his indulgence of an individual personality which provides the main dramatic energy of the play. After Bolingbroke's ringing couplets of prepared rhetoric, Richard provides the deflating comment which as arbiter he should eschew:

> How high a pitch his resolution soars!

Both of course are intensely conscious of the political issues which lie behind the ritual pomp: Bolingbroke's attack on Mowbray is in fact an oblique attack upon Richard himself. A moment later, under the pretext of assuring Mowbray that he may speak freely, Richard reminds Bolingbroke of how far he stands from the throne:

> Were he my brother, nay, my kingdom's heir,
> As he is but my father's brother's son.

The excitement Richard feels in this intellectual play and in his first memorable image as he mentions his individual soul leads to a confusion of pronouns as he wavers between the royal plural and a more individual address:

> Such neighbour nearness to our sacred blood
> Should nothing privilege him nor partialise
> The unstooping firmness of my upright soul.
> He is our subject, Mowbray; so art thou:
> Free speech and fearless I to thee allow.

Richard is put to the test in a political situation immediately: the situation requires firm handling. Instead, Richard pleads for an end to the quarrel with a feebleness and a nervous jest which are perfectly caught in the hollow couplets:

> This we prescribe, though no physician;
> Deep malice makes too deep incision.
> Forget, forgive, conclude and be agreed:
> Our doctors say this is no month to bleed.

Predictably, open defiance follows Richard's failure to play consistently his royal role; his belated resumption of it with his reminder at the end of the scene that 'We were not born to sue but to command' comes too late to solve the problem on the spot.

The second scene, in which Gaunt is urged towards revenge by Gloucester's widow, is clumsily written, but its placing between the two scenes in which Richard conducts the elaborate ritual which ends in the banishment of Mowbray and Bolingbroke is significant. Here is a reminder that underneath the brilliant costume and courtesies of Richard's court lurk murder, bitterness and danger. Whatever the trappings of Gallic splendour around Richard's throne, he is surrounded by powerful barons, and unless he can sustain successfully the role of *primus inter pares* he will not survive. Bolingbroke's understanding and eventual assertion of this role lead him to Richard's crown.

Beneath the formal pageantry of the lists in the next scene there develops the drama deriving from a personality which does not fit the kingly role Richard should be playing. There is surely a sardonic note in Richard's acknowledgement of Bolingbroke:

> Cousin of Herford, as thy cause is right,
> So be thy fortune in this royal fight!

Richard, enjoying the political posturing which he knows to be hollow, delays his intervention until the last possible moment, though it is a previously agreed Council decision he has to announce. The exchanges between Richard and the two contestants which follow are significant. The strain of Richard's public role is telling and his individuality flashes out. His reaction to the faithful Mowbray, who realises as well as Richard that his banishment is part of a political bargain the King has had to strike, is cruel and careless:

> It boots thee not to be compassionate;
> After our sentence plaining comes too late.

The banishment reminds us of Lear's abrupt dismissal of Kent years later; Richard like Lear can ill afford the loss of such a sturdy and vigorous supporter in the troubled times ahead.

Significantly, the reduction of Bolingbroke's banishment from ten to six years, which is a Council decision in Froissart, is made by Shakespeare a stroke of Richard's alone: he is shown as responding with the warmth of individual sympathy to Gaunt's distress but also whimsically undoing a carefully weighed Council decision. Typically, the unpredictable Richard, a prey to each passing fancy, has treated his supporter harshly and his political opponent generously; public and private man have moved out of phase with each other.

This instinctive generosity of Richard's is the more marked because he more than anyone else on stage is aware of the dangerous ambition lurking in this Bolingbroke whose sentence he commutes. In the next scene he shows he has not only observed Bolingbroke's courtship of the common people but deduced its political direction:

> Off goes his bonnet to an oyster-wench;
> A brace of draymen bid God speed him well,
> And had the tribute of his supple knee,
> With 'Thanks, my countrymen, my loving friends' —
> As were our England in reversion his,
> And he our subjects' next degree in hope.

The passage is followed immediately by an example of Richard's own political recklessness as he plans to replenish his coffers wasted by 'too great a court' by farming his royal realm and leaving sweeping powers of taxation in the hands of his favourites as he goes off to his Irish wars. His reception of Gaunt's grievous sickness is characteristically witty, unguarded and misguided:

> Come, gentlemen, let's all go visit him.
> Pray God we may make haste, and come too late!

The foolishness of this is immediately emphasised by the scene which follows, in which the dying Gaunt's warning against Richard's 'rash fierce blaze of riot' and invocation of England's glory develops an increasingly chorus-like quality. Richard, ever intelligent and ever sensitive to the power of words, is clearly moved, but his reaction as his great nobles watch anxiously is disastrously personal. As Gaunt's manner becomes increasingly that of an Old Testament prophet, Richard rounds on him peevishly:

*Gaunt*: Landlord of England art thou now, not king,
Thy state of law is bondslave to the law,
And thou —

*Richard*: A lunatic lean-witted fool,
Presuming on an ague's privilege,
Darest with thy frozen admonition
Make pale our cheek, chasing the royal blood
With fury from his native residence.
Now by my seat's right royal majesty,
Wert thou not brother to great Edward's son,
This tongue that runs so roundly in thy head
Should run thy head from thy unreverent shoulders.

It is noticeable here how Richard asserts his majesty with the royal plural, but slips back into the singular immediately in mid-speech. When York intervenes to try to terminate the increasingly bitter exchanges between Richard and Gaunt on a more forgiving note, he tactlessly shows his ignorance of the political issues which underlie the situation by comparing Gaunt's loyalty to that of his son. Richard rounds on him with the terse impatience which makes the political breach open for all to see:

Right, you say true; as Herford's love, so his;
As theirs, so mine; and all be as it is.

This abrupt dismissal of York's ill-chosen attempt at peacemaking reminds us that despite his self-conscious wordiness later in the play, Richard can be as curt and elliptical as anyone, as he shows throughout this scene. His folly is to consider sharp intellect a substitute for policy rather than merely an element in it. His very incisiveness becomes a handicap rather than an aid to him because of this. Not once in the play does he mask a reaction or contain his appraisal of a situation until he has formulated a plan of action which takes all considerations into account. Either he has no comprehension of the effect of his actions upon those around him, or he has a contempt for those who even consider such effects.

Richard's worst moment in the play, politically as well as ethically, comes with the news of Gaunt's death. The conventional grief is expressed with a rhyme which marks the platitude; then the language springs immediately away with the cynical seizure of Gaunt's possessions without even a pretence of justice:

The ripest fruit first falls, and so doth he;
His time is spent, our pilgrimage must be.
So much for that. Now for our Irish wars:
We must supplant those rough rug-headed kerns,
Which live like venom where no venom else,
But only they, have privilege to live.
And for these great affairs do ask some charge,
Towards our assistance we do seize to us
The plate, coin, revenues, and moveables,
Whereof our uncle Gaunt did stand possess'd.

Gaunt of course is a political enemy and Richard no doubt detects an element of humbug in his stance. As John Palmer[2] points out: 'Richard saw in this Galahad of the sceptred isle a political enemy masquerading as a patriot, a cantankerous nobleman whose son had already made mischief in the land and was to make more.' Richard's resentment is thus understandable in one who so easily sees the political realities beneath public protestations which deceive less incisive onlookers at the game. His mistake is that he will not consent to play that game himself: he makes here no attempt to dissemble private feeling with any of the public shows which he needs to make.

He shows indeed a deliberate contempt for such considerations. When the patient York is driven to remind him of the implications of his seizure of what are now Bolingbroke's possessions, Richard refuses even to attempt justification of his conduct:

Think what you will, we seize into our hands
His plate, his goods, his money and his lands.

When even York loses patience with his headstrong failure to recognise the responsibilities of the crown, his response combines the swift irony of private argument with the strain of political crassness we by now expect: he creates the ageing, easily confused York Lord Governor of England in his absence.

Within four lines of this foolish punishment of York with an office which he does not want, Northumberland moves briskly forward with his plans for insurrection as the King sweeps out. As so often in Shakespeare, the retribution for mistaken policy follows with the swiftness of dramatic irony. Whether Northumberland's rallying call to 'Make high majesty look like itself' springs from a real sense of outrage or political manoeuvre, Richard has given him a genuine case with which to move honest men and left a feeble representative to resist them.

Events from this point move swiftly. The interest throughout the play lies not in the facts of history but in what Coleridge called 'a history of the human mind'. It is necessary to appreciate this to savour the drama in this apparently static play. The tension derives not from the events which surround the rise of one great man at the expense of another but from the juxtaposition of the two contrasting minds and approaches to private and public life which are involved. The climax of this kind of drama is of course in the great deposition scene in Act IV, in which the two men, each intensely conscious of the other and the issues involved, confront each other over the crown.

Here there are notable differences from Marlowe's *Edward II*, the play with which this one is most often compared. Though Edward, like Richard, is a flawed individual whose downfall and sufferings we are asked to pity, there is no contrasting and balancing figure to maintain the dramatic impetus of the play. Mortimer, who brings down Edward, is the conventional Machiavellian villain whose characteristic cry at the height of his villainy,

Fear'd am I more than lov'd, let me be fear'd

seems to come directly from Chapter 17 of *The Prince*. The convention is an excuse for Marlowe to ignore all psychological investigation of the character, so that Mortimer's abrupt and unconvincing changes become merely devices of plot. In this he is a great contrast to the enigmatic but utterly convincing Bolingbroke.

Because he does not investigate the issues of kingship and authority involved in deposition, Marlowe's Edward becomes a pathetic rather than a tragic figure, as the author in the closing scenes heaps almost every sordid detail of the chroniclers upon him. In Shakespeare, the crux is seen to be the individual personality's relationship with power: Richard can be brought face to face with his accusers as Edward never is, and the claims of both sides examined throughout.

Act II contrasts the hand-wringings and confusions of Richard's favourites and of York with the steady efficiency of the rebels. The more major contrast which is to dominate the rest of the play, that between Richard and Bolingbroke, is also made manifest. Bolingbroke re-enters with a practical question, 'How far is it, my lord, to Berkeley now?' and Northumberland's effusive declarations of friendship which follow receive the briefest acknowledgement:

> Of much less value is my company
> Than your good words.

Not until he is confronted by York and forced to justify his invasion does he speak at length. Then he speaks with the logic he always displays on such occasions, the kernel of his argument being exactly what York had warned Richard it might be:

> If that my cousin King be King in England,
> It must be granted I am Duke of Lancaster.

Having stated his case, he lets Northumberland do his blustering for him as York tries to remonstrate. York's collapse before the steady pressure applied to him underlines Richard's disastrous decision in making him his representative to gratify a personal pique:

> Well, well, I see the issue of these arms.
> I cannot mend it, I must needs confess,
> Because my power is weak and all ill left.

Within twenty lines Bolingbroke has consolidated his position, shrewdly blaming the country's ills on the friendless 'caterpillars of the commonwealth', and won the royal representative York to bewildered neutrality.

At the beginning of Act III the favourites provoke one of Bolingbroke's longer speeches in which Tillyard notes 'a plain and understandable passion as he recounts his wrongs'.[3] He seizes the opportunity to blame the seizure of his own lands and other ills on them rather than directly on Richard. In the forty-four lines of this scene Bolingbroke moves confidently into three decisive actions, sending Northumberland off to see to the execution of the favourites, sending messengers to reassure the Queen and moving purposefully off to fight Glendower. The contrast of this brisk despatch of affairs with what follows could hardly be more stark.

Where Bolingbroke is conscious always of his next objective, Richard suggests a world where elegant means may matter more than ends. Dover Wilson suggested that although Bolingbroke acts forcefully, he 'appears to be borne upwards by a power beyond his own volition'.[4] The truth is that Richard is so little conscious of political cause and effect and so much concerned with his own emotions at any particular moment that he becomes almost an active instrument in the success of Bolingbroke's opportunism.

Thus Richard, landing in his own kingdom where he knows the rebels are already dangerously strong, is already rehearsing his role of ill-used King and tender caretaker of his realm, despite his careless and selfish use of it until now:

> Needs must I like it well: I weep for joy
> To stand upon my kingdom once again.
> Dear earth, I do salute thee with my hand,
> Though rebels wound thee with their horses' hoofs.
> As a long-parted mother with her child
> Plays fondly with her tears and smiles in meeting,
> So weeping, smiling, greet I thee, my earth,
> And do thee favours with my royal hands.

As Palmer has it, 'Narcissus is already absorbed in the contemplation of his own image.'[5] Though he is briefly aware of the reaction of his supporters,

> Mock not my senseless conjuration, lords,

he brushes aside Aumerle's uncomfortable reminder that Bolingbroke is growing strong through their inaction.

Shakespeare concentrates our attention on Richard's mind by denying us any obvious surprises of plot: as Richard's fortunes decline before our eyes with the long catalogue of bad news, we know before the scene begins the worst piece of news, that of York's collapse. Richard's mind, said Dowden,[6] is 'merely dazzled by phenomena instead of perceiving things as they are . . . He satiates his heart with the tenderness, the beauty or the pathos of situations.' In this scene he behaves as an artist, seizing on the stuff of circumstance and exercising all his energy and creative power to make poetry of it. His self-indulgent abandonment to his nature makes the world of a discontented people and warring nobles which constantly intrudes seem unreal to him. The contrast with Bolingbroke makes the delineation of the issues involved more effective. Bolingbroke deliberately subdues all his emotions to political expediency, permitting us only the occasional vivid flash of feeling where it can perhaps assist his progress, such as the glimpse of him 'eating the bitter bread of banishment' in the previous scene.

Shakespeare sets himself a considerable task in portraying Richard thus, and for the first time his language is equal to such demands. As hope and despair follow in bewildering alternation in Act III Scene ii,

Richard's mind reels in a dazzling confusion of bright conceits. It is the kind of writing which the author might have wished to employ in *Henry VI*, but of which he was not then capable.

Ure[7] thinks that we meet in the scene for the first time the new, expressive Richard. In fact, Shakespeare's conception is all of a piece. Richard's swift starts and sharp irresponsible jests of the early scenes are quite consistent with his later behaviour. The key thing is that as power drops from him and kingship by degrees become a mere token, Richard is ever more confident in giving rein to his individual character and feelings. His consciousness of the drama and pathos of his personal situation and his indulgence of this vision increase as his fortunes decline. In the harsh world of turbulent barons and cynical power politics, Richard is the increasingly lonely spokesman for a different set of values. Shakespeare shows by lustrous images, which are wholly appropriate to Richard's Gallic temperament and love of ornament, what is going on in his mind and heart. His concern is wholly with himself and not at all with his realm, which is mentioned only where it can emphasise the tragedy of his personal situation.

Shakespeare's powers, as I say, are now equal to the demanding task of delineating such a man. This is the point in the play where the situation runs closest to that of *Edward II*, and those recent commentators who have seen Marlowe's play as superior should study how dazzlingly Shakespeare handles this section. Edward, like Richard, responds to images which rise and will not be denied whatever the facts which surround him:

> But when I call to mind I am a king,
> Methinks I should revenge me of the wrongs,
> That Mortimer and Isabel have done
> But what are Kings, when regiment is gone.
> But perfect shadows in a sun-shine day?
> My nobles rule, I bear the name of King
> I wear the crown, but am controlled by them.

But, as Richard's bright vision beguiles him in a similar way, it is Shakespeare who perfectly encapsulates the man:

> Not all the water in the rough rude sea
> Can wash the balm off from an anointed King;
> The breath of worldly men cannot depose
> The deputy elected by the Lord;

> For every man that Bolingbroke hath press'd
> To lift shrewd steel against our golden crown,
> God for his Richard hath in heavenly pay
> A glorious angel: then, if angels fight,
> Weak men must fall, for heaven still guards the right.

As always, Richard's power over words has its readiest audience in himself, but reality cannot long be held off with images, and poetry is no substitute for action in a desperate political situation. Salisbury and Scroop with their news

> Of Bolingbroke covering your fearful land
> With hard bright steel, and hearts harder than steel

swiftly crush Richard's brittle optimism. Richard's venomous reception of what he mistakenly supposes to be the treachery of his favourites shows both the degree to which emotion rules his reeling mind and the kind of role which he is unconsciously adopting for himself.

> Three Judases, each one thrice worse than Judas!
> Would they make peace? Terrible hell,
> Make war upon their spotted souls for this!

Such anger in a political man would be translated into immediate action. Richard, surrounded by supporters looking for a military lead, indulges in his most famous and most marvellous outpouring of individual melancholia, culminating in the appropriately medieval image of Death keeping his court. If Shakespeare's mastery of language surpasses Marlowe's, so does his dramatic construction; Richard interweaves a private and public tragedy, until the two become for him one fabric:

> No matter where — of comfort no man speak.
> Let's talk of graves, of worms, and epitaphs,
> Make dust our paper, and with rainy eyes
> Write sorrow on the bosom of the earth.
> Let's choose executors and talk of wills.
> And yet not so — for what can we bequeath
> Save our deposed bodies to the ground?
> Our lands, our lives, and all, are Bolingbroke's,
> And nothing can we call our own but death;
> And that small model of the barren earth

Which serves as paste and cover to our bones.
For God's sake let us set upon the ground
And tell sad stories of the death of kings:
How some have been depos'd, some slain in war,
Some haunted by the ghosts they have deposed,
Some poisoned by their wives, some sleeping kill'd,
All murthered — for within the hollow crown
That rounds the mortal temples of a king
Keeps Death his court, and there the antic sits,
Scoffing his state and grinning at his pomp,
Allowing him a breath, a little scene,
To monarchize, be fear'd, and kill with looks;
Infusing him with self and vain conceit,
As if this flesh which walls about our life
Were brass impregnable; and, humour'd thus,
Comes at the last, and with a little pin
Bores through his castle wall, and farewell king!

When Carlisle reminds him that 'wise men ne'er sit and wail their woes'
Richard rallies briefly, only for Scroop to heap on him the final blow of
York's desertion. His cup is full and as the scene ends he turns to
Aumerle with no attempt now to mask the attraction to him of a
picturesque despair:

Beshrew thee, cousin, which didst lead me forth
Of that sweet way I was in to despair!
What say you now? What comfort have we now?
By heaven, I'll hate him everlastingly
That bids me be of comfort any more.

Shakespeare chooses to let Richard dominate his play with his
assertion of an individuality that is by turns dazzling, moving and
irritating. Bolingbroke is subordinated to him, made to strike a subdued
note in the language which is the central dynamism of the play as his
political fortunes rise ever higher. This is writing which Shakespeare is
to develop with full subtlety in Anthony and Octavius some fifteen
years later. Yet the juxtaposition is effective enough here: Bolingbroke's
flatness and deliberate obscurity of language are cultivated as aspects of
his character, as part of the stock in trade of the cautious but clear-
sighted opportunist. The deposition scene is the most sustained example
of the skill with which Shakespeare uses this juxtaposition of language

to convey wholly different worlds and aspirations. Until then, he sets examples of the conduct of each side by side.

Thus as we move now to Bolingbroke's army all is brisk efficiency. Growing more secure and more assertive as his power increases, Bolingbroke brusquely checks his uncle York and concludes the exchange with a splendidly ambivalent sentiment:

> *Bol.*: Mistake not, uncle, further than you should.
> *York*: Take not, good cousin, further than you should,
> Lest you mistake: the heavens are o'er our heads.
> *Bol.*: I know it, uncle; and oppose not myself
> Against their will.

His instructions to Northumberland as he sends him to treat with Richard are a mixture of conciliation and military threats which curiously foreshadow his son's approach to a different situation at Harfleur a generation later. The approach springs directly from his sense of political reality. Though he swiftly arrives at a situation where Richard's defeat in war is assured, he is aware throughout the rest of the play of the danger that even a defeated and humiliated Richard may embody and of the desirability of some form of public reconciliation.

Much of the dramatic tension of the play now springs from the fact that the person who most clearly apprehends what Bolingbroke is about is Richard himself. Always acutely aware of what is in men's minds even when political facts elude him, Richard uses this knowledge to discomfort Bolingbroke whenever an audience is available.

Thus Richard begins the parley by bearing himself like the King many still hope to see as he subdues the incautious Northumberland:

> We are amaz'd, and thus long have we stood
> To watch the fearful bending of thy knee,
> Because we thought ourself thy lawful king;
> And if we be, how dare thy joints forget
> To pay their awful duty to our presence?
> If we be not, show us the hand of God
> That hath dismiss'd us from our stewardship.

But the strain of maintaining the mien of impersonal royalty soon tells. Richard becomes excited by his own conceits, the royal plural deserts him with his sense of political reality, and his threats become vaguer as he seeks to banish harsh realities by attractive images of the mind:

> Yet know, my master, God omnipotent,
> Is mustering in his clouds, on our behalf,
> Armies of pestilence, and they shall strike
> Your children yet unborn, and unbegot,
> That lift your vassal hands against my head,
> And threat the glory of my precious crown.

As Northumberland returns from Bolingbroke, Richard is so excited by the pathos of his humiliation and the aesthetic consolations he derives from expressing it that he cannot wait to hear the message. He strings together a glittering array of contrasts and cadences:

> What must the kind do now? Must he submit?
> The king shall do it. Must he be depos'd?
> The king shall be contented. Must he lose
> The name of king? a God's name, let it go.
> I'll give my jewels for a set of beads;
> My gorgeous palace for a hermitage;
> My gay apparel for an almsman's gown;
> My figur'd goblets for a dish of wood;
> My sceptre for a palmer's walking staff;
> My subjects for a pair of carved saints,
> And my large kingdom for a little grave,
> A little little grave, an obscure grave,
> Or I'll be buried in the king's highway,
> Some way of common trade, where subjects' feet
> May hourly trample on their sovereign's head.

The weeping Aumerle provokes Richard's most contrived image, that of twin graves fretted by their tears, but the loneliness he feels is suddenly bleakly upon him as he looks at those around him:

> Well, well, I see
> I talk but idly and you laugh at me.

As Richard comes submissively and symbolically down from the walls, his fortunes are almost at their lowest, yet Shakespeare gives us a reminder of his quality. Bolingbroke's enthronement, whatever its necessity, began the Wars of the Roses and the darkest era of English political life. It is Richard who apprehends the horrors which are to come most clearly, and he apprehends them not through political foresight but through the vaguer but more telling medium of his imagination. In a single searing image, Richard foresees the long nightmare which will follow his deposition:

Down, court! down, king!
For night owls shriek where mounting larks should sing.

Despite his situation, Richard enjoys his first meeting with Bolingbroke since the latter's banishment, for he reads his opponent's heart as accurately as ever, and knows he can outmatch him in word-play. He lures Bolingbroke into a mention of his deserts and rounds upon him to dismiss all political claptrap with an analysis of the situation which might be the guideline for political conduct for the ensuing century:

Well you deserve. They well deserve to have
That know the strong'st and surest way to get.

Though Bolingbroke protests 'I come but for my own,' Richard knows what is in prospect — a deposition and a coronation, which must be achieved in London — and makes it apparent to all:

What you will have, I'll give, and willing too,
For do we must what force will have us do.
Set on towards London, cousin, is it so?

Only the garden scene, with its elaborate symbolism, separates these taut exchanges from the deposition scene which is the climax of the play's theme.

In the great Westminster Hall scene this larger theme of the nature and qualities of man dominates. There is no interest in the struggle for political power between Richard and Bolingbroke: this is already decided. All the interest lies in the contrast in temperament between the two and between the philosophies they embody. For all the irritation Richard arouses both in his audience of nobles on stage and in the audience in the theatre by his wilful lethargy in urgent political situations, we are never unconscious of the worth of the world which he represents. For the first time with consistent effect, Shakespeare is able to suggest the major theme of much of his greatest work: the idea that while a certain kind of personality may be necessary for the successful exercise of power, the mind which rejoices in its individuality, however wilful and dangerous such a course may be, may in fact have more to offer the total world of man than that of a politically well equipped opponent.

Richard's language responds to Shakespeare's intention: its greatest heights of lyricism and most memorable images are achieved as his political fortunes ebb and his personal tragedy flows. Here one should mention a factor which has sometimes hindered rather than helped effective criticism: this is the dispute as to whether Richard himself is or is not an effective poet or artist. Fashions in literature as elsewhere change and ours is an age which estimates the lyrical strain which is Richard's dominant effect less highly than some previous ones. But the language in which Richard speaks is a dramatic medium, not a piece of poetry divorced from a character. Once we accept this, it is clear that Richard's language is highly effective dramatic poetry, since it matches perfectly, and itself largely creates, the personality behind it. Richard is a poet not because he speaks in what for most of us is verse of magnificent imagery and music, but because of his faith in words, his determination to force every emotional moment immediately into language.[8]

Similarly the cautious economy of Bolingbroke's speeches as his fortunes rise marks his lack of interest as a private man to whom other men can give an immediate and instinctive response, his subjugation of his personality into a purely public role. The price he pays for this careful abnegation is not fully apparent until *Henry IV*, but the process of the discipline is perfectly mirrored in his language in *Richard II*.

The clash of language and minds is the whole drama of the abdication scene. First Bolingbroke deals decisively with exactly the same situation which confronted Richard at the beginning of the play. As Bolingbroke firmly quells the unruly nobles, he uses the royal plural for the first time:

Your differences shall all rest under gage
Till we assign to you your days of trial.

Before Richard enters there is a chilling demonstration of the iron of the police state, the confusion of might and right, which Henry's reign will usher in. As Bolingbroke, carefully waiting for a message from Richard through York, ascends the throne, the Bishop of Carlisle protests. There is no attempt to refute his arguments. The Himmler-like Northumberland makes his move cynically and unemotionally,

Well have you argued, sir, and, for your pains,
Of capital treason we arrest you here.

As always, Bolingbroke stands by without comment whilst Northumberland performs the harshest deeds in his name. Into the framework of this brutal new state is set Richard's last and greatest public appearance. Bolingbroke's instructions to York make it clear to all that a formal public statement of abdication is what he plans:

> Fetch hither Richard, that in common view
> He may surrender; so we shall proceed
> Without suspicion.

This wary consciousness of political necessity and subjugation of private emotion to public image is the foil for Richard's final, most vivid display of defiant, self-indulgent individuality. Both men are conscious of the issues at stake, for Richard, despite his carelessness, even scorn, for the larger issues of statesmanship, is too acute not to realise what his opponents are about. He will make them appear crude and insensitive and strip bare the truth about their ultimate designs. Bolingbroke arranges this dangerous meeting with Richard because he knows that, if he is to consolidate his position, the anointed King must willingly and publicly release his crown; Richard consents because in exposing the mummery involved he can for the last time dramatise his own pathos and expose Bolingbroke's deficiencies of spirit and imagination in public. What should be a formal abdication and confession of crimes becomes, because of the audience of peers, a taut battle of wits and words which Richard wins, despite his loss of every conceivable political position and his departure under armed guard to the Tower.

Richard begins with a shameless appeal to his audience about the pathos of his personal situation:

> Alack, why am I sent for to a king
> Before I have shook off the regal thoughts
> Wherewith I reign'd? I hardly yet have learn'd
> To insinuate, flatter, bow, and bend my knee.
> Give sorrow leave awhile to tutor me
> To this submission.

There is no doubt now how highly he rates the martyrdom he seems determined upon:

> Yet I well remember
> The favours of these men. Were they not mine?

Did they not sometime cry 'All hail!' to me?
So Judas did to Christ. But he, in twelve,
Found truth in all but one; I, in twelve thousand, none.

Richard directs his taciturn opponent into his stage position, holding
the other side of the crown, and embarks on the daring image of himself
and Bolingbroke as two buckets, the one ascending and ever more full
of tears as the other, empty one rises ever higher in consequence. This
draws from Bolingbroke the tight-lipped 'I thought you had been willing
to resign' which elicits only Richard's determination to set his griefs
before his audience:

My crown I am, but still my griefs are mine.
You may my glories and my state depose,
But not my griefs; still am I king of those.

The scene as a public demonstration of Richard's willing resignation
is going sadly awry for Bolingbroke, and he is drawn into an irritated
direct question, 'Are you contented to resign the crown?' Richard is
ready for this; his immediate response is to tease his opponent with
riddles but then he moves into the elaborate inverted ritual of his
deconsecration:

Ay, no; no, ay; for I must nothing be.
Therefore no 'no', for I resign to thee.
Now, mark me how I will undo myself.
I give this heavy weight from off my head,
And this unwieldy sceptre from my hand,
The pride of kingly sway from out my heart;
With mine own tears I wash away my balm,
With mine own hands I give away my crown,
With mine own tongue deny my sacred state,
With mine own breath release all duteous oaths;
All pomp and majesty I do forswear;
My manors, rents, revenues, I forgo;
My acts, decrees, and statutes I deny.
God pardon all oaths that are broke to me,
God keep all vows unbroke are made to thee!
Make me, that nothing have, with nothing griev'd,
And thou with all pleas'd, that has all achiev'd.
Long may'st thou live in Richard's seat to sit,

And soon lie Richard in an earthy pit.
God save King Henry, unking'd Richard says,
And send him many years of sunshine days!

Though the action is what Bolingbroke wants, Richard succeeds by his determinedly personal rendering of it in striking exactly the note of sympathy which is disastrous for his opponent.

Bolingbroke now leaves the worst business as usual to the callous Northumberland: Richard must be made to read a prepared confession. Northumberland's insensitivity provokes Richard to a superb one-line dismissal of his hectoring, after which he turns back to the theme of his personal fortunes:

No lord of thine, thou haught insulting man;
Nor no man's lord. I have no name, no title;
No, not that name was given me at the font,
But tis ursurp'd.

The death-wish which is upon him now finds release in perhaps the most striking of all his images:

O that I were a mockery king of snow,
Standing before the sun of Bolingbroke,
To melt myself away in water-drops!

Richard's contempt for the usurper is growing ever more open, and no one realises better than Bolingbroke how the scene is going astray. He calls off the insistent Northumberland and, as Richard achieves his most outrageous stroke in shattering the looking-glass, he has no alternative but to be drawn into a verbal exchange with him. This man of such calculation has not foreseen Richard's high emotional appeal through the projection of his own suffering, because it is not within his own range of action or understanding. Bewildered but dogged, he seems at times not to understand Richard; yet for all the fact that the scene is played to Richard's tune, Bolingbroke loses neither his grasp of political issues nor his coolness. He is even able to respond to Richard's claim that his sorrow has destroyed his face as the mirror lies shattered before him with a verbal quibble of his own:

The shadow of your sorrow hath destroy'd
The shadow of your face.

Richard, however, having drawn his opponent for once into a verbal contest, is not to be denied his triumphs of word-play in the lines which follow. After this, nervous exhaustion overtakes him and as usual he makes no attempt to dissemble this private distress. He asks peevishly to go

Whither you will, so I were from your sights.

As Richard leaves on a final note of defiance, Bolingbroke reasserts political reality with a swiftness that reminds us again of the gulf between the old King and the new:

*Bol.* :    Go some of you, convey him to the Tower.
*Rich.* :   O, good! Convey! Conveyers are you all,
            That rise thus nimbly by a true king's fall.
                        (*Exeunt Richard and Guard.*)
*Bol.* :    On Wednesday next we solemnly set down
            Our coronation. Lords, prepare yourselves.

As Richard and his Queen confront each other for the only time in the play at the beginning of Act V, Richard is too concerned with his own tragedy to show real warmth for his Queen or concern for her anguish. His egotism intrudes even as he orders her away to France:

Tell thou the lamentable tale of me
And send the hearers weeping to their beds.

Without an audience of nobles, Richard is reduced to an uninspired prolixity and his conversation with his Queen is no more than a cold exchange of clever couplets. Northumberland dismisses Richard's warning of disasters to come with the abrupt contempt of the man without imagination:

My guilt be on my head, and there an end.
Take leave and part, for you must part forthwith.

Despite this joyless scene, Richard has become more attractive in his own person as the trappings of power have passed from him, in a manner that is to become familiar to us in Shakespeare's greatest work. In his final soliloquy at Pomfret he confronts his own folly and himself.

Ruined and weary, with death at hand, Richard's way is still that of the artist. He is still concerned to model the force and pressure of his inward vision into its exact expression in words and the scene opens with his most explicit statement of this artist's approach to experience:

> I have been studying how I may compare
> This prison where I live unto the world;
> And, for because the world is populous
> And here is not a creature but myself,
> I cannot do it. Yet I'll hammer it out.

Richard ends his life thinking of others, blessing the anonymous provider of the music and warning the faithful groom as the murderers enter that 'tis time thou wert away'.

There remain only a few more examples of Bolingbroke's effortless despatch of political business and his characteristically enigmatic reception of Exton's arrival with Richard's body. The play closes with his rhyming couplets which express the appropriate measured political sentiments. The elaboration of the metre may suggest a prepared speech ready for the occasion:

> They love not poison that do poison need,
> Nor do I thee. Though I did wish him dead,
> I hate the murtherer, love him murthered.
> The guilt of conscience take thou for thy labour,
> But neither my good word nor princely favour;
> With Cain go wander through shades of night,
> And never show thy head by day nor light.
> Lords, I protest my soul is full of woe
> That blood should sprinkle me to make me grow.
> Come mourn with me for what I do lament,
> And put on sullen black incontinent.

Memorable lines such as 'With Cain go wander thorough shades of night' are wrapped here in the artificiality of the couplets, and the ambivalence of the new King's sentiments as he stands over the blood-stained corpse of the old one is thus perfectly reflected in his language. The last picture we have of Bolingbroke in the play leaves the private man as elusive to us as ever.

## Henry IV, Part 1

*Henry IV* develops the ambivalence of the successful public figure into a wider examination of aspects of power and the individual mind. The most important of the various analyses of themes in the play remains Danby's brilliant exposition[9] of the difference between the ethical worlds of the earlier histories and of the later tetralogy. He dismisses the popular view of the plays which sees them as portraying England as a heroic composite thing: 'If this is so, it is an England seen in her most unflattering aspects — an England pervaded throughout court, tavern and country retreat by pitiless fraud.' It is a kingdom governed now by purely secular motives. As Danby says, whereas in the earlier histories the major issue was 'Is the King right or wrong?' the questions now are reduced and vulgarised to 'Is the King strong or weak? Is the state secure or insecure?'

A. R. Humphreys[10] develops this view: 'The Henry IV plays inhabit the Tudor Erastian world. Religious references are mostly perfunctory.' Certainly it is notable that Henry's never-fulfilled intention to lead a crusade to the Holy Land, for instance, has a clear political purpose to which religion must always take second place. The sense of compelling and often sordid reality reaches its climax with Prince John's conduct in Act IV Scene ii of Part 2, on which his 'God, and not we, hath safely fought today' is Shakespeare's surely ironic epitaph. The only guiding principle evident is that oft-repeated piece of sixteenth-century pragmatism which asserts that 'The King must rule.'

In the face of this clearly demonstrable framework, attempts to find other approaches to the plays seem of secondary importance. The most common of these is that which sees Falstaff as bestriding and unbalancing the plays in a way which Shakespeare did not originally intend. The theory has some distinguished adherents, among whom Chambers[11] is one of the most extreme: 'Chronicle-history becomes little more than a hanging, dimly wrought with horses and footmen, in their alarums and excursions . . . [which] becomes the setting of a single great comic figure.' However much the immortal sprite catches our imagination, this is not a summary of the construction of the plays nor of the way that construction is worked out. As Humphreys[12] points out, 'the historical themes are urged upon us with Shakespeare's utmost vigour'.

The truth is surely that Shakespeare is examining and setting before us, by means of the contrasts through which he so often works, the nature of power, its exercise, and its effects upon individual man. Thus Palmer,[13] though we may take a more or a less charitable view of Hal, concentrates our attention correctly on the use of the major figures in the plays:

> In the first and second parts of *Henry IV,* Shakespeare, in three major characters, contrasts the Prince's invincible priggery with just the qualities most fitted to set it off . . . Hotspur and Falstaff are alike incapable of any form of humbug . . . The third person to bring out the essential quality of the Prince is his father, Henry, the King.

The issues which the Prince has to resolve to become an effective king in this world of blood and iron are starkly set out in the two plays. Both the attractions and the delusions of the worlds of Hotspur and Falstaff are set before us; as the fortunes of each decline in turn, so Hal moves nearer to kingship. His use of the rejection of Falstaff at the end of Part 2 shows at once the public recognition of the way in which a monarch must act and the wanton cruelty in private relationships which marks the decline of our sympathy for the individual.

The King's opening speech shows him as cautiously conscious of political issues as we left him in *Richard II,* though Shakespeare skilfully suggests in the rhythms of the lines the passage of time and the strain of power exercised under constant challenge:

> So shaken as we are, so wan with care,
> Find we a time for frighted peace to pant,
> And breathe short winded accents of new broils
> To be commenc'd in stronds afar remote:
> No more the thirsty entrance of this soil
> Shall daub her lips with her own children's blood,
> No more shall trenching war channel her fields,
> Nor bruise her flow'rets with the armed hoofs
> Of hostile paces.

This strain of weariness has another purpose. It contrasts with the note of energy which is to become Hal's dominant note by the time of *Henry V,* and helps to explain why he chafes at this court of anxious and unremitting seriousness. When it is threatened and action is demanded he will respond; meanwhile his restless spirit will find outlets in whatever transient diversions are at hand. Gadshill may teach him how to secure the allegiance of all the good lads of Eastcheap; it also helps to explain his exultant confidence throughout *Henry V* as his prodigious desire to organise and indulge in physical movement finds almost continuous outlet.

Henry's political brain is as alert as ever and the proposed crusade is an obvious attempt to cement the uneasy peace: his physical decline is again evident as he dully acknowledges the collapse of the scheme:

> It seems then that the tidings of this broil
> Brake off our business for the Holy Land.

Despite his awareness of political situations, Henry is not acute about people. He has lived his adult life in political calculation; he now seems unable to judge men by the wider considerations which must be applied in more general estimations of character. The speech by which he arouses the audience's curiosity about Hotspur and Hal shows not only Shakespeare's developing powers of language but also Henry's over-simplified judgements of men by appearance:

> A son who is the theme of honour's tongue,
> Amongst a grove the very straightest plant,
> Who is sweet Fortune's minion and her pride;
> Whilst I by looking on the praise of him
> See riot and dishonour stain the brow
> Of my young Harry. O that it could be prov'd
> That some night-tripping fairy had exchang'd
> In cradle-clothes our children where they lay,
> And call'd mine Percy, his Plantagenet!
> Then would I have his Harry, and he mine.

The scenes which follow show not only that Hal has enough of his father. in him to make the paternal anxiety unnecessary but also that Hotspur, however secure his honour, would hardly sustain Henry's parental enthusiasm for very long as an heir apparent.

From this speech of Henry's we move to our first sight of Falstaff; within just over a hundred lines the three approaches to power and its responsibilities which dominate Part 1 are under way. Quiller-Couch[14] drew attention to Falstaff's role in the morality-structure of the play which he saw as 'the contention between Vice and Virtue for the soul of a Prince'. Dover Wilson[15] pointed out that 'Hal associates Falstaff in turn with the Devil of the miracle play, the Vice of the morality, and the Riot of the interlude, when he calls him "that villainous abominable misleader of Youth, that old white-bearded Satan", "that reverend Vice, that grey Iniquity, that father Ruffian, that Vanity in years", and "the tutor and feeder of my riots". "Riot", again is the word that comes most readily to King Henry's lips when speaking of his prodigal son's misconduct.' All this is scholarly and instructive, and probably justifies Dover Wilson's contention that an Elizabethan audience 'knew, from the beginning, that the reign of this marvellous Lord of Misrule must have an end, that Falstaff must be rejected by the Prodigal Prince, when the time for reformation came'.

Indeed, Hal, in his opening words, pins on Falstaff the familiar Vice-qualities of gluttony, intemperance, idleness and lechery:

> Thou art so fat-sitted with drinking of old sack, and unbuttoning thee after supper, and sleeping upon benches after noon, that thou hast forgotten to demand that truly which thou wouldst truly know. What a devil hast thou to do with the time of the day? Unless hours were cups of sack, and minutes capons, and clocks the tongues of bawds, and dials the signs of leaping-houses, and the blessed sun himself a fair hot wench in flame-coloured taffeta, I see no reason why thou shouldst be so superfluous to demand the time of the day.

Yet the view that the recognition of the morality play derivations in the structure will demonstrate to us how we should react to Falstaff is plainly absurd. As always, Shakespeare has taken whatever was convenient from his surroundings and made quite original use of it. His departure from the morality tradition is immediately evident in the exchanges of this scene. While Hal's waggery is skin deep and relies largely on invective, his opponent in the contest has a fertility of imaginative invention that immediately gives him an individual vitality quite outside the morality structure:

> O, thou hast damnable iteration, and art indeed able to corrupt a saint: thou has done much harm upon me, Hal, God forgive thee for it: before I knew thee, Hal, I knew nothing, and now am I, if a man should speak truly, little better than one of the wicked. I must give over this life, and I will give it over: by the Lord, and I do not, I am a villain, I'll be damned for never a king's son in Christendom.

Moreover, the Prince's much analysed soliloquy at the end of this scene shows the deficiency of the Vice against Virtue motivation thesis. There is no tension in this supposed struggle: Hal is aware from the start of what he is doing and will have no difficulty in dispensing with his supposed tempter whenever he pleases. As Tillyard[16] puts it: 'The Prince is aloof and Olympian from the start and never treats Falstaff any better than his dog, with whom he condescends once in a way to have a game. It is not the Prince who deceives, it is Falstaff who deceives himself by wishful thinking.' There is a complete absence of that tension within an individual which characterises the tragedies as Hal allies the calculation of his father with a greater degree of subtlety:

> I know you all, and will awhile uphold
> The unyok'd humour of your idleness.
> Yet herein will I imitate the sun,
> Who doth permit the base contagious clouds
> To smother up his beauty from the world,
> That, when he please again to be himself,
> Being wanted he may be more wonder'd at
> By breaking through the foul and ugly mists
> Of vapours that did seem to strangle him.

Henry has always been the opportunist who uses political occasions with great skill as they arise. Hal has all the coolness of his father and also a touch more imagination; he may in due course make his own occasions. Already perhaps it is Falstaff rather than this clear-sighted and unsentimental young Prince who is in danger. Danby[17] points to this passage as evidence of the changed ethics of the political world of *Henry IV*: 'The process ends in the Machiavel of goodness Prince Hal. Hal is no longer aware that society might be wicked. He espouses the aims and the means of the Society to hand, he equips himself to be good in accordance with the terms of the State he will ultimately govern.'

> I'll so offend, to make offence a skill,
> Redeeming time when men think least I will.

Technique is the thing, let the ends look after themselves.

In the next scene, the King's opening speech shows the old knowledge of the moment to assert himself, though the strain is also suggested:

> My blood hath been too cold and temperate,
> Unapt to stir at these indignities,
> And you have found me — for accordingly
> You tread upon my patience: but be sure

I will henceforth rather be myself,
Mighty, and to be fear'd, than my condition,
Which hath been smooth as oil, soft as young down,
And therefore lost that title of respect
Which the proud soul ne'er pays but to the proud.

The royal plural is absent but appears in his dismissal of Worcester, which recalls the decisive treatment of overweening barons in *Richard II*:

Worcester, get thee gone, for I do see
Danger and disobedience in thine eye:
O sir, your presence is too bold and peremptory,
And majesty might never yet endure
The moody frontier of a servant brow.
You have good leave to leave us; when we need
Your use and counsel we shall send for you.

Hotspur's first speech stamps his imprint firmly on the play. He projects private thoughts into public conduct as eagerly as the Richard he helped to unseat:

My liege, I did deny no prisoners,
But I remember, when the fight was done,
When I was dry with rage, and extreme toil,
Breathless and faint, leaning upon my sword,
Came there a certain lord, neat and trimly dress'd,
Fresh as a bridegroom, and his chin new reap'd
Show'd like a stubble-land at harvest-home.
He was perfumed like a milliner,
And 'twixt his finger and his thumb he held
A pouncet-box, which ever and anon
He gave his nose, and took't away again —
Who therewith angry, when it next came there,
Took it in snuff — and still he smil'd and talk'd:
And as the soldiers bore dead bodies by,
He call'd them untaught knaves, unmannerly,
To bring a slovenly unhandsome corse
Betwixt the wind and his nobility.
With many holiday and lady terms
He question'd me, amongst the rest demanded

My prisoners in your Majesty's behalf,
I then, all smarting with my wounds being cold,
To be so pester'd with a popinjay,
Out of my grief and my impatience
Answer'd neglectingly, I know not what,
He should, or he should not, for he made me mad
To see him shine so brisk, and smell so sweet,
And talk so like a waiting-gentlewoman
Of guns, and drums, and wounds, God save the mark!

When Blunt voices the general reaction of sympathy, it is Henry who cuts shrewdly through the emotion to the political situation with 'Why yet he doth deny his prisoners'.

In the face of this realism, Hotspur shows the same tendency to let what he wished were the case supplant reality as did Richard; his account of Mortimer's meeting with Glendower rings with medieval chivalry:

He never did fall off, my sovereign liege,
But by the chance of war: to prove that true
Needs no more but one tongue for all those wounds,
Those mouthed wounds, which valiantly he took,
When on the gentle Severn's sedgy bank,
In single opposition hand to hand,
He did confound the best part of an hour
In changing hardiment with great Glendower.
Three times they breath'd, and three times did they
    drink
Upon agreement of swift Severn's flood,
Who then affrighted with their bloody looks
Ran fearfully among the trembling reeds,
And hid his crisp head in the hollow bank,
Bloodstained with these valiant combatants.

Henry's cool dismissal of the whole episode is a warning of the political dangers of such lyrical indulgences:

Thou dost belie him, Percy, thou dost belie him,
He never did encounter with Glendower:
I tell thee, he durst as well have met the devil alone
As Owen Glendower for an enemy.

Art thou not asham'd? But sirrah, henceforth
Let me not hear you speak of Mortimer:
Send me your prisoners with the speediest means,
Or you shall hear in such a kind from me
As will displease you.

The King's exit is the signal for the outburst of emotional excitement which shows how ill-fitted is Hotspur's approach to the balance of power. He sees issues in the blacks and whites of youth rather than in the various shades of grey more commonly apparent in rulers. His father and uncle — his own commitment is conveniently ignored at this point — have conspired

To put down Richard, that sweet lovely rose,
And plant this thorn, this canker, Bolingbroke.

Hotspur shows himself to be in his own more virile way as egotistical as Richard before him; like Richard he makes no distinction between public and private thoughts, and an audience encourages him to exaggerate his private feelings into public stances:

By heaven, methinks it were an easy leap
To pluck bright honour from the pale-fac'd moon,
Or dive into the bottom of the deep,
Where fathom-line could never touch the ground,
And pluck up drowned honour by the locks,
So he that doth redeem her thence might wear
Without corrival all her dignities.

Amidst the careful plotting around him, his statecraft extends no further than this vague and fanciful pursuit of military glory. Although he affects to despise them where Richard frankly embraced them, words are as heady a draught to him as they were to Richard. His idea of teaching a starling to shout Mortimer's name is as bizarre as any of Richard's flights. More seriously, his self-satisfied despatch from his thoughts of the 'sword and buckler Prince of Wales' as 'poisoned with a pot of ale' shows an underestimation of a political opponent which that cautious assessor of men never makes, despite his later satirical lines about Hotspur. His account of the way Henry wooed him to his cause at Berkeley is winning and accurate but shows a naive ignorance of the way rebellions must proceed to win support:

Why, what a candy deal of courtesy
This fawning greyhound then did proffer me!
'Look when his infant fortune came to age'
And 'gentle Harry Percy', and 'kind cousin':
O, the devil take such cozeners!

Worcester is much more in touch with the minds of men who owe a political debt in a world which is increasingly favouring the survival of the fittest:

For, bear ourselves as even as we can,
The King will always think him in our debt,
And think we think ourselves unsatisfy'd,
Till he hath found a time to pay us home.

Hotspur, oblivious to advice he does not wish to hear, ends the scene on a note which shows how little he apprehends the issues in which he has involved himself with these dangerous elders of his:

O let the hours be short
Till fields, and blows, and groans applaud our sport.

He enters conspiracy with the political awareness with which public schoolboys entered the 1914–18 War.

The scene switches to Falstaff and the Gadshill business, the juxta-position that will become familiar during the play. Both Hotspur and Falstaff indulge what Shelley called the 'generous error' of living life by a vision of it; in both cases their vision of life takes over when they are on stage because it is the vivid and essential part of them. A vision of life, if pursued so relentlessly, must, almost by definition, collide with real life eventually, but visions are as important in showing the range and possibilities of mankind as the facts of history. If Hotspur sees a naked struggle for the spoils of rebellion in terms of a righteous crusade, Falstaff has a contempt for all such issues. He punctures the pompous protestations of aspirants to power so easily that he refuses to entertain seriously any notion of the responsibilities of office. There is no attempt by Shakespeare to disguise the squalor of his conduct, but the vigour and invention of his humour is such that while he is on stage we suspend moral judgement in admiration of his vision of the enjoyment of life. His explanation of why he continues to associate with Poins might well be our verdict on Falstaff himself:

I have forsworn his company hourly any time this two and twenty years, and yet I am bewitched with the rogue's company. If the rascal have not given me medicines to make me love him, I'll be hanged. It could not be else, I have drunk medicines.

As is to be the pattern throughout, he is more than Hal's equal in wit and has much the better of their exchanges. The Prince's final words give a vivid picture of Falstaff's distress but scant evidence of royal compassion:

> Falstaff sweats to death,
> And lards the lean earth as he walks along.
> Were't not for laughing I should pay him.

The beautifully written little scene between Hotspur and Lady Percy which follows shows Hotspur's attraction and affection, but also his immaturity. The exictement of war as sport is still with him; it is heady enough to make him thrust away even his delicious Kate:

> Love! I love thee not,
> I care not for thee, Kate; this is no world
> To play with mammets, and to tilt with lips;
> We must have bloody noses, and crack'd crowns.

From this cameo of Hotspur we move to perhaps the greatest of all the tavern scenes in which the richness of Falstaff's comic invention is lavishly displayed. As Walter Raleigh[18] put it: 'Falstaff is a comic Hamlet, stronger in practical resource, and hardly less rich in thought. He is in love with life, as Hamlet is out of love with it.' Men with this open and essentially personal reaction to life are always vulnerable in the political world with which Shakespeare surrounds them; the vulnerability of both Falstaff and Hotspur is made clear in these central scenes of the play.

The prince's laboured jest whereby he and Poins call the drawer from different rooms emphasises the paucity of his wit without Falstaff's stimulation. In contrast, the breadth and resource of Falstaff's humorous imagination lift the scene immediately on his entry. His exuberantly escalating fiction of the eleven buckram men he fought, his nimble extrication of himself from the corner into which the truth should confine him, his inverted caricature of his own way of life ('a plague of sighing and grief, it blows a man up like a bladder'), are part of that marvellously fertile enlargement of life which is his attraction to Hal as to us. The Henry who will lead his ragged cross-section of English man-hood to the famous victory at Agincourt has need of this experience; Falstaff's infinite capacity for enjoyment at his own as readily as at others' expense is a necessary text for anyone who wishes to move the hearts and minds of all men.

Hal as usual is aware of these issues:

> and when I am King of England I shall command all the good lads of Eastcheap . . . I am now of all humours that have showed themselves since the old days of goodman Adam.

There follows immediately his satire on Hotspur:

> I am not yet of Percy's mind, the Hotspur of the North, he that kills me some six or seven dozen of Scots at a breakfast, washes his hands, and says to his wife, 'Fie upon this quiet life, I want work'.

The placing of the passage emphasises Hal's contempt for Hotspur, as a man who has so signally failed to comprehend the catalogue of humanity and thus equip himself to rule.

In the parody of the King and Prince at court, Hal is driven to mere invective. Falstaff defends himself and the wider part of man for which he stands with equal facility as King and Prince. As Northrop Frye[19] puts it:

> Falstaff is a mock king, a lord of misrule, and his tavern is a Satur-nalia. Yet we are reminded of the original meaning of the saturnalia, as a rite intended to recall the golden age of Saturn. Falstaff's world is not a golden world, but as long as we remember it we cannot forget that the world of Henry V is an iron one.

Both worlds are set before us as Falstaff defends himself with conviction and unwonted dignity:

> But to say I know more harm in him than in myself were to say more than I know. That he is old, the more the pity, his white hairs do witness it, but that he is, saving your reverence, a whoremaster, that I utterly deny. If sack and sugar be a fault, God help the wicked! If to be old and merry be a sin, then many an old host that I know is damned: if to be fat be to be hated, then Pharaoh's lean kine are to be

loved. No, my good lord; banish Peto, banish Bardolph, banish Poins —
but for sweet Jack Falstaff, kind Jack Falstaff, true Jack Falstaff,
valiant Jack Falståff, and therefore more valiant, being as he is old
Jack Falstaff, banish not him thy Harry's company, banish not him
thy Harry's company: banish plump Jack and banish all the world.

Amidst the pandemonium which ends the exchanges as the Sheriff
hammers at the door, Hal's 'I do, I will' stills us as it does Falstaff, the
cold steel of its determination cutting through the banter and confusion.
For the time being, however, he will protect Falstaff against the
Sheriff, though those who make much of Hal's lie to save Falstaff —
'The man I do assure you is not here' — ignore the fact that the truth
would reveal his own part in the escapade as well as Falstaff's.

The following scene shows Hotspur as attractive and as vulnerable as
Falstaff in his different sphere. His crossing of Glendower is always
immensely effective on stage. It springs from the forthright attitude to
pretentious posturing which we should all like to adopt, which explains
Hotspur's perennial attraction. It is also a sign of hopeless political
immaturity, which Mortimer and Worcester immediately remark:
without the Welsh wizard and his army the conspirators have little
chance of success.

By the time of this middle section of the play, the macrocosm of the
state and the microcosm of individual man are alike in confusion, and
anarchy seems imminent. The issues in relation to the individuals
involved are, however, becoming clearer, and the lines of the eventual
resolution have already been laid. Henry, ageing and anxious, is as
shrewd as ever, but the driving physical energy which carried him to
power is in decline. Perhaps because of the strait-jacket in which he has
for so long constrained his individual feelings, he is now proving as King
less adept at shaping circumstances to his purpose than he was during
his rise to power at shaping his own attitudes and conduct to emerging
circumstances.

Hotspur has already shown himself an engaging personality but no
ruler. He is malleable in the hands of unscrupulous men like Worcester
and Northumberland, and too prone to substitute rhetoric for policy to
be a reliable leader. Above all, he is too little aware of the distinctions
which may be necessary between private feelings and public avowals
to succeed in the world in which he is operating. He is always intensely
conscious of the image he is presenting, but his anxiety is to present
his private spirit in all the bright aura he feels around it rather than to
shape that image to what is required by the great events around him.

Hal is at this point an enigma. His father and Hotspur have spoken of him in the most disparaging terms and we have seen him so far only in the dissolute company which his father so abhors. It is beguiling company because of the Promethean comic figure who dominates it, but Hal appears to be neglecting his place at court whilst a power vacuum develops. Yet we have heard a clear enunciation of a strain of cold calculation at the beginning of the play which marks him as his father's son; moreover he has just declared anew his intention to reject Falstaff, when that Lord of Misrule was at his most attractive. Clearly if he has the energy to go with this cool and ruthless brain he may yet emerge as a successful man of action and the resolution of the chaos in the state. The demonstration of this energy will drive forward the second half of this play and most of Part 2. In full force and with the authority and trappings of majesty, it will be the subject of prolonged celebration in *Henry V.*

There now follows the first private scene in which Henry has been shown in two plays in which he has been almost wholly concerned with his public effects. Even here, his language springs to greatest life and flexibility as he describes to his son how aspirants to power should bear themselves in public. There is almost an affectionate nostalgia in his account of what was the nearest medieval equivalent of a presidential election campaign:

By being seldom seen, I could not stir
But like a comet I was wonder'd at,
That men would tell their children, 'This is he!'
Others would say, 'Where, which is Bolingbroke?'
And then I stole all courtesy from heaven,
And dress'd myself in such humility
That I did pluck allegiance from men's hearts,
Loud shouts and salutations from their mouths,
Even in the presence of the crowned King.
Thus did I keep my person fresh and new,
My presence, like a robe pontifical,
Ne'er seen but wonder'd at, and so my state,
Seldom, but sumptuous, show'd like a feast,
And won by rareness such solemnity.

The development of Shakespeare's style into the mature instrument adaptable for his every purpose is clearly apparent in this passage; as Henry's excitement is kindled by his theme, image is heaped upon image in quick succession and rhythms quicken despite the relentless logic of the syntax. The force of this speech shows us Henry at his frankest; in private with his son he reveals how carefully his effects were planned, a factor which he could never reveal publicly and one of which only Richard himself was aware at the time. There is a paradox of course: Henry is most alive and moved in private when speaking of his public effects and his careful creation of a public image. He has acquired the art of success in public situations at the expense of effectiveness in more private and intimate relationships. Here he is so rapt with the recollection of how cleverly he secured popular support that when Hal, genuinely moved, interrupts with the simple directness with which Shakespeare almost invariably denotes this reaction, he scarcely hears him:

*Prince*:   I shall hereafter, my thrice gracious lord,
            Be more myself.
*King*:                  For all the world
            As thou art to this hour was Richard then
            When I from France set foot at Ravenspurgh,
            And even as I was then is Percy now.

There is an irony in that Henry fails to realise how much of himself there is in Hal. His opening metaphor to his son in the passage quoted above,

By being seldom seen, I could not stir
But like a comet I was wondered at

and his later references to 'sun-like majesty' which dazzles most when it shines seldom are echoes of Hal's thoughts and language in his Act I soliloquy.

So little does Henry know his son, and so secretive is that son, that he has no idea how closely their political approaches tally. Despite his now habitual political awareness, Henry is so little at home in assessing private relationships that he envisages the spectre of his son fighting against him under Percy's pay. Curiously, Hal makes no attempt to reassure his father by expounding his own political philosophy, which the latter would immediately understand. Throughout his meteoric career, Hal admits to no one but himself what his innermost thoughts are. His private relaxation is not with any of his obvious intimates or with his family but with the tavern companions who can be kept at a distance and discarded when it suits him. Thus, in refuting his father's charges, he is utterly convincing and clearly stirred, but his refutation is curiously distanced: it has the effectiveness of a more public speech as well as the familiar calculation of how Hotspur's reputation might be turned to advantage:

> Do not think so, you shall not find it so;
> And God forgive them that so much have sway'd
> Your majesty's good thoughts away from me!
> I will redeem all this on Percy's head,
> And in the closing of some glorious day
> Be bold to tell you that I am your son,
> When I will wear a garment all of blood,
> And stain my favours in a bloody mask,
> Which, wash'd away, shall scour my shame with it;
> And that shall be the day, whene'er it lights,
> That this same child of honour and renown,
> This gallant Hotspur, this all-praised knight,
> And your unthought-of Harry chance to meet.
> For every honour sitting on his helm,
> Would they were multitudes, and on my head
> My shames redoubled! For the time will come
> That I shall make this northern youth exchange
> His glorious deed for my indignities.
> Percy is but my factor, good my lord,
> To engross up glorious deeds on my behalf.

From the urgent military action with which this scene closes, there is an immediate move of contrast to the indolent but beguiling Falstaff, contemplating himself and pretending a reform which, unlike the Prince's reform we have just seen, will be stillborn:

> Bardolph, am I not fallen away vilely since this last action? Do I not bate? Do I not dwindle? Why, my skin hangs about me like an old lady's loose gown. I am withered like an old apple-john. Well, I'll repent, and that suddenly, while I am in some liking; I shall be out of heart shortly, and then I shall have no strength to repent.

Though the scene may have its origins in the morality Vice, Misleader of Youth, this is no caricature. Moral stances are undermined by the nimbleness of Falstaff's wit in his villainy, the treasure-house of his imagination as he contemplates Bardolph's face, his turning of the tables in argument upon Hal. Eventually we are almost prepared to accept his argument: 'Thou see'st I have more flesh than another man, and therefore more frailty'.

Bradley,[20] analysing Falstaff's attractions, pointed out that he is no sot and that we never see him for an instant with his brain dulled by sack; this freedom from slavery to drink makes his enjoyment contagious and prevents our sympathy with it from being disturbed. He performs 'not with the discontent of a cynic but with the gaiety of a boy'. Nevertheless, his parody of the Prince's rallying couplet as he goes off to the serious business of war shows that he does not recognise the moment for a change of mood; his failure to recognise such moments will eventually lead to his downfall:

*Prince*: The land is burning, Percy stands on high,
And either we or they must lower lie.
*Fal.*: Rare words! Brave world! Hostess, my breakfast, come!
O, I could wish this tavern were my drum.

There is another interpretation of this interweaving of comic commentary and serious events which grows ever closer as the play proceeds. This is put at its most extreme by L. C. Knights[21] who, noting how Henry manipulates the symbols of majesty with a calculating concern for ulterior results, concludes that the comedy should be taken as a devastating satire on war and on government. The audience, he writes, should feel a jeering response when Henry declares sonorously after Shrewsbury 'Thus ever did rebellion find rebuke.' This approach would surely have been impossible for the Elizabethans, who would have been more in sympathy with C. L. Barber's[22] almost opposite view 'that the dynamic relation of comedy and serious action is saturnalian rather than satiric, that the misrule works, through the whole dramatic rhythm, to consolidate rule'.

Shakespeare's aim is not to moralise. There are searing insights on power and its exercise by individuals, some of which are manifested through satire and ironic juxtapositions. But what he does is to set before us political situations in which people move, to investigate the reasons why they are successful or unsuccessful and the interaction of these processes with individual temperaments. He does not direct us to adopt particular attitudes, which may depend as much on our own temperaments as on what he portrays.[23]

The superbly efficient alternation of comic and serious plot continues

with Worcester's reception of Northumberland's sickness, which shows
the assessment of reality in the face of Hotspur's desperate optimism:

> But yet I would your father had been here:
> The quality and hair of our attempt
> Brooks no division; it will be thought,
> By some that know not why he is away,
> That wisdom, loyalty, and mere dislike
> Of our proceedings kept the Earl from hence.

Hotspur shows his now familiar determination to frame unpleasant facts
in the way he wishes to see them:

> I rather of his absence make this use:
> It lends a lustre and more great opinion,
> A larger dare to our great enterprise,
> Than if the Earl were here.

Vernon's description of the Prince is the first authentic glimpse of
the effulgent leader-by-example of Agincourt:

> I saw young Harry with his beaver on,
> His cuisses on his thighs, gallantly arm'd,
> Rise from the ground like feather'd Mercury,
> And vaulted with such ease into his seat
> As if an angel dropp'd down from the clouds
> To turn and wind a fiery Pegasus,
> And witch the world with noble horsemanship.

Hotspur's reaction is as out of touch with real events as was Richard's
at Berkeley Castle, though his escapism is not through mystical melancholia but through the bloodlust of war:

> No more, no more! Worse than the sun in March,
> This praise doth nourish agues. Let them come!
> They come like sacrifices in their trim,
> And to the fire-ey'd maid of smoky war
> All hot and bleeding will we offer them:
> The mailed Mars shall on his altar sit
> Up to the ears in blood.

The intricate reticulation of connections among the main characters of the play is now almost complete: A. R. Humphreys gives a detailed textual account of this network[24] and points out how Hal is determined to live in the real world whilst Hotspur and Falstaff live their fantasies. Both are dangerously attractive and Shakespeare confuses the issue, deliberately and gloriously, by making their attractions seem worth more than all that calculation can offer. Yet neither can see things in proportion: Falstaff aims no further than sensuality and Hotspur no further than battle honours.

Now Falstaff's ragged army and damnable misuse of the King's press are set between the two scenes of Hotspur's misplaced optimism, and not merely for contrast. Both attitudes to great events are inadequate. Hotspur's assessment of the odds is forced to fit the needs of his private personality. Falstaff's would no doubt be more dispassionate and more accurate, but he fails to see the need for any such assessment, being content to take what pickings he can wherever he finds himself.

Hotspur's assessment of Henry when Blunt comes as messenger again demonstrates the evolution of Shakespeare's mastery of blank verse. Despite his contempt for 'mincing poetry' Hotspur gives us a vivid condensed picture in sinewy verse:

The King is kind, and well we know the King
Knows at what time to promise, when to pay:
My father, and my uncle, and myself
Did give him that same royalty he wears,
And when he was not six and twenty strong,
Sick in the world's regard, wretched and low,
A poor unminded outlaw sneaking home,
My father gave him welcome to the shore:
And when he heard him swear and vow to God
He came but to be Duke of Lancaster,
To sue his livery, and beg his peace
With tears of innocency, and terms of zeal,
My father, in kind heart and pity mov'd,
Swore him assistance, and perform'd it too.

The full speech shows how ill-fitted Hotspur still is at this last stage for political dealings: he artlessly attributes to his relatives and friends a warmth and spontaneity of response that is his own.

In contrast to Hotspur's over-exposure of his own personality in rhetoric, the Prince's gesture at the beginning of Act V in paying full tribute to his rival and offering to settle the issue by single combat is effective in restoring him further in the eyes of those around him:

> Tell your nephew,
> The Prince of Wales doth join with all the world
> In praise of Henry Percy: by my hopes,
> This present enterprise set off his head,
> I do not think a braver gentleman,
> More active-valiant or more valiant-young,
> More daring or more bold, is now alive
> To grace this latter age with noble deeds.
> For my part, I may speak it to my shame,
> I have a truant been to chivalry,
> And so I hear he doth account me too;
> Yet this before my father's majesty —
> I am content that he shall take the odds
> Of his great name and estimation,
> And will, to save the blood on either side,
> Try fortune with him in a single fight.

When we consider the policy the Prince outlined for himself in his early soliloquy and his more recent exchange with his father, we may be conscious of a man delaying this gesture until the moment of maximum effect. If it is coldly calculated, it argues a political awareness and capacity that are as much instinctive and hereditary as the product of experience. Hal has a capacity to move men with words which his father has never had, despite his political acuity; he uses it with a sense of the supreme moment for its application which is as sure and confident as his father's.

Falstaff's catechism on honour is set within twenty-five lines of Hal's shining challenge, an ironic commentary on the fine poses being struck all around it. The ethical situation is by now highly confused: a usurper sits on an uncertain throne, having left the obvious heir to Richard's crown deliberately unransomed in Wales. The rebels, despite their newly declared sense of Richard's wrongs, are the very men who helped Bolingbroke to the throne and have now deserted him in the hope of better pickings. All the talk of honour on both sides has thus a hollow ring, and Hotspur and Hal are both intent upon their personal reputations. Falstaff's analysis of this elusive concept of honour that is so freely invoked around him is totally in character; within the larger context of the Henry plays it is also a cool denunciation of the sham with which men cloak greed with the loftiest and vaguest of abstracts. Falstaff's argument arriving at the conclusion that 'Honour is a mere scutcheon' is skilfully placed to make its maximum effect in the tapestry of the tetralogy. As if to echo Falstaff's devastating logic, Shakespeare places immediately after it the most despicable action of the play, Worcester's failure to disclose to Hotspur the King's offer of grace. The wariness of a politician reluctant to rest his security on the good faith of another dominates Worcester's thinking:

It is not possible, it cannot be,
The King should keep his word in loving us;
He will suspect us still, and find a time
To punish this offence in other faults . . .
Look how we can, or sad or merrily,
Interpretation will misquote our looks,
And we shall feed like oxen at a stall,
The better cherish'd still the nearer death.

There remains only the field of Shrewsbury, on which the major threads of the play are finally brought together. Once again, 'Shakespeare makes brilliant use of the long-standing tradition of comic accompaniment and counterstatement by the clown.'[25] Falstaff may well have led his troops where the battle was hottest for base reasons, as the Arden editor suggests,[26] but it seems unfair to gainsay his courage, for he has certainly led them, not sent them. His conduct here is consistent with Poins' opinion before Gadshill that he would fight no longer than he saw reason and the stage direction indicating that he struck a blow or two there and fled only when clearly outnumbered. Falstaff stands by his own creed that discretion is the better part of valour, but there is no reason to suppose that he shirks a fight once his reason is convinced, as his speech at the end of the scene confirms:

Well, if Percy be alive, I'll pierce him. If he do come
in my way, so: if he do not, if I come in his willingly,
let him make a carbonado of me. I like not such
grinning honour as Sir Walter hath. Give me life,
which if I can save, so: if not, honour comes unlooked
for, and there's an end.

The most succinct summary of Falstaff's attitude is that of Palmer:[27] 'To the horrors and hazards of war he brings the chill verdict of common sense and the defensive mechanism of humour. His dreadful levity is that of the hardened warrior.'

When Hal rescues his father from Douglas, the King's words indicate how little he has trusted his son's fine words until they were confirmed by deeds:

> Stay and breathe a while:
> Thou hast redeem'd thy lost opinion,
> And show'd thou mak'st some tender of my life,
> In this fair rescue thou has brought to me.

His private personality and capacity for day-to-day intimate relationships have now been totally subsumed into his public role. He places so little value upon assurances of faith and love that his disregard of them is now automatic; his bleak words here show surprise that his eldest son should after all have some love for him.

If Henry's personal responses are almost entirely withered away, his son can still be moved, though his public bearing is by now so calculated that it is only when entirely alone that he will acknowledge it in words. Standing over the dead Hotspur, he feels generosity towards a gallant fallen opponent, a need to moralise on 'ill-weav'd ambition' in his declamatory strain, and a wry recognition that were Hotspur 'sensible of courtesy' he would not offer it. When he turns to the apparently dead Falstaff, his ambivalence is not the considered public caution which we now expect from son as from father, but the genuinely mixed emotion of one who will miss Falstaff and his world but has long been determined to set them aside:

> What, old acquaintance, could not all this flesh
> Keep in a little life? Poor Jack, farewell!
> I could have better spar'd a better man:
> O, I should have a heavy miss of thee
> If I were much in love with vanity:
> Death hath not struck so fat a deer today,
> Though many dearer, in this bloody fray.

The self-conscious disclaimer 'If I were much in love with vanity' and the callous jest of the last two lines show the blunted sensibility to the normal affections of friendship which will characterise the more direct rejection at the end of Part 2.

## Henry IV, Part 2

Most commentators have noted the generally darker tone of the second part of *Henry IV*. This derives almost entirely from the quelling of those wider aspects of human potential which were apparent in *Richard II* and in Part 1. Hotspur's bright optimism and spontaneous reactions were crushed at Shrewsbury and there is no replacement for him in the rebel camp in this play. The emerging Hal is almost entirely separated from that other representative of more universal enjoyments, Falstaff: they are seen together only once before the rejection. Moreover, as the Prince grows more grave as he feels the approach of his great office, Falstaff, though his humour and resource never flag, shows more of his seamy side.

This further lowering of tone is marked from the outset; Rumour's prologue creates the atmosphere of anarchy, suspicion and desperate pragmatism which is to mark the play. Ethics will be almost entirely absent, except as they are invoked to provide a political platform for courses of action determined by less elevated considerations.

The impression is reinforced in the first scene. With the news of the death of Hotspur, Northumberland casts aside his crafty sickness; he spends no time in mourning a son whose quality he never understood:

> For this I shall have time enough to mourn.
> In poison there is physic; and these news,
> Having been well, that would have made me sick,
> Being sick, have in some measure made me well.

Morton frankly admits the dressing of the rebels' squalid cause in high thoughts which none of them now treat seriously; even Richard is now reduced to a propaganda emblem:

> But now the bishop
> Turns insurrection to religion:
> Suppos'd sincere and holy in his thoughts,
> He's follow'd both with body and with mind,
> And doth enlarge his rising with the blood
> Of fair King Richard, scrap'd from Pomfret stones;
> Derives from heaven his quarrel and his cause.

The familiar alternation of serious and comic strains is taken up with the entry of Falstaff, whose humour soon shows a darker and more desperate strain. He is re-introduced with the imagery of disease which is to be so predominant in Part 2:

*Falstaff*: Sirrah, you giant, what says the doctor to my water?

*Page*:     He said sir, the water itself was a good healthy water; but, for the party that owed it, he might have more diseases than he knew for.

Falstaff rallies immediately with one of his best defences of himself and his world:

Men of all sorts take a pride to gird at me; the brain of this foolish-compounded clay, man, is not able to invent anything that tends to laughter, more than I invent or is invented on me: I am not only witty in myself, but the cause that wit is in other men.

Yet the format of the scene reminds us that the quality and range of his wit will struggle ever harder against the tone of events around him in this play. The Lord Chief Justice, for instance, now gives us a vivid picture of Falstaff's physical decline:

Do you set down your name in the scroll of youth, that are written down old with all the characters of age? Have you not a moist eye, a dry hand, a yellow cheek, a white beard, a decreasing leg, an increasing belly? Is not your voice broken, your wind short, your chin double, your wit single, and every part about you blasted with antiquity, and will you yet call yourself young? Fie, fie, fie, Sir John!

Falstaff's defence is as spirited, ingenious and outrageous as ever:

My lord, I was born about three of the clock in the afternoon, with a white head, and something a round belly. For my voice, I have lost it with hollaing, and singing of anthems. To approve my youth further, I will not: the truth is, I am only old in judgment and understanding; and he that will caper with me for a thousand marks, let him lend me the money, and have at him!

But we feel that he cannot hold out for ever against a world whose temper has moved so much against him, however spiritedly he reverses the Lord Chief Justice's pious hope into 'God send the companion a better Prince!' The scene closes with the disease symbol on which it began: Falstaff, although he is fighting a battle for the world of good fellowship and enjoyment against the world of increasingly tawdry political stances which will dominate this play, is himself in decay and becoming more desperate:

A pox of this gout! or, a gout of this pox! for the one or the other plays the rogue with my great toe. 'Tis no matter if I do halt; I have the wars for my colour, and my pension shall seem the more reasonable. A good wit will make use of anything; I will turn diseases to commodity.

The Archbishop of York's lines in the next scene on the way the populace now think of Richard could hardly contrast more starkly with the tone of Hotspur's invocation of that hallowed name at the same stage of Part 1:

So, so, thou common dog, didst thou disgorge
Thy glutton bosom of the royal Richard,
And now thou wouldst eat thy dead vomit up,
And howl'st to find it.

Hotspur, like Falstaff, had the seeds of political destruction within him. Yet if we ever think that Shakespeare's only or even primary purpose was to show this, we need only look in this play at numerous passages such as the above one to remind us of the worth in the total life of mankind of Hotspur's values and aspirations. This was the man whose 'great imagination' Lord Bardolph has just described as 'proper to madmen'.

At the opening of Act II, Falstaff is shown in an unamiable light immediately before our first sight of the Prince in this play. Hal on his entry is uninspired and unattractive, in harmony with the generally pessimistic note so far prevailing. As he moves towards the highest office, he narrows the range of his private emotions as his father did before him. His first lines show him much aware of his public image:

*Prince*:  Before God, I am exceeding weary.
*Poins*:  Is it come to that? I had thought weariness durst not have attached one of so high blood.
*Prince*:  Faith, it does me, though it discolours the complexion of my greatness to acknowledge it. Doth it now show vilely in me to desire small beer?

He feels the need to offer gratuitous passing insult to Poins even as he unburdens himself, addressing him as 'one it pleases me, for fault of a better, to call my friend', and generally appears at his least attractive in this low-life scene without Falstaff.

The next scene gives us a brief reminder through the loving eyes of Lady Percy of the qualities that are so conspicuously undervalued as civil war gnaws at the vitals of the land. In a speech which foreshadows Ophelia's in a different kind of agony, she takes us like Ophelia outside the prevailing themes of the play into a brighter and more optimistic world:

> and by his light
> Did all the chivalry of England move
> To do brave acts: he was indeed the glass
> Wherein the noble youth did dress themselves:
> He had no legs that practis'd not his gait;
> And speaking thick, which nature made his blemish,
> Became the accents of the valiant;
> For those that could speak low and tardily,
> Would turn their own perfection to abuse,
> To seem like him: so that, in speech, in gait,
> In diet, in affections of delight,
> In military rules, humours of blood,
> He was the mark and glass, copy and book,
> That fashion'd others.

It is a brief, bitter-sweet moment; the prevailing tone is restored by the end of the scene as the treacherous and ageing Northumberland resolves upon further cowardly retreat:

> Fain would I go to meet the archbishop,
> But many thousand reasons hold me back.
> I will resolve for Scotland: there am I,
> Till time and vantage crave my company.

We move appropriately from the squalid manoeuvres of the political world to Falstaff, that 'living criticism of the world of policy'.[28] John Masefield considered this 'the finest tavern-scene ever written'.[29] Amidst the mixture of low comedy, horseplay and high wit, there are searing examples of Shakespeare's universal touch, all of which remind us of how the events and atmosphere outside the tavern are moving ever closer to its joys. Doll Tearsheet puts an abrupt end to her opening exchanges with Falstaff as this suddenly strikes her:

> Come, I'll be friends with thee, Jack: thou art going to the wars; and whether I shall ever see thee again or no, there is nobody cares.

After he has banished the drunken bragadoccio Pistol, she looks at him with even more affection and foreboding, in words which foreshadow the Prince's brutal 'the grave doth gape for thee' as he rejects Falstaff at the end of the play. With a superbly chilling stroke, Shakespeare brings in the agent of the rejection Falstaff refuses to consider, to stand silent and observing behind him at this moment:

> Thou whoreson little tidy Bartholomew boar-pig, when wilt thou leave fighting o'days, and foining o'nights, and begin to patch up thine old body for heaven?
> (*Enter behind the Prince and Poins, disguised like Drawers.*)

*Falstaff*: Peace, good Doll! do not speak like a death's head: do not bid me remember mine end.

This moment, like the Prince's 'I do. I will' in his mock-banishment of Falstaff in Part 1, intrudes a profound shaft of darkness at the height of the humorous development of the scene. We are reminded that in an increasingly insecure world light and gaiety are ever more threatened.

Though Falstaff extricates himself as nimbly as ever from the situation when the Prince and Poins reveal themselves, his wit is rudely interrupted by the wars. The Prince's final words to Falstaff have none of the warmth of his words on the battlefield of Shrewsbury at the end of Part 1. He moves immediately and automatically to his public role:

> By heaven, Poins, I feel me much to blame,
> So idly to profane the precious time,
> When tempest of commotion, like the south,
> Borne with black vapour, doth begin to melt
> And drop upon our bare unarmed heads.
> Give me my sword and cloak. Falstaff, good night.

No scene supports more graphically Palmer's[30] view that 'Falstaff is a point of contrast between two worlds. In him the larger life of humanity, at its most genial and exuberant, is brought into touch with the narrow life of the public person at its most calculating and unscrupulous.' That Falstaff himself should never suspect that he will be rejected shows how wide and deep is the gulf between spontaneous human nature and political conduct.

Henry's soliloquy at the beginning of Act III is one of the very few private moments permitted to him in two plays. His complete

subordination of his private temperament into the public role of King
has meant that there is little private consolation for him. That greatest
of Shakespearian balms, sleep, is denied to him; he can convince us
easily enough of his concluding sentiment that 'Uneasy lies the head
that wears a crown.' However, his private mind is too limited, his
personality too narrow, for him to move us as Macbeth, for instance,
is to move us when he is upon a similar mental rack. Henry moves more
easily in his public role, where his private puzzlements are necessarily
set aside; he is as cautious as ever in protesting that he had originally no
designs upon the crown:

> Though then, God knows, I had no such intent,
> But that necessity so bow'd the state
> That I and greatness were compelled to kiss.

After the sick King and his troubled court, the scene of Falstaff's
recruiting his company in Gloucestershire provides glorious comic relief
and a breath of the outdoors. It has another purpose, deriving from its
insertion between the anxious preparations of the careworn King and
the two scenes in Act IV in which the rebels are undone by the most
cynical piece of treachery perpetrated in the tetralogy. Falstaff's
undisguised comic zest in his manipulation of the war machinery to his
own advantage provides an ironic comment on the military aspirations
of the serious world, which are now being exposed in their full squalor.

In the first of these scenes, the Archbishop of York, in the characteristic imagery of the play, expresses the plight of the country more clearly
than he can construct a high-minded cause:

> We are all diseas'd;
> And, with our surfeiting and wanton hours
> Have brought ourselves into a burning fever,
> And we must bleed for it: of which disease
> Our late king, Richard, being infected, died.

John of Lancaster has the family penchant for letting agents conduct
his dirtiest work. Westmoreland is sent to set up the false parley; when
Mowbray suspects that the offer 'proceeds from policy, not love' he is
assured that it 'comes from mercy'.

Lancaster's long moralising address to the Archbishop which opens
the following scene is the rankest hypocrisy, concerned only with the
basest of the politician's effects, creating an impression which is exactly

the opposite of his real intentions so as to bemuse the opposition. It recalls Hotspur's contrasting of 'Richard, that sweet lovely rose' with the 'vile politician, Bolingbroke' and the qualities which so irked him in Lancaster's father. There is no attempt at ambivalence: straightforward deceit will serve the purpose:

> My lord, these griefs shall be with speed redress'd;
> Upon my soul, they shall. If this may please you,
> Discharge your powers unto their several counties,
> As we will ours: and here between the armies
> Let's drink together friendly and embrace,
> That all their eyes may bear those tokens home
> Of our restored love and amity.

When he is assured that the rebel army is dispersed, Westmoreland moves forward to perform his sinister business as decisively and brutally as Northumberland arresting the Bishop of Carlisle at the same stage in Part 1:

> I do arrest thee, traitor, of high treason:
> And you, lord archbishop, and you, Lord Mowbray,
> Of capital treason I attach you both;

Lancaster concludes the proceedings with couplets whose rhyme emphasises their humbug:

> Most shallowly did you these arms commence,
> Fondly brought here and foolishly sent hence.
> Strike up our drums! pursue the scatter'd stray:
> God, and not we, hath safely fought to-day.
> Some guard these traitors to the block of death;
> Treason's true bed, and yielder up of breath.

Clearly there is less and less room for Falstaff in such a world. His musings after he has failed to amuse cold young Lancaster are an argument not just for drink but for the enjoyment of life and good fellowship in which he has so continuously indulged; his argument for the balanced personality achieved by various kinds of experience is as convincing as his demolition of the chivalric myth of honour at the same stage of Part 1:

> Good faith, this same young sober-blooded boy doth not love me;
> nor a man cannot make him laugh; but that's no marvel, he drinks
> no wine . . . Hereof comes it that Prince Harry is valiant; for the cold
> blood he did naturally inherit of his father, he hath, like lean, sterile,
> and bare land, manured, husbanded, and tilled, with excellent en-
> deavour of drinking good and good store of fertile sherris, that he is
> become very hot and valiant. If I had a thousand sons, the first
> human principle I would teach them should be, to forswear thin
> potations and to addict themselves to sack.

Falstaff ignores the fact that his Prince is cool and ruthless enough to
discard him after savouring and using the kind of experience he can
offer simply because such calculation is totally outside his own conceptions of conduct, for all his lack of scruple.

Warwick, being of that world in which the Prince moves, can summarise his conduct more accurately than the increasingly vulnerable
Falstaff:

> The prince but studies his companions
> Like a strange tongue, wherein, to gain the language,
> 'Tis needful that the most immodest word
> Be look'd upon, and learn'd; which once attain'd,
> Your highness knows, comes to no further use
> But to be known and hated. So, like gross terms,
> The prince will in the perfectness of time
> Cast off his followers.

'Studies his companions' is an accurate description of the clinical
approach to the Eastcheap scenes which Hal has employed. J. H. Walter[31]
claims that the above passage is a 'defence of the Prince's essential
integrity'. This can be an integrity only in terms of the pragmatic
political world of which he is both the product and the proponent;
there is no integrity in his treatment of his tavern companions.

There is more evidence of this in the scene which follows. The
Prince, supposing that his dying father is indeed dead, is, even in this
most private of moments, more excited by the sight of the crown
upon his pillow than by the grief which would in other men override
at this moment all other considerations:

> My due from thee is this imperial crown,
> Which, as immediate from thy place and blood,

Derives itself to me. Lo! here it sits,
            *(Putting it on his head)*
Which heaven shall guard; and put the world's whole
   strength
Into one giant arm, it shall not force
This lineal honour from me.

Hal has prepared himself with such thorough calculation for his public role that his individual feelings, by the time of this supreme emotional moment, have been so strongly subdued that they scarcely trouble him as he practises the public demeanour he will assume. It is a moment which has been less closely examined than the rejection of Falstaff: in its own way it is just as chilling.

The incident is rather clumsily contrived so that the scene from Part 1 in which father and son confront each other may be almost directly repeated, but Shakespeare characteristically makes virtue of necessity to show us the preoccupation of the Prince with the great office now at hand. As he convinces the King of his good faith, his choice of the supreme way to demonstrate his allegiance is significant:

        if I do feign,
O! let me in my present wildness die
And never live to show the incredulous world
The noble change that I have purposed.

Searching for the thing nearest to his heart, he chooses the plan which he has cherished since the beginning of Part 1 to play the reformed reprobate: the choice argues that the heart is a cold and ruthless one. Hal's protestations of unwillingness to receive the crown are out of tune with the excitement and exaltation of the response quoted above:

But if it did infect my blood with joy,
Or swell my thoughts to any strain of pride;
If any rebel or vain spirit of mine
Did with the least affection of a welcome
Give entertainment to the might of it,
Let God for ever keep it from my head.

He shows his usual trick of putting the best complexion for himself on an action.

The King's final words as he is borne away to die in the Jerusalem chamber are on the usurpation which has never ceased to trouble him. His son's dismissal of the thought is as illogical as it is confident and steadfast: possession is now the whole of the law in public life:

> How I came by the crown, O God, forgive!
> And grant it may with thee in true peace live.
> *Prince*:  My gracious liege,
> You won it, wore it, kept it, gave it me;
> Then plain and right must my possession be:
> Which I with more than with a common pain
> 'Gainst all the world will rightfully maintain.

Again the couplets, unusual in the Henry plays, may mark the shallowness of the intellectual argument.

It has been said that the Henry plays end at this point and that Act V is consecrated to the downfall of Falstaff: if we view the design of the plays as that of the 'Fortunes of Falstaff' this is logical. Certainly this act reads like an extended prologue to *Henry V,* and the epilogue shows that this may have been in Shakespeare's thoughts. Yet, if we take Hal's ideas and conduct to be the central theme of the two *Henry IV* plays, this act may be seen as a culmination: it is the one in which Hal makes public the image he has so long prepared in private.

He uses the grief of children for a dead father as his first device in unfolding his reformation. The speech is too elaborately constructed for us to see Hal genuinely riven by grief, and the image of clothing which he uses is to become a familiar Shakespearian indication of the disguise of true feeling:

> Yet be sad, good brothers,
> For, to speak truth, it very well becomes you:
> Sorrow so royally in you appears
> That I will deeply put the fashion on
> And wear it in my heart. Why then, be sad;
> But entertain no more of it, good brothers,
> Than a joint burden laid upon us all.
> For me, by heaven, I bid you be assur'd,
> I'll be your father and your brother too;
> Let me but bear your love, I'll bear your cares:
> Yet weep that Harry's dead, and so will I;
> But Harry lives that shall convert those tears
> By number into hours of happiness.

The gracious treatment of the Lord Chief Justice is then played out at indulgent length, as a prologue to the new King's more general message:

> The tide of blood in me
> Hath proudly flow'd in vanity till now:
> Now doth it turn and ebb back to the sea,
> Where it shall mingle with the state of floods
> And flow henceforth in formal majesty.

Whatever our reactions to the new monarch, the next scene shows why Falstaff must be rejected. His lack of all discrimination and justice in his pursuit of enjoyment would be fatal to a ruler. The kind of reward to favourites he promises is the same want of policy which made Richard II so unpopular and thus so vulnerable. The mention of the Lord Chief Justice is introduced to make a deliberate contrast with Hal's statesmanlike gesture which has preceded it:

> Let us take any man's horses: the laws of England are at my commandment. Happy are they which have been my friends, and woe unto my Lord Chief Justice!

There is a contrast also in the reactions to Hal's accession: Hal falls easily into the stance he has carefully rehearsed for two plays, whereas Falstaff is all immediate and unthinking excitement.

In the last scene of the play, Falstaff is deliberately shown at his most attractive before the rejection:

> Come here, Pistol; stand behind me. O! if I had had time to have made new liveries, I would have bestowed the thousand pound I borrowed of you. But 'tis no matter; this poor show doth better: this doth infer the zeal I had to see him . . . But to stand stained with travel, and sweating with desire to see him; thinking of nothing else; putting all affairs else in oblivion, as if there were nothing else to be done but to see him.

The King's rejection is more harsh because we have seen Falstaff as so eager and so pathetically vulnerable; it could hardly be more abrupt and savage:

> I know thee not, old man: fall to thy prayers;
> How ill white hairs become a fool and jester!
> I have long dream'd of such a kind of man,

So surfeit-swell'd, so old, and so profane;
But, being awak'd, I do despise my dream.
Make less thy body hence, and more thy grace;
Leave gormandising; know the grave doth gape
For thee thrice wider than for other men.
Reply not to me with a fool-born jest:
Presume not that I am the thing I was;
For God doth know, so shall the world perceive,
That I have turn'd away my former self;
So will I those that kept me company.
When thou dost hear I am as I have been,
Approach me, and thou shalt be as thou wast,
The tutor and the feeder of my riots:
Till then, I banish thee, on pain of death,
As I have done the rest of my misleaders,
Not to come near our person by ten mile.

The scriptural overtones of the opening of this[32] may have their origin in a formal rejection of Vice in the morality-structure. But if this is so, Shakespeare again makes a greater use of it: Henry for the period of his kingship draws about him the aura and ritual of religion at every possible opportunity. *Henry V* is full of such references as the King attempts through them to restore the mystical overtones to the monarchy which have been conspicuously dispersed in the two *Henry IV* plays. This is merely the first example of a consistent attempt to suggest a larger approval of his temporal power and actions.

What Falstaff has failed to recognise is the distinction Hal has always made between the public and the private man. Had he come to the King in private, no doubt he would have had gentler treatment and a better explanation of why he must be set aside: presenting himself in public he is treated as no more than the apparatus for demonstrating the royal reform. But Falstaff has never made the smallest distinction between his own public and private conduct. His zest for life, his outrageous lies, have been manifested alike in the tavern and on the battlefield. Because he would be contemptuous of such distinctions himself, he has not realised how ruthless and how emotionless Hal will be in his public role. He is simply unaware that the bonds of a private affection might complicate the King's conduct, just as Hal seems insensitive to any responsibility deriving from years of good fellowship. Not until after the rejection does the broken Falstaff realise duly the distinction between public and private conduct which might have mitigated his humiliation:

Do not you grieve at this: I shall be sent for in private to him. Look
you, he must seem thus to the world.

The hope is immediately doused as the Lord Chief Justice returns to
take him to the Fleet. The immediate comment on the action of the
scene has its bitter irony stressed by its placing in the mouth of that
ruthless hypocrite John of Lancaster:

I like this fair proceeding of the King's.

Although he explains away the harshness of the treatment, the emphasis
remains on public appearances rather than private ethics:

He hath intent his wonted followers
Shall all be very well provided for;
But all are banish'd till their conversations
Appear more wise and modest to the world.

The rejection itself we have long seen as inevitable; the manner of it
is still a shock. Hal is conscious only of making the maximum public
effect and Falstaff is used as an instrument in that effect. The rejection
is as ruthlessly executed as anything Hal's father perpetrated, and
Bolingbroke would never have incurred the private obligations to
Falstaff which his son so contemptuously ignores. The new King's
rejection of Falstaff for his own political purpose shows at once the
recognition of the public attitudes a monarch must strike and the
effortless disregard of personal relationships which marks the decline
in our sympathy for him as an individual. It is a superbly effective
dramatic stroke which is made possible by the clarity with which
Shakespeare has kept the developing public and the diminishing private
roles of Hal before us.

## Henry V

We need not spend long on the opposing critical estimates of Shakespeare's
pageant-king: the development of the character is consistent through
three plays and much of the detail has already been treated. At one
pole are those who see Henry as 'the mirror of all Christian Kings' and
the play as devoted to the depiction of what the late nineteenth century
generally saw as 'Shakespeare's only hero'. At the other are those who
follow John Masefield's[33] estimate:

> Henry is not a hero, he is not a thinker, he is not even a friend; he is
> a common man, whose incapacity for feeling enables him to change
> his habits whenever interest bids him . . . There is no goodfellowship
> in him, no sincerity, no wholeheartedness . . . He impresses one as
> quite common, quite selfish, quite without feeling.

Modern criticism has tended to look for a middle point between these
two extremes. In fact, the apparently contrasting qualities of Henry are
fused rather than left in contradiction, to give us a ruler perfectly fitted
for the situation he meets. As M. Manheim[34] puts it:

> First, despite the objections of some critics (once more on the
> increase), Henry is intended to be a successful, admirable, and heroic
> figure; second, Henry is as consummate a Machiavel as any King
> represented in these plays . . . What was in *Richard III* an image of
> horror and malignancy bent on power by any means possible has
> become an image of practical politics cast in a beautiful, heroic
> mould.

Henry V is in all Shakespeare's work the man with the clearest distinction
between private feelings and political conduct. He is the less winning
because his solution to this clearly perceived dilemma costs him so
little effort of conscience or feeling: it is to frame all his conduct in
terms of the public persona which he desires to create and which he
succeeds in becoming through his continuous pursuance of the task.
This is why R. J. Dorius[35] finds him 'one of the few protagonists in
Shakespeare outside of the comedies who succeeds without much
suffering' and why Bradley thought him 'Shakespeare's most efficient
character'.

There is then to be no inner tension within Henry to give interest
to the play, which is a prolonged celebration of patriotic military success.
Henry has the rhetoric to accompany his remarkable physical and
mental dynamism, and he is given a splendid reinforcement in the Chorus.
The ostensible reason and probable starting-point for Shakespeare's most
prolonged use of this ancient device is the difficulty of the dramatic
material for the Elizabethan stage; as usual Shakespeare seizes other
and more important possibilities which his Chorus offers. The nearest
approach to this theme of the celebration of military conquest in
English drama is Marlowe's *Tamburlaine* of a decade earlier, in which
Shakespeare may well have acted. Marlowe's Prologue sets out his
author's stall with similar sentiments to Shakespeare's:

From jigging veins of rhyming mother wits,
And such conceits as clownage keeps in pay,
We'll lead you to the stately tent of war,
Where you shall hear the Scythian Tamburlaine
Threatening the world with high astounding terms.

Shakespeare takes the hint of this fragment in Marlowe and turns it to thrilling effect. The Chorus sets the ambience and tone of the play in his prologues to each act, exhorting us to raise our thoughts above individual men to the lofty plane fitting for this glittering spectacle:

Suppose within the girdle of these walls
Are now confin'd two mighty monarchies,
Whose high upreared and abutting fronts
The perilous narrow ocean parts asunder:
Piece out our imperfections with your thoughts;
Into a thousand parts divide one man,
And make imaginary puissance;
Think, when we talk of horses, that you see them
Printing their proud hoofs i' the receiving earth;
For 'tis your thoughts that now must deck our kings.

Henry's first major speech in the play, at the beginning of its second scene, is an apparently impressive display of conscience, with no less than three mentions of God and several other religious references. In fact, it is an elaborate public display of rectitude for the benefit of the onlookers. His father's last advice to his son was to 'busy giddy minds with foreign wars' and Lancaster's closing lines in *Henry IV* made this more specific:

I will lay odds, that, ere this year expire,
We bear our civil swords and native fire
As far as France. I heard a bird so sing,
Whose music, to my thinking, pleas'd the King.

In this play, Canterbury has already spoken of the King's intention. Henry, quite certain of his own intentions, is using his father's trick of hanging back in declaring his policy until his supporters have come out firmly for him. Canterbury voices the common feeling in most unclerical terms:

> Gracious Lord,
> Stand for your own, unwind your bloody flag;
> Look back into your mighty ancestors:
> Go, my dread lord, to your great-grandsire's tomb,
> From whom you claim; invoke his war-like spirit,
> And your great uncle's, Edward the Black Prince,
> Who on the French ground play'd a tragedy,
> Making defeat on the full power of France;
> Whiles his most mighty father on a hill
> Stood smiling to behold his lion's whelp
> Forage in blood of French nobility.

Ely, Exeter and Westmoreland reinforce this, and Henry is able to do for the first time what he does so superbly in this play, to voice the feelings of a united party in a speech which fires the imaginations of those around him:

> Now are we well resolv'd; and by God's help,
> And yours, the noble sinews of our power,
> France being ours, we'll bend it to our awe
> Or break it all to pieces: or there we'll sit,
> Ruling in large and ample empery
> O'er France and all her almost kingly dukedoms,
> Or lay these bones in an unworthy urn,
> Tombless, with no remembrance over them.

When the ambassadors deliver the Dauphin's insult, Henry develops this note into the torrent of force and energy which will sweep all before it in the play, which pauses for a moment only when he solemnly invokes God to his cause yet again:

> But tell the Dauphin I will keep my state,
> Be like a king and show my sail of greatness
> When I do rouse me in my throne of France:
> For that I have laid by my majesty
> And plodded like a man for working-days,
> But I will rise there with so full a glory
> That I will dazzle all the eyes of France,
> Yea, strike the Dauphin blind to look on us.
> And tell the pleasant prince this mock of his
> Hath turn'd his balls to gun-stones; and his soul

Shall stand sore charged for the wasteful vengeance
That shall fly with them: for many a thousand widows
Shall this his mock mock out of their dear husbands;
Mock mothers from their sons, mock castles down;
And some are yet ungotten and unborn
That shall have cause to curse the Dauphin's scorn.
But this lies all within the will of God,
To whom I do appeal; and in whose name
Tell you the Dauphin I am coming on,
To venge me as I may and to put forth
My rightful hand in a well-hallow'd cause.

Henry was of course determined upon war before the receipt of the
Dauphin's ill-chosen message; the incident gives him an opportunity
which he seizes with relish to stir the blood of his followers and invoke the
deity on his side. It is a strain we have now learned to expect in eager
nationalists, but it is so well produced that it is heady stuff none the
less.

The invocatory tone of the second Chorus speeech which follows
immediately reinforces the effect of Henry's call to arms:

Now all the youth of England are on fire,
And silken dalliance in the wardrobe lies:
Now thrive the armourers, and honour's thought
Reigns solely in the breast of every man.
They sell the pasture now to buy the horse,
Following the mirror of all Christian kings,
With winged heels, as English Mercuries.

There is now no Falstaff to question the elusive nature of this honour
which so excites, and the scene which follows only undermines the
loss. Comic horseplay will provide a straightforward contrast to the
more serious theme of the play, but there will be none of the breadth
and profundity of wit and humour that Falstaff brought. Lest we be
too much dazzled by the panoply of military majesty, Shakespeare
reminds us here of the price of Henry's public image in private terms:
as Falstaff lies grievously sick off-stage, the Hostess, Nym and Pistol all
remind us of how 'The King has killed his heart.'

The next scene, in which the traitors are unmasked, is another
example of Henry's penchant for stage-managing an event to maximum
public effect. The King, knowing of their treachery and impending arrest,

forces them to play a charade before him, and likens their crime to 'another fall of man', a phrase last used by Queen Isabel in the garden scene of *Richard II*. The deity is again continually introduced, and Henry even uses the squalid event to hint at a holy war:

> We doubt not of a fair and lucky war,
> Since God so graciously hath brought to light
> This dangerous treason lurking in our way
> To hinder our beginnings. We doubt not now
> But every rub is smoothed on our way.
> Then forth, dear countrymen: let us deliver
> Our puissance into the hand of God,
> Putting it straight in expedition.

As Palmer[36] says, Falstaff has to be excluded from this play for the same reason as Mercutio has to be killed off in *Romeo and Juliet*: the design of the play is not large enough to contain him. His power of humorous redefinition of the serious action of the play would be fatal to Shakespeare's purposes here. The last mention of the old rogue is placed significantly, immediately after the rallying-call just quoted, and Shakespeare lingers lovingly over it. The hostess's lament shows an ear for the universality of English common speech which only Hardy has rivalled; it brings a sudden stroke of human profundity:

> a' parted even just between twelve and one, even at the turning o' the tide: for after I saw him fumble with the sheets and play with flowers and smile upon his fingers' end, I knew there was but one way; for his nose was as sharp as a pen, and a' babbled of green fields. 'How now, Sir John?' quoth I: 'what, man! be o' good cheer.' So a' cried out 'God, God, God!' three or four times: now I, to comfort him, bid him a' should not think of God, I hop'd there was no need to trouble himself with any such thoughts yet. So a' bade me lay more clothes on his feet: I put my hand into the bed and felt them, and they were as cold as any stone; then I felt to his knees, and so upward, and upward, and all was as cold as any stone.

Lest in an access of sentiment we underrate the virtues of strong monarchy, Shakespeare sets before us at this point the vacillations and vanities of the French court. The contrast is not that of the long, lyrical lament of Richard, nor of the bright optimism of Hotspur (whose virtues Henry has by now assimilated as he does those of other men), nor even of the dark plans of self-seeking nobles, but of an effete and ineffective court. There is no tension or clash of our loyalties in the two pictures, and the Dauphin is no rival to set off Henry if we compare him to Hotspur: Shakespeare wishes to detract in no way from the martial splendour of the mirror of all Christian kings in the May-morn of his youth. The French court is used merely to underline the judgement, and above all the energy, of the English King. Thus the Dauphin's view of Henry as 'a vain, giddy, shallow, humorous youth' is not an arguable alternative view but the exact opposite of what we know to be true from what we have already seen. Should we be in any doubt, Exeter arrives to confirm the fierce resolve that is Henry's real keynote:

> for if you hide the crown
> Even in your hearts, there will he rake for it:
> Therefore in fierce tempest is he coming,
> In thunder and in earthquake like a Jove,
> That, if requiring fail, he will compel;
> And bids you, in the bowels of the Lord,
> Deliver up the crown.

Separated only by the Chorus's third invocatory address, Henry now follows these speeches of Exeter's with his own greatest speech in a similar vein. It is evidence of Shakespeare's confidence in his powers over language that the imagery is more resourceful, the rhythms more varied, the music more sustained, and the total effect more thrilling:

> Once more unto the breach, dear friends, once more,
> Or close the wall up with our English dead.
> In peace there's nothing so becomes a man
> As modest stillness and humility:
> But when the blast of war blows in our ears,
> Then imitate the action of the tiger;
> Stiffen the sinews, conjure up the blood,
> Disguise fair nature with hard-favour'd rage;
> Then lend the eye a terrible aspect;
> Let it pry through the portage of the head
> Like the brass cannon: let the brow o'erwhelm it
> As fearfully as doth a galled rock
> O'erhang and jutty his confounded base,
> Swill'd with the wild and wasteful ocean,
> Now set the teeth and stretch the nostril wide,

Hold hard the breath, and bend up every spirit
To his full height!

Henry inherited his father's judgement of when and how to act; he has
added to it a capacity to urge men with moving words to follow a
simplified cause, which is a crucial quality of the political and military
leader, as the Nuremberg rallies of the nineteen-thirties and Churchill's
war speeches have evidenced in our own time.

The parody of Henry's call to arms by Bardolph, Nym and Pistol is
no more than low comedy; the boy's cool denunciation of them underlines their villainy. Falstaff might have undermined Henry's fine words
as effectively as he did those of Hotspur, and thus confused the uncomplicated consistency of Shakespeare's portrait of the hero of Agincourt.

Henry parades his army before the walls of Harfleur very much as
his father did before the walls of Richard's Berkley Castle sixteen years
earlier. His threat is more explicit than his father's, his speech overflowing
with a dynamism that is this time full of menace:

If I begin the battery once again,
I will not leave the half-achiev'd Harfleur
Till in her ashes she lie buried.
The gates of mercy shall be all shut up,
And the flesh'd soldier, rough and hard of heart,
In liberty of bloody hand shall range
With conscience wide as hell, mowing like grass
Your fresh-fair virgins and your flowering infants.
What is it then to me, if impious war,
Array'd in flames like to the prince of fiends,
Do, with his smirch'd complexion, all fell feats
Enlink'd to waste and desolation?
What is't to me, when you yourselves are cause,
If your pure maidens fall into the hand
Of hot and forcing violation?
What rein can hold licentious wickedness
When down the hill he holds his fierce career?
We may as bootless spend our vain command
Upon th' enraged soldiers in their spoil
As send precepts to the leviathan
To come ashore. Therefore, you men of Harfleur,
Take pity of your town and of your people,
Whiles yet my soldiers are in my command.

There is an interesting comparison herewith with Marlowe's *Tamburlaine*. In a similar situation at Damascus, Tamburlaine not only slaughters the virgins and hoists their bodies upon the walls of the city, but indulges his sadistic temperament by toying with them beforehand. Henry, with a wider vision of individual horror, uses it only as a public effect to achieve the surrender of the city, deflowered virgins for him being one item in a catalogue of horrors with which he can threaten the elders of the city.

We have already seen Henry following Machiavelli's instruction to his ruler to use God and the Church wherever possible to strengthen his position. Machiavelli's lion was never more evident than in the intensity of Henry's images of rapine, murder and destruction at Harfleur. The speech recalls Yeats' comment that Henry is 'as remorseless and undistinguished as some natural force'. Henry gets his way of course; the manner of it underlines the prophetic insight of Richard's bitter aphorism on the new political morality a generation earlier:

> Well you deserve. They well deserve to have
> That know the strong'st and surest way to get.

The exultant conqueror who now wears the crown with such confidence could hardly have moved further from the timorous action and indulgent reverie of Richard. Yet Richard would have recognised and responded to Henry's gift for words. Henry has fused the driving energy which Richard always lacked with a talent for language which is different from but as effective for his very different purposes as was Richard's. For the world of the Wars of the Roses and military adventure for which Richard was so patently ill-fitted, Henry is the ideal ruler. The private self which Richard paraded so relentlessly before us is now almost totally concealed by Henry, as submerged now under his public persona as Richard's kingship was submerged under his private tragedy.

Henry is now most at home in the most public context. Playing the most formal of public scenes in front of his army with Montjoy, he stage-manages the event with instinctive skill to make the most of the ritual defiance he must send. First he sets the scene in which a hero might best emerge:

> Though 'tis no wisdom to confess so much
> Unto an enemy of craft and vantage,
> My people are with sickness much enfeebled,
> My numbers lessen'd, and those few I have
> Almost no better than so many French.

In such a setting, his message cannot fail to lift the spirit:

> Go therefore, tell thy master here I am;
> My ransom is this frail and worthless trunk,
> My army but a weak and sickly guard;
> Yet, God before, tell him we will come on,
> Though France himself and such another neighbour
> Stand in our way.

The greatest of the Chorus speeches, that preceding Act IV, heightens this effect, the characteristic fire imagery now muted to the general note of expectancy. No hero has ever had a more vividly painted back-cloth against which to play, and the lines evoke an atmosphere as well as setting a scene:

> Now entertain conjecture of a time
> When creeping murmur and the poring dark
> Fills the wide vessel of the universe.
> From camp to camp through the foul womb of night
> The hum of either army stilly sounds,
> That the fix'd sentinels almost receive
> The secret whispers of each other's watch:
> Fire answers fire, and through their paly flames
> Each battle sees the other's umber'd face;
> Steed threatens steed, in high and boastful neighs
> Piercing the night's dull ear; and from the tents
> The armourers, accomplishing the knights,
> With busy hammers closing rivets up,
> Give dreadful note of preparation.
> The country cocks do crow, the clocks do toll,
> And the third hour of drowsy morning name.
> Proud of their numbers, and secure in soul,
> The confident and over-lusty French
> Do the low-rated English play at dice;
> And chide the cripple tardy-gaited night
> Who, like a foul and ugly witch, doth limp
> So tediously away. The poor condemned English,
> Like sacrifices, by their watchful fires
> Sit patiently, and inly ruminate
> The morning's danger, and their gesture sad
> Investing lank-lean cheeks and war-worn coats

Presenteth them unto the gazing moon
So many horrid ghosts.

The long scene in which Henry wanders round the various sections
of his army shows the value of the range of experience he has so carefully
gathered to him: he has the common touch as well as the power to
inspire the great men of his realm. Yet it is for the most part tedious
stuff. Henry has never been most at home in private conversation, as we
have seen, and only when there was the enormous comic intellect and
presence of Falstaff to raise the level of interchange were the low-life
scenes memorable. At the end of the scene, he is given the one moment
in the play in which he reveals his private self. His meditation upon the
burdens of kingship is conventional and uninspired when it is compared
with the great public set-pieces of the play. This is not to say that
Shakespeare has failed, but rather that he has been consistent. The
great King, so continuously effective in a succession of different public
situations, is curiously uninteresting as a private man, largely because
there is so little indecision. The same trait will be seen in two Caesars,
whilst Antony's reservation to himself of his intense private existence
will lead to his public disasters. Henry has put all his formidable force
and intelligence into creating his public figure: he has done it so successfully, Shakespeare suggests, that there is little of interest left in the
private man. He would be everyone's choice as military leader and royal
autocrat, no one's as confidant or philosopher. There is little tension in
this situation, no great sense of a price being paid for public success.
Henry has been shown from the outset as fitted by temperament for
his present role; he has merely developed and matured with devastating
logic into the character he now displays to all.

Again there is an intriguing comparison with *Tamburlaine*. Marlowe's
conqueror, like Henry, excels in infusing his companions with his own
confidence in his destiny. At exactly the same point in the first part
of *Tamburlaine* as Henry's St Crispin's speech occurs in this play,
Tamburlaine too is exhorting his troops:

Awake, ye men of Memphis! hear the clang
of Scythian trumpets; hear the basilisks,
That roaring shake Damascus' turrets down.
The rogue of Volga holds Zenocrate,
The soldan's daughter, for his concubine,
And with a troop of thieves and vagabonds,
Hath spread his colours to our high disgrace,

While you faint-hearted, base Egyptians,
Lie slumbering on the flowery banks of Nile,
As crocodiles that unaffrighted rest
While thundering cannons rattle on their skins.
                              (*Tamburlaine,* Pt. 1, IV, i, 1-11)

It is stirring stuff, and it needs to be, for Tamburlaine speaks for a third of the two plays; in his search for an elevated style, Marlowe uses 1,410 proper names, of which 454 gain stress by being placed at the end of the line.[37] Yet Tamburlaine has no private self to subdue; his only qualities are the public ones of limitless ambition and vaunting confidence. His effective but unvarying method of expressing these is in the high style of 'Marlowe's mighty line'. Because of this, he is becoming by this key stage of the play montonous and unconvincing.

Shakespeare's Henry far surpasses Tamburlaine in his extraordinary mesmerism for his followers because we have seen how private experience has been assimilated into this devastating public performance. Moreover, Shakespeare is able to suggest this knowledge of private emotions, of what moves a vast range of individual men, in a style of which the flexibility and vigour leaves Marlowe's bombast far behind:

This day is call'd the feast of Crispian:
He that outlives this day, and comes safe home,
Will stand a tip-toe when this day is nam'd,
And rouse him at the name of Crispian.
He that shall see this day, and live old age,
Will yearly on the vigil feast his neighbours,
And say, 'Tomorrow is Saint Crispian':
Then will he strip his sleeve and show his scars,
And say, 'These wounds I had on Crispin's day'.
Old men forget; yet all shall be forgot,
But he'll remember with advantages
What feats he did that day. Then shall our names,
Familiar in his mouth as household words,
Harry the king, Bedford and Exeter,
Warwick and Talbot, Salisbury and Gloucester,
Be in their flowing cups freshly remember'd.
This story shall the good man teach his son;
And Crispin Crispian shall ne'er go by,
From this day to the ending of the world,
But we in it shall be remembered;

We few, we happy few, we band of brothers;
For he to-day that sheds his blood with me
Shall be my brother; be he ne'er so vile
This day shall gentle his condition:
And gentlemen in England now a-bed
Shall think themselves accurs'd they were not here,
And hold their manhoods cheap whiles any speaks
That fought with us upon Saint Crispin's day.

Henry's talent for words is, like everything else about him, supremely fitted to the task in hand; it is never reflective, like that of Richard or Hamlet. Shakespeare's other men of action, such as Macbeth, Othello, Antony, even Coriolanus, all have their moments of inner doubt which are magnificently conveyed in words. Henry's great imaginative moments are always when action beckons and excites; his intrinsic vitality and power of spirit in such situations make him the supreme communicator of his own excitement and the supreme inspirational leader. The fusing of political insight with the capacity to motivate action through words is present so effectively only in the Antony of 'Julius Caesar'. Henry dies at the height of his fame whilst still a young man; Antony survives into middle age, to develop as an individual and to fail as a leader.

## Notes

1. *Ideas of Good and Evil* (1903).
2. *Political Characters of Shakespeare*, p. 141.
3. *Shakespeare's History Plays*, p. 259.
4. Introduction to Cambridge edition (1939).
5. *Political Characters of Shakespeare*, p. 153.
6. *Shakespeare – his Mind and Art* (1875).
7. Introduction to Arden edition (1956).
8. Poets themselves, notably Coleridge, Dowden and Yeats, have been among the greatest admirers of Richard's verse. Swinburne, in a typically exuberant piece in *Three Plays of Shakespeare* (1909), takes an opposite view, but is arguing chiefly for the demonstrably mistaken view that this is 'unmistakably the author's first attempt at historic drama'.
9. In *Shakespeare's Doctrine of Nature*.
10. Introduction to Arden *Henry IV Part 1* (1960).
11. *Shakespeare, a Survey*.
12. Introduction to Arden *Henry IV Part 1*, p. xlv.
13. *Political Characters of Shakespeare*, pp. 186–7.
14. *Shakespeare's Workmanship* (1918).
15. *The Fortunes of Falstaff* (Cambridge University Press, Cambridge, 1943).
16. *Shakespeare's History Plays*.
17. *Shakespeare's Doctrine of Nature*.

18. *Shakespeare* (1909).

19. *The Argument of Comedy* (1948), quoted in R. J. Dorius (ed.), Twentieth Century Interpretations volume on *Henry IV Part One* (Prentice-Hall, Englewood Cliffs, New Jersey, 1970), p. 91.

20. *Oxford Lectures on Poetry* (1909).

21. 'A Note on Comedy' in F. R. Leavis (ed.), *Determinations* (1934).

22. 'Rule and Misrule in Henry IV', pp. 192-213 in *Shakespeare's Festive Comedy* (1972).

23. For instance there has been an increasing tendency since the horrors of the 1914-18 War to dismiss the great rallying speeches of Henry V in phrases such as 'patriotic rant'; other centuries have not generally found them this, nor is there agreement in our own.

24. Introduction to Arden *Henry IV Part I*, p. xlvii.

25. Barber, 'Rule and Misrule in Henry IV'.

26. Footnote, p. 153.

27. *Political Characters of Shakespeare*, p. 193.

28. Kenneth Muir, *Scrutiny* (1951).

29. *Shakespeare* (1911).

30. *Political Characters of Shakespeare*, p. 184.

31. Introduction to Arden *Henry V*, p. xxii.

32. Luke 13, 27: 'But he shall say, I tell you, I know not whence ye are; depart from me, all ye workers of iniquity.'

33. *Shakespeare*.

34. *The Weak King Dilemma in the Shakespearean History Play*, p. 167.

35. Introduction to Twentieth Century Interpretations of *Henry IV Part One*, p. 2.

36. *Political Characters of Shakespeare*, p. 226.

37. See H. Levin, *Christopher Marlowe: the Overreacher* (Faber, London, 1965), p. 61.

# THE PROBLEM PLAYS: *TROILUS AND CRESSIDA, ALL'S WELL THAT ENDS WELL* AND *MEASURE FOR MEASURE*

I have chosen to follow what I think is now a useful convention in designating a group of Shakespeare's plays written in the first years of the seventeenth century as 'problem plays'. Yet after almost a century of attempts at definition, the term remains a vague one; I have set down beside my chapter heading the three plays I determine to constitute the group.

It was F. S. Boas in 1896 who first used the term. In *Shakspere and his Predecessors* he wrote:

> All these dramas introduce us into highly artificial societies, whose civilization is ripe unto rottenness . . . Dramas so singular in theme and temper cannot strictly be called comedies or tragedies. We may therefore borrow a convenient phrase from the theatre of today and class them together as Shakespeare's problem-plays. (p. 345)

The plays Boas thus distinguished were the three to which this chapter is given over plus *Hamlet*. His mention of the theatre of his own day, in which Shaw was championing the virtues of Ibsen and producing his own social drama, indicates that Boas was using the term to stress a theme of social commentary in these Shakespeare plays, an idea which he developed in his analysis of the plays. He maintained that the presentation of the moral issues was straightforward and unequivocal, that Isabella, for instance, in *Measure for Measure*, was not 'torn by the conflict between sisterly love and her ideal of duty' because Shakespeare eschewed 'blurring the line between right and wrong'. The plays, he thought, stemmed primarily from a criticism of particular societies.

This was too vague to meet general acceptance. *King Lear*, for instance, is often thought Shakespeare's most devastating criticism of society, yet it is never cited as a problem play. Subsequent critics have found the term 'problem plays' useful, but have chosen their own definitions and their own groups of plays. W. W. Lawrence published *Shakespeare's Problem Comedies* in 1931, excluding *Hamlet* as I have done from Boas' original four. He applied the term 'to those productions which clearly do not fall into the category of tragedy and yet are too serious and analytic to fit the commonly accepted conception of comedy'. This is clear enough, though it would allow a case for more than the three plays he accepted.

The best known of more modern works on these plays is E. M. W. Tillyard's *Shakespeare's Problem Plays* (1961), which accepts Boas' original four plays and sees them as 'powerfully united by a serious tone amounting at times to sombreness; they show a strong awareness of evil, without being predominantly pessimistic' (p. 5). Tillyard dismisses the view that the plays are essentially bitter and satirical and is convinced that the themes of mercy and forgiveness are sincerely and not ironically presented. He is also quite frank about the vagueness of his definition of what constitutes a problem play. The culmination of this line of criticism is W. B. Toole's *Shakespeare's Problem Plays: Studies in Form and Meaning* (1966), which sees the four as religious plays, deriving quite directly from medieval morality drama.

E. Schanzer, in *The Problem Plays of Shakespeare* (1963), comments on the vagueness of all previous definitions and offers as his own designation:

> A play in which we find a concern with a moral problem which is central to it, presented in such a manner that we are unsure of our moral bearings, so that uncertain and divided responses to it in the minds of the audience are possible or even probable.

Although Schanzer has much that is stimulating to say about his chosen plays, his definition, relying as it does upon 'divided responses . . . in the minds of the audience' seems to me less precise than some of the others. What of *Henry V*, for instance, who as I said in my last chapter has brought a sharply divided response in our own century? Schanzer chose as his three problem plays *Julius Caesar*, *Measure for Measure* and *Antony and Cleopatra*, an arbitrary grouping of plays constructed over about a decade.

The chronology of construction seems important in this instance. There is now general agreement that *Hamlet, Troilus and Cressida, All's Well that Ends Well* and *Measure for Measure* were constructed close to each other in the early years of the seventeenth century. It used to be fashionable to detect a crisis in Shakespeare's own life that is reflected in these plays; as Chambers confidently put it:

> for a period in Shakespeare's history near the beginning of the seventeenth century the rose-red vision gave place to the grey

. . . if he still wrote as an idealist, it was as an idealist into whose imagination had passed the ferment of doubt and the bitterness of disillusion.[1]

It is now almost equally fashionable to decry such an approach as romantic or indulgent, yet there is much evidence in the plays of their author's disillusion. Particularly in the plays' imagery of disease and food, and in their treatment of women, there is a sharp change from the mature comedies and histories which immediately precede them. Yet we are unlikely now ever to learn more of Shakespeare's personal trauma, if trauma there was. The theory can be little more than a fascinating speculation, and we must disregard it as a key to the problem plays because ultimately it leads away from the plays rather than into them. If we had a Pepys' diary of Shakespeare's life around the turn of the century, we should still have to come back to an estimation of the plays; even if we understood them better, we should still find them problems in the theatre.

The same might be said of another kind of speculation, that concerning the audience for which they were written. It is quite possible that the three works I have grouped as problem plays were all written with an Inns of Court audience in mind rather than the 'vulgar' and wider audience of the Globe. There is much evidence both in theme and treatment that this is so, and a thorough investigation of the theory might help us to understand the plays better. But even if it could be proved positively, as it probably never will be, that these plays were designed for Inns of Court performances, we should still wish to assess them as products for our modern theatre and as works of art. We understand perfectly the occasions and the conditions for which elaborate seventeenth-century masques were devised, but our theatrical verdict is that they are interesting historical oddities, representatives of a form that is now obsolete. It would illuminate our knowledge of *Troilus and Cressida* to know that the Trojans' debate was designed for an audience of young legal bloods, or to know that the man who penned Thersites' bitter satire was passing through a personal crisis, but in the end the play's reputation will stand or fall on its text.

When we look at the texts of the problem plays, certain elements emerge which seem to justify treating them as a group. They are full of material which looks both backwards, to the comedies, as in the resolution of Isabella and Helena, and forward to the tragedies and beyond, for Shakespeare is beginning to grapple with the themes of forgiveness and mercy which will dominate his final plays. In this watershed of ideas there are inevitable confusions. Traversi, who took Boas' original four plays as the problem group but saw *All's Well* as merely a preliminary sketch for *Measure for Measure*, saw them as plays

> in which the heroes are actuated by no clear motives, but rather grope in a kind of spiritual darkness, seeking to clarify their own impulses ...almost all the themes of the great tragedies make their appearance in the obscure and difficult plays of these years . . . All these plays are concerned, each after its fashion, with the effort to arrive at some kind of personal order in a world dominated by contradiction and obscurity.[2]

The problems of existence in a complex world, of great abstractions like justice and mercy, seem to have interested Shakespeare more than the possible solutions. All this implies an experimental approach, and experiment is the key to the problem plays. My concern in this book is the development of a particular aspect of Shakespeare's dramatic technique. But the development of the public-private counterpoint as a key factor in dramatic structuring goes alongside the development of other aspects of his craftsmanship. Principal among these is his increasing control over the language and verse-structure he employs as a medium for his dramatic material. As Shakespeare experiments with dramatic method and different kinds of material, he develops his mastery of the iambic pentameter and his capacity to suggest wider imaginative worlds through his imagery; the language in which his characters speak becomes the most sinuous and effective medium the stage has seen.

The problem plays are a forging-house of development and experiment. And as we would expect in such circumstances, success is incomplete and coherence is lacking. Many critics who have agonised over the problem plays and sought in them complex allegories seem to ignore the simple fact that the three plays I am considering are among the least popular in the canon. Were they prepared to accept that they are not very effective works, many of the problems would disappear and they would be freer to accept them as flawed but interesting plays, lacking both the joy of the mature comedies and the profundities of the great tragedies, but instrumental in the playwright's development.

Such judgements are of course subjective. The nearest we can come to an objective measure on theatrical works is the critical and com-mercial reception of productions of the plays over the years. *Measure for Measure* has probably enjoyed more productions over the last twenty years than in any previous period, but it has not had such attention previously. Although the play, with its questioning of office and the effects of it on individuals, has much contemporary appeal, reviews of performances almost always begin with comments on the difficult nature of the play and the necessity to search for its rewards. *Troilus and Cressida* has never been a popular play; with its uneven tone and joyless humour, it has always been a play to quote from rather than to admire as a whole. Almost every review of the 1981 BBC television production began with a comment on the difficulties of approaching the play's strengths. They might have been a repeat performance of the reviews accorded to *All's Well* earlier in the year, for these too felt it necessary to comment on the play's imperfections before attempting an assessment of the television production. The production of *All's Well* mounted at Stratford in 1981 was the first for fourteen years, a significant fact in itself and a frequency that is typical of the play's fortunes over the centuries.

The three plays I designate as problem plays, then, are not conspicuous artistic or theatrical successes. They are characterised by experiment in dramatic form and in language. But what then are we to make of the fourth play which was written at this time, which is set with these three among the problem plays by Boas, Tillyard and Traversi? For *Hamlet* has been a conspicuous and often dazzling success both in theatre and study ever since it was written. And there is much in the imagery of the play and the attitudes of its hero to argue a grouping with the other plays. When Hamlet tells his mother not to comfort herself with the illusion that he is mad, because:

> It will but skin and film the ulcerous place,
> Whilst rank corruption, mining all within,
> Infects unseen

the words could well come from Thersites in *Troilus and Cressida*. His treatment of Ophelia could be that of a dissilusioned Troilus. Laertes is as callow and suggestible as is Claudio in *Measure for Measure.*

Yet *Hamlet,* despite its similarities with the other three plays written at about the same time, despite its many loose ends and the evidence of haste in construction, has a coherence which is missing in the other three. It is a coherence which derives from its dramatic construction. Perhaps the other three plays were devised for an Inns of Court audience and *Hamlet* benefited by its design for the rough and tumble and the wider cross-section of audience in the Globe. Perhaps Shakespeare's adoption of the convention of the revenge-play imposed fortuitously upon him a framework which drove him forward to an artistic unity despite the uncertainties and sidetrackings of his hero. What is certain is that *Hamlet* is one of the most dramatically effective of all plays; this is a fact which familiarity with its plot and the attraction for the reader of its hero's metaphysical delights have tended to obscure. In my next chapter I shall try to show why the play works so effectively as a drama. Here I distinguish it from the three plays which are now my concern because it has a dramatic coherence which they lack.

These three plays, I have said, are experimental and not wholly successful. Shakespeare tries out various techniques, and some of the difficulties come when he applies techniques to material to which they are not wholly suited. Many of the stresses of *All's Well* and *Measure for Measure* come from the application of a realistic approach to material that lends itself to a less direct treatment; no doubt lessons of the experiment conducted here were learned and applied in the late romances. In *Troilus and Cressida* the debates of the Greeks and Trojans are conducted as intellectual exchanges between characters who only intermittently engage our sympathies, so that their outcomes are arbitrary and unconvincing.

Yet Shakespeare is in these plays extending his range of character and dramatic intervention, though he does so with the unevenness that denotes experiment rather than confident assertion. Most importantly, he passes from the straightforward deceptions which men like Richard of Lancaster practise upon others in their public roles, to the self-deceptions men practise upon themselves. Claudio and Angelo, Bertram and Troilus, acquire knowledge of themselves and the world around them as these plays proceed. They are experiments which prepare the way for the great voyages of self-discovery and the moral questioning of the great tragedies.

## Troilus and Cressida

No work better illustrates the uneven quality of the problem plays than *Troilus and Cressida*. Troilus, in the double part of military commander and romantic, unfortunate lover is unconvincing. We are told several times in the play of how 'blood' prevails over 'judgement', how emotions rule understanding of the realities of life. Yet Shakespeare is normally unsurpassed in winning our sympathy for such men even whilst we recognise that they are unfitted for the *realpolitik* of political life; H- Hotspur and the ageing Antony are only the most notable of h-

Troilus moves us only at certain moments in the play, partly because the construction does not lend itself to a full investigation of his agonies; partly because the overwhelming pessimism of the play falls like a blanket over any brighter stirrings; partly because Shakespeare's language is experimental and patchy rather than consistent in its effects. The play's theme, its often obscure diction, its passionate and intellectually demanding love poetry in the manner of Donne, its occasional legal jokes, and the obliquity of its intentions, all argue that it may have been written for an Inns of Court audience. What Shakespeare does not succeed in doing is weaving the varied strands of this work into a consistent or convincing dramatic fabric. Traversi is right when he says that the intention of the play 'consists in uniting, in a manner mutually illuminating, a personal theme and its public "social" extension'.[3] But Shakespeare has not brought the thing off convincingly. The play's attractions are more obvious in the study, its defects more obvious in the theatre.

Troilus' indecision in the opening speech of the play ushers in the theme of public and private aspirations at the outset:

Call here my varlet; I'll unarm again:
Why should I war without the walls of Troy,
That find such cruel battle here within?
Each Trojan that is master of his heart,
Let him to field; Troilus, alas! hath none.

But the development of this dual theme is stuttering. The clumsy scene, reminiscent of an older drama, in which Pandarus parades the Trojan warriors before her, is not an auspicious introduction to Cressida. When Shakespeare gives her a soliloquy, that key moment in character development shows her in an unattractive light. She has an understanding of the courtesan's art without Cleopatra's grandeur or breadth of vision; rhyming couplets emphasise her shallow cleverness:

But more in Troilus thousand-fold I see
Than in the glass of Pandar's praise may be;
Yet hold I off. Women are angels, wooing:
Things won are done, joy's soul lies in the doing:
That she belov'd knows naught that knows not this —
Men prize the thing ungain'd more than it is.

Once this pair of rather unconvincing lovers have been introduced, Shakespeare sets about showing the political world which is to be their context. The debate in the Greek camp consists of a series of public attitudes struck in appropriately inflated styles: there is little or nothing of the private men behind these attitudes. Ulysses' speech on degree has sometimes been thought an earnest piece of political philosophy. But it is no more than the rhetorical statement of conventional Elizabethan dogma, possibly intended to reassure an Elizabethan near death or an insecure James the First just before or after his accession:

> O, when degree is shak'd,
> Which is the ladder to all high designs,
> The enterprise is sick! How could communities,
> Degrees in schools, and brotherhoods in cities,
> Peaceful commerce from dividable shores,
> The primogenitive and due of birth,
> Prerogative of age, crowns, sceptres, laurels,
> But by degree, stand in authentic place?
> Take but degree away, untune that string,
> And, hark, what discord follows!

Perhaps Ulysses is meant to be a bore in this long, contrived speech. Nestor and Agamemnon react to it with prompt and thoughtless sycophancy: if the writing here is not meant to be satirical, then it is poor. Tillyard argues that the spirit of criticism which plays on the minor political characters in *Henry V,* like the Archbishop of Canterbury, comes into the open and is intensified in *Troilus and Cressida,* so that the whole of the Greek debate is written in a deliberately inflated style.[4]

The entry of Aeneas, his challenge to Agamemnon and the replies of Agamemnon and Nestor develop inflation into outright bombast. We are reminded of Richard II's sardonic 'How high a pitch his resolution soars' as Hereford and Mowbray strike similar attitudes. There is no one as vivid and intelligent as Richard in this political arena. When Ulysses reduces the challenge to farce by arranging that 'blockish Ajax' shall be tricked up as their champion, it is left to the oafish Nestor, relishing the sport, to emphasise the distasteful nature of the whole proceeding in the scene's final couplet:

> Two curs shall tame each other: pride alone
> Must tarre the mastiffs on, as 'twere their bone.

The Trojan debate in Act II Scene ii, which counterbalances the Greek one, is a more convincing piece of drama. There is general agreement with Tillyard that 'The Trojans have more capacious minds, deeper feelings and a freer speech than the Greeks, yet they achieve less.'[5] This is promising material for Shakespearian drama: it is on these very issues that plays like *Richard II*, *Hamlet* and *Antony and Cleopatra* turn, and they are present in most of the greatest works. Yet here Shakespeare, having set up in the framework of his play such opportunities, curiously fails to make very much of them. Perhaps the contrasts are diffused through too many characters in each camp: it is notable in *Richard II* how effectively Richard and Bolingbroke embody the virtues and vices of their different worlds, how in *Antony and Cleopatra* Octavius encapsulates the cold efficiency of Rome and Cleopatra the sensual grandeurs of Egypt. But there is a failure too in a construction in *Troilus* which does not make much use of the tensions between great affairs of state and private passions, as these other plays continually do.

Thus, though the Trojans' debate promises a better investigation of the puzzles of power and the individual, Troilus is given little interplay of public and private inclinations. He begins with a statement of the militarist's view, dispensing with reason in favour of aggression in one of the play's vivid flashes of imagery:

> You fur your gloves with reason. Here are your reasons:
> You know an enemy intends you harm;
> You know a sword employ'd is perilous . . .
>           Nay if we talk of reason
> Let's shut our gates and sleep.

Troilus knows how to subjugate reason to a more sensual drive. The issue of the debate, of course, is whether to return Helen to the Greeks. He dwells not upon the morality of the case but on the charms of Helen:

>          whose youth and freshness
> Wrinkles Apollo's and makes stale the morning . . .
> Whose price hath launch'd above a thousand ships,
> And turn'd crown'd kings to merchants.

In Elizabethan terms, Troilus is defective in wit but strong in will, and by now he has so subjugated his reason that the culmination of his argument has a splendid irony as he calls in ringing terms for the retention of the spoils of what he acknowledges as theft:

>          O theft most base,
> That we have stolen what we fear to keep!

Shakespeare ends this curious line of argument with an even more curious intervention, denoted by the stage direction, 'Enter Cassandra, raving.' Cassandra's prophecy is in the manner of Thisbe's death-speech in *A Midsummer Night's Dream*:

> Add to my clamours! let us pay betimes
> A moiety of that mass of moan to come.
> Cry, Trojans, cry! practise your eyes with tears!
> Troy must not be nor goodly Ilion stand;
> Our firebrand brother, Paris, burns us all.
> Cry, Trojans, cry! an Helen and a woe:
> Cry, cry! Troy burns, or else let Helen go.

This episode can only be intended as a deliberate intrusion of broad farce into the Trojan debate, for there is no convention that prophecy must be couched in this vein: by comparison, the Soothsayer's warning to Caesar, 'Beware the Ides of March,' shows a masterly economy. Perhaps Shakespeare could not resist a round of applause from the young men gathered at the Inns of Court. Probably it indicates the satirical intention of the whole scene. We have to remember that Shakespeare's audience, both intellectuals and others, knew the story of this play beforehand: 'as true as Troilus' and 'as false as Cressida' were proverbial. The interest was in how the author would treat his material: the fact that Cassandra was expected may explain the panto-mime effect the author chooses to make with her.

The debate is soberly resumed. Hector puts Troilus' lack of reason clearly before us:

> Is your blood
> So madly hot that no discourse of reason,
> Nor fear of bad success in a bad cause,
> Can qualify the same?

Paris further confuses reason by his preoccupation with appearances and loss of face:

> But I would have the soil of her fair rape
> Wip'd off in honourable keeping her.
> What treason were it to the ransack'd queen,
> Disgrace to your great worths, and shame to me,
> Now to deliver her possession up
> On terms of base compulsion!

Hector succinctly summarises the arguments of Troilus and Paris and asserts the importance of the law:

> The reasons you allege do more conduce
> To the hot passion of distemper'd blood
> Than to make up a free determination
> 'Twixt right and wrong . . .
> There is a law in each well-order'd nation
> To curb those raging appetites that are
> Most disobedient and refractory.

Yet he immediately succumbs improbably to the arguments of saving public face, in despite of private morality:

> Yet ne'ertheless,
> My sprightly brethren, I propond to you
> In resolution to keep Helen still;
> For 'tis a cause that hath no mean dependence
> Upon our joint and several dignities.

There remains only self-deception: Troilus asserts a desperate lust for glory, and, as so often in Shakespeare, a disastrous course begins when public man asserts himself over individual ideas of justice. But this time the arguments have failed either to convince or to move us: it is an appropriately abrupt ending to an unconvincing debate.

Elizabethan sympathies were Roman rather than Greek, so that Shakespeare's savage caricature of the Greek generals no doubt met with amused approval. But there is not much evidence for the general view that he portrays the Trojans much more sympathetically. Thersites in the next scene puts the Trojan as well as the Greek stance in perspective:

> Here is such patchery, such juggling and such knavery! All the argument is a cuckold and a whore.

The writing in the Trojan scenes is as uneven as in the rest of the play. Although the distinction between private morality and public conduct is clearly pointed, we see no one character riven by the knowledge, as we see men as different as Macbeth and Antony riven.

Indeed, the characters in this play are not generally aware of their failures, and much dramatic interest is thereby sacrificed. *Hamlet,* written at almost the same time as *Troilus,* is an outstanding dramatic success partly because the hero's agonising over his failure to act constantly heightens the emotional temperature. This feature of the dramatic slackness of *Troilus* is underlined if we consider a feature in its construction that is apparently paralleled in *Antony and Cleopatra.* Thersites, commenting on the action at important points in the development, has a similar function to Enobarbus and others in the later play: indeed Thersites' 'All the argument is a cuckold and a whore' foreshadow Philo's opening words on Antony, 'the triple pillar of the world transformed / Into a strumpet's fool'. But in *Antony and Cleopatra* there is continuous dramatic tension because Enobarbus, Caesar and the rest voice criticisms which are only extreme views of what Antony sees in himself. The dramatic interest indeed revolves around this individual tension, and we are kept continually aware of the interplay between Antony's public conduct with his Roman colleagues and his private predilections towards Egypt. In *Troilus and Cressida,* although we are several times reminded explicitly of the conflict between 'blood' and 'judgement', there is no individual who is much disturbed by the conflict; although Thersites provides a bitter commentary upon the action, the play lacks tension because the characters have too little self-awareness to present us with individual dilemmas of private and public conduct.

Here it is necessary to say a little about the part of Thersites in the play's construction. Tillyard says: 'To make Thersites into a chorus, the authentic commentator on the play's action, is ridiculous. His function is that of a Fool, to give a twist to every action and every motive.'[6] But the roles of chorus and fool, as Shakespeare was shortly to show in *King Lear,* need not be far apart. Thersites accompanies all the major scenes of the play on the barest of excuses and, in considering its construction, I have to agree with Bertrand Evans who sees him as an 'adviser of our awareness' and 'the strongest force of unity in the play; perhaps the sole unifying force'.[7] A. L. Birney sees Thersites as an instrument of satiric catharsis.[8] Certainly he is the strongest embodiment of the play's prevailing tone of disillusioned satire.

He disappears to make way for the ponderous humour of the strange scene in which the Greeks try vainly to call Achilles forth from his tent, in which the stupid Agamemnon and Ajax deplore the pride which is their own besetting sin and Ulysses contributes to the cumbersome device of praising the wisdom of the brutish Ajax.

There follows the first meeting of Troilus and Cressida. There is an extravagant conventionality in the string of similes in which Troilus declares his love which shows him working hard upon himself and the idea of himself as romantic lover:

> True swains in love shall, in the world to come,
> Approve their truths by Troilus: when their rhymes,
> Full of protest, of oath, and big compare,
> Want similes, truth tir'd with iteration, —
> As true as steel, as plantage to the moon,
> As sun to day, as turtle to her mate,
> As iron to adamant, as earth to the centre —
> Yet, after all comparisons of truth,
> As truth's authentic author to be cited,
> As true as Troilus shall crown up the verse,
> And sanctify the numbers.

It is all a little too elaborate. Troilus neglects the real Cressida to create for himself the woman he wishes to see. Cressida subscribes readily enough to the illusion, subsuming any doubts about her real character in a lengthy parallel to Troilus' series of comparisons:

> If I be false, or swerve a hair from truth,
> When time is old and hath forgot itself,
> When waterdrops have worn the stones of Troy,
> And blind oblivion swallow'd cities up,
> And mighty states characterless are grated
> To dusty nothing; yet let memory
> From false to false, among false maids in love,
> Upbraid my falsehood! when they have said — as false
> As air, as water, wind or sandy earth,
> As fox to lamb, as wolf to heifer's calf,
> Pard to the hind, or stepdame to her son;
> Yea, let them say, to stick the heart of falsehood,
> As false as Cressid.

To say that this is elaborate is not to say that it fails to move: the opening lines in particular have that sense of timelessness and breadth which characterise Shakespeare at his most memorable. But the passage is most moving when we take it from its context; its most important dramatic significance is that it parallels Troilus' declaration, showing Cressida more excited by the picture Troilus paints of her than by reality. It is the worthless Pandarus who pronounces the bargain sealed, and closes the scene upon the play's more characteristic note of transient physical pleasure:

> Whereupon I will show you a chamber and a bed; which bed, because it shall not speak of your pretty encounters, press it to death: away!

The love affair of Troilus and Cressida is framed within the tawdry context of the older affair which is the cause of the wars. At the opening of Act IV, Paris asks Diomedes to distinguish who 'merits fair Helen best', himself or Menelaus. Diomedes' estimation of the rival suitors and Helen is in the vein of Thersites and strikes the now familiar note of jaded disillusion:

> He, like a puling cuckold, would drink up
> The lees and dregs of a flat tamed piece;
> You, like a lecher, out of whorish loins
> Are pleas'd to breed out your inheritors:
> Both merits pois'd, each weighs nor less nor more;
> But he as he, each heavier for a whore.

Within ten lines of this, we see Troilus and Cressida, briefly and tenderly together before the news comes of Cressida's removal. Their parting produces from Troilus the most famous passage of the play:

> We two, that with so many thousand sighs
> Did buy each other, must poorly sell ourselves
> With the rude brevity and discharge of one.
> Injurious time now, with a robber's haste,
> Crams his rich thievery up, he knows not how:
> As many farewells as be stars in heaven,
> With distinct breath and consign'd kisses to them,
> He fumbles up into a loose adieu;
> And scants us with a single famish'd kiss,
> Distasted with the salt of broken tears.

This is marvellous stuff in the metaphysical vein. It is also excellent dramatic poetry, for it suggests not only the intensity of Troilus' emotion but also, through the imagery of the palate and the scenes, the fragility of the relationship. L. C. Knights points out, in an interesting essay on the play,[9] that the expression of Troilus' idealism through the imagery of taste underlines its insubstantiality and its subjection to time.

There is no doubt that Troilus feels the brittleness of the relationship, for within a few lines he has descended from his high note to fears about Cressida's fidelity:

> The Grecian youths are full of quality;
> They're loving, well compos'd, with gifts of nature flowing,
> And swelling o'er with arts and exercise.

Within a few moments, we see how far the Cressida he loved existed only in the mind of Troilus. Earlier Cressida has responded briefly to the love-speeches of Troilus by direct imitation; for the rest, she is presented as the wanton of tradition. As she arrives with Diomedes in the Greek camp, she is handed round like a puppet, to be kissed by each of the generals in a mime of her prostitution. It is another element of stylisation in the play's presentation; like the earlier scene in which Pandarus displayed the charms of the Trojan generals to Cressida, it recalls an older and cruder drama. This scene, of course, ironically echoes that earlier presentation of Cressida. Ulysses' reaction to Cressida's conduct here points the way that the scene must be played:

> Fie, fie upon her!
> There's language in her eye, her cheek, her lip,
> Nay, her foot speaks: her wanton spirits look out
> At every joint and motive of her body.
> O, these encounterers, so glib of tongue,
> That give a coasting welcome ere it comes,
> And wide unclasp the tables of their thoughts
> To every ticklish reader! set them down
> For sluttish spoils of opportunity,
> And daughters of the game.

From this point to the end of the play, Shakespeare hurries on events remorselessly, as if anxious to be finished with a satire that had become tedious to him. There is some careless writing. Hector's introduction to the famed Greek warriors, which could in a different play be a tense dramatic moment, is treated in lines dangerously close to doggerel:

> The worthiest of them tell me name by name;
> But for Achilles mine own searching eyes
> Shall find him by his large and portly size.

Nick Bottom's Pyramus is not far away from this!

Similarly, Cressida's couplets at the moment of her betrayal of Troilus are vapid stuff:

> Troilus, farewell! one eye yet looks on thee;
> But with my heart the other eye doth see.
> Ah, poor our sex! this fault in us I find,
> The error of our eye directs our mind:
> What error leads must err; O, then conclude,
> Minds sway'd by eyes are full of turpitude.

If straightforward robust satire is the intention, this is no doubt effective enough, but it is thin stuff to engage our dramatic interest for very long. More importantly, it is evidence again of the uneven texture of the play and its confusing mixture of styles. The Troilus-Cressida love theme has earlier been treated seriously: we cannot sustain interest in its decline because there is no progress in Cressida's descent from virtue. We follow each agonising stage of Macbeth's descent into the abyss, of Othello's decline from the pillar of state. Here the only interest is the ambiguity between what the characters publicly declare themselves to be and what they really are. Although Shakespeare makes us share the play's confusions, the dramatic method he employs is ineffective because it does not allow for character development.

The most striking example of this is that Troilus is never shown alone after the revelation to him of Cressida's infidelity, although the speech of his discovery in Act V Scene ii is the best-written passage of this unsatisfactory final section of the play. Troilus recovers his public poise, but the fact that we are not shown his private agony playing against it detracts from the dramatic impact of the individual man and restricts the emotional intensity in a way uncharacteristic of Shakespeare. The characters' earlier lack of awareness of their own shortcomings restricts the dramatic range of the play.

Hector's death at the end of the play is a treacherous travesty of heroic arms, and no doubt meant to be so. Achilles' brief speech of celebration recalls the style of the Player's Hecuba speech in *Hamlet*:

> The dragon wing of night o'erspreads the earth,
> And, stickler-like, the armies separate.
> My half-supp'd sword, that frankly would have fed,
> Pleas'd with this dainty bait, thus goes to bed.
> Come, tie his body to my horse's tail;
> Along the field I will the Trojan trail.

This dark-toned, bitter play ends appropriately with Pandarus' epilogue devoted to venereal diseases.

What Shakespeare has failed to do is to fuse his love-story with the background of the wars to provide effective drama, whether serious or satirical. In *Othello*, the hero's plangent dedication of himself and his romantic military history to his 'fair warrior' is the starting-point for the tragedy, and as it develops we are constantly aware how his easy command of men in war is no match for Iago's more intimate wiles. In *Antony and Cleopatra*, Antony's military decline both mirrors and deepens the tragedy of the principals. In *Troilus and Cressida* the love story remains obstinately separate from the public events around it, and this construction contributes to a lack of intensity and a sense of incompleteness in both areas.

I have tried to show why *Troilus* has remained over the centuries an unsatisfactory work. This savage satire on war remains patchy in its effects even in our own time, when its theme is so relevant. Traversi summarised the matter as well as anyone: 'The verse and construction of *Troilus and Cressida* are clearly experimental; they do not, like those of *Macbeth*, imply a natural fusion of theme and emotion in a finished work of art.'[10] I am left wondering whether much older critical thought is not perhaps best; I cannot agree with Tillyard when he writes: 'The old interpretation of the play as an outburst of unrestrained bitterness against life, to be overcome later, is fantastically false.'[11] It is true that it is unproductive to hypothesise a trauma in the author's personal life and project this into the texts of the problem plays. I have tried to show from the text how *Troilus* is an uneven, incoherent and ineffective drama, despite short bursts of splendid language. It does seem that the play's defects of coherence derive from an all-pervading pessimism in the writer, which prevents him from developing its best elements thoroughly, whether those elements be elevated, satiric, or more broadly comic.

### All's Well that Ends Well

I said earlier that one of the least subjective yardsticks of assessment amidst the confusions of the problem plays is that of success or otherwise in the theatre over the years. It is fitting therefore to begin by noting the Arden editor's words: '*All's Well that Ends Well* is not a play that is often read or performed, and on the rare occasions when it is seen or heard it does not seem to give much general pleasure.'[12]

Imperfect plays often stretch wide a director's ingenuity. Trevor Nunn's Royal Shakespeare Company production of 1981-2 transferred the action to Edwardian days, used a set which suggested Marylebone station, and put both the Florentine wars and Countess Rossillion's house by the railway. The production was generally well received, and had some splendid things in it, but the series of desperate inventions around the edge of the text often seemed a laudable attempt to disguise the deficiencies in dramatic construction.

There is much that is interesting in the play, but it is often interesting in relationship to other works rather than within the boundaries of this one. As in all the problem plays, the mixture of styles and material leads to a lack of coherence. The differences in thought and expression were strong enough for Coleridge to argue that the play 'was written at two different, and rather distinct, periods of the poet's life'. There are some speeches which have the lyrical tone of the earlier comedies, but much language which is the supple dramatic medium of the greatest work. The play is now fairly reliably dated at 1603-4, but some of the writing may of course date from much earlier. G. K. Hunter accepts an unusual amount of variation in the verse-levels of both *All's Well* and *Measure for Measure* but suggests: 'Both these plays may be seen as efforts to reconcile a sense of divine purpose with a salty practical wisdom, and this mixture may be held responsible for the mixture of styles.'[13]

Although the dramatic development of *All's Well* is more consistent than that of *Troilus and Cressida,* it is still uneven, with lurches not so much in the movement of the plot as in the tones of different scenes. Shakespeare had by this time developed not only psychological subtlety of characterisation but the sinewy, compressed language, full of wider suggestion, which is the greatest glory of his maturity. Here he fits a highly realistic set of principal characters into a plot which derives from the fantastic world of folk-lore.

Tillyard calls Bertram 'a close and not very friendly study of unlicked aristocracy'. He is a far more detailed and convincing observation than the more amiable pictures of Bassanio and Orlando. Similarly, Helena is far closer to real life than the charming, psychologically untroubled heroines of the earlier comedies: she is closer to the Cordelia soon to come than to Viola, created not long before her. Yet in the folklore material on which so much of the play depends, psychological subtlety is a distraction rather than a help, for it invites us to measure deliberately unrealistic material against the yardstick of realism we apply to character.

Shakespeare learnt by the experiments conducted in the problem plays, for when he treats similar material in the late romances, he steadily sacrifices studies of character to the wider consideration of his plot, so that young couples like Miranda and Ferdinand, and Perdita and Florizel, become instruments of a greater purpose rather than important in themselves.

The key scene in which the King emerges cured by Helena (Act II Scene iii) illustrates these tensions. The device of the sovereign elixir which saves the King's life has the miraculous felicity of folk-tale and is taken straight from Bocaccio's *Decameron*, Shakespeare's source. For a hundred lines, the fable proceeds smoothly, until the King awards Helena her prize, Bertram; then the indignant Bertram halts that progress with harsh disdain:

> I know her well:
> She had her breeding at my father's charge.
> A poor physician's daughter my wife! Disdain
> Rather corrupt me ever.

The King, newly restored to health, sees through the trappings of public man and the delusions of rank in lines which foreshadow the purged Lear:

> Good alone
> Is good, without a name; vileness is so:
> The property by what it is should go,
> Not by the title.

With the King's anger, the language springs away from couplets into a freer verse. In a speech full of interesting ironies, he invokes the power and rank he has just derided to secure the good he cannot persuade Bertram to accept:

> My honour's at the stake, which to defeat,
> I must produce my power. Here, take her hand,
> Proud, scornful boy, unworthy this good gift,
> That dost in vile misprision shackle up
> My love and her desert; that canst not dream
> We, poising us in her defective scale,
> Shall weight thee to the beam; that wilt not know
> It is in us to plant thine honour where

We please to have it grow. Check thy contempt;
Obey our will which travails in thy good;
Believe not thy disdain, but presently
Do thine own fortunes that obedient right
Which both thy duty owes and our power claims.

This is the kind of material which Shakespeare investigates with such piercing insight in the tragedies, where public and private man continually wrestle for supremacy: here it is an abrupt change of gear from a less direct kind of drama.

Most of the play's problems derive from stresses of this kind. One of the major difficulties is Bertram. Hunter feels that as a surface portrait of a Renaissance nobleman he is credible, 'but when the moral dimension of natural man choosing Sin but saved by Grace is added . . . the superstructure of meaning becomes too heavy for the basis of character and the whole topples dangerously near incoherence, and virtually separates out into its constituent elements'.[14]

The difficulty extends to most of the major characters. The Countess of Rossillion, which Shaw called 'the most beautiful old woman's part ever written' gives us a convincing picture of the noble household she rules, through her conversations with the clown, steward, Lafew and Helena. Parolles is a brilliant Jonsonian caricature,[15] the clothes-imagery, as usual in Shakespeare, a means of suggesting a difference between appearance and reality. His unmasking in Act IV Scene iii is a beautifully managed scene, in which Shakespeare's skill as a practical dramatist runs for a while free of larger concerns. But Parolles is depicted by means which hardly suit with the vaguer suggestions of an older magic which we are given at important points in the play.

The difficulty extends to the principals. Bertram's only relieving characteristic is the glimpse we are allowed of his genuine courage in battle. Peter Ure, noting his 'reality of stubbornly consistent shabbiness and lack of bounty', says that his depiction clashes with that of Helena: 'Two characters from two quite disparate kinds of fiction are pretending that they belong to the same world.'[16] But even within Helena there are contrasts: the miracle-worker of the first half of the play is transformed into the brisk business-woman of the later part.

W. W. Lawrence[17] pointed out that the main plot is clearly related to folk-tale and fairy-tale, being built around two traditional episodes, 'the healing of the king' and 'the fulfilment of the tasks'. There is no doubt that the bed-trick, so difficult for a modern audience, was familiar to Shakespeare's contemporaries as a piece of fairy-lore that could be accepted without question. R. S. Forsyth in *The Relations of Shirley's Plays to the Elizabethan Period* (1914) cited 21 plays of the period in which the device occurs. But the greatest difficulty is Shakespeare's setting of the episode in a section of the play which is dominated by a realistic treatment of character. As Hunter says:

> The psychological reality of Helena and the realism of the background make the facile substitution of one body for another seem irrelevant and tasteless, while the satiric stratum of the play seems to underline those elements in the trick which modern criticism finds abhorrent . . . The Christian and gnomic overtones of the play again seem to raise issues which cannot easily be resolved by plot-manipulation.[18]

Helena comes nearest to uniting the two kinds of material in the play. There are moments in the first part of the play where she manages to unite the suggestion of more than mortal strength in the folklore heroine with a personality that is believable. Such a moment comes after she has stood silent and humiliated through the storm which follows Bertram's rejection of her and the King's anger; with an inner strength and simple dignity worthy of Viola or Cordelia she says to the King:

> That you are well restor'd, my lord, I'm glad.
> Let the rest go.

Similarly, Helena's great speech of love and resolution in III ii which closes the first half of the play unites intense personal feeling with an independence suggesting the strength of a grace from outside the realities of the situation:

> O you leaden messengers,
> That ride upon the violent speed of fire,
> Fly with false aim; move the still-piecing air
> That sings with piercing; do not touch my lord.
> Whoever shoots at him, I set him there;
> Whoever charges on his forward breast,
> I am the caitiff that do hold him to't;
> And though I kill him not, I am the cause
> His death was so effected. Better 'twere
> I met the ravin lion when he roar'd
> With sharp constraint of hunger; better 'twere

That all the miseries which nature owes
Were mine at once. No; come thou home, Rossillion,
Whence honour but of danger wins a scar,
As oft it loses all; I will be gone;
My being here it is that holds thee hence . . .
　　　　　　Come, night; end, day;
For with the dark, poor thief, I'll steal away.

The night she invokes is to be her medium of salvation; it is a curious reversal of the fate of that other invoker of darkness from the other end of the spectrum of good and evil, Lady Macbeth. But the busy plotting and deception, her final subjection of Bertram by the bed-trick, sit uneasily with the role of an instrument of grace. This role is clearly set out by the Countess at the beginning of the second half of the play, when she hears of Bertram's treatment of his bride:

He cannot thrive
Unless her prayers, whom Heaven delights to hear
And loves to grant, reprieve him from the wrath
Of greatest justice.

At the end of the play, the climax is meant to be seen not as the achievement of a husband, as it might be in the earlier comedies, but the redemption of wickedness by the supreme power of mercy. But the psychological realism of the second half of the play in particular, the skilled plot-contrivances of Parolles' unmasking and the twists of the last act, the use of the bed-trick rather than some more mysterious and elevated device, all militate against the function of Helena as an instrument of divine grace. It is no wonder that she has often been seen as Shakespeare's loveliest heroine in his unloveliest comedy.

As with the other problem plays, we have to wait for the last plays for the solutions to the experiments Shakespeare begins in *All's Well*; only there are the problems of technique and the stylistic tensions he sets up here successfully resolved.

## Measure for Measure

Probably no play of Shakespeare's has produced such divided responses as *Measure for Measure*. The divisions go back at least as far as the great Romantic critics. Whilst Hazlitt wrote in 1818, 'This play is as full of genius as it is of wisdom,'[19] Coleridge thought in 1827, 'It is a hateful work. Our feelings of justice are grossly wounded in Angelo's escape. Isabella herself contrives to be unamiable, and Claudio is detestable.'[20] Nor has our own century come much nearer to consensus. Wilson Knight found the play full of the spirit of the Gospels, an extended dramatic parable exemplifying the passage in Christ's Sermon on the Mount, which begins 'Judge not, that ye be not judged.'[21] Una Ellis-Fermor a few years later thought it a cynical play, in which

> The lowest depths of Jacobean negation are touched . . . with the exception of the kindly, timid Provost, there is no character who is not suspect, and those whose claims to goodness or decency seem most vigorous are precisely those in whom meanness, self-regard, and hyprocrisy root deepest.[22]

A problem play, indeed! In the last twenty years 'Christian' interpretations have proliferated among critics, but each new production of the play has drawn responses from theatre critics which stress the seamier side of the play as the major problem of stage presentation.

The truth as well as the problem is that the play attempts to combine apparently intractable elements, with a realistic stage investigation of psychological motivation running alongside the great abstracts of sin and forgiveness. Shakespeare is experimenting again: on the basis, says Traversi, of the Duke's statement in Act IV that 'All difficulties are but easy when they are known.' In investigating justice and mercy by means of a play which centres on sexual passion, he has set himself a formidable task. Traversi offers the key both to the construction of this play and its place within the canon: 'The theme of *Measure for Measure* is still the interdependence of good and evil within human experience as centred in the act of passion. The mature tragedies which follow are to separate the elements within this complexity.'[23]

Part of the uneasiness modern readers and audiences feel comes from the plot of the play, which depends upon our acceptance of the black and white extremes of Victorian melodrama. As far as the outline of the plot goes, Isabella, Angelo and the Duke might spring from *East Lynne*. Of course Shakespeare makes more of them than Mrs Henry Wood could ever have done, but in investigating the psychological complications which lie behind the stances the plot demands, he explains behaviour without achieving a satisfying coherence in the play. As in *All's Well*, most of the difficulties stem from a realistic treatment of material which in his last plays he will deliberately treat less directly.

Commentators have often been so beguiled by the parable strain in *Measure for Measure* that they have overlooked the presence of Shakespeare's most consistent preoccupation, that of power and its relation to the individual, considered here through another variation of his investigation of the differences between appearance and reality. The Duke in the opening line of the play speaks of unfolding 'the properties of government': the first three acts are relentless expositions of how public life finds out Angelo, just as the last four acts of *Othello* show how private life undermines the Moor. Isabella, in the later stages of the play in particular, may well act as instrument of divine mercy; it is indisputable that as Angelo misuses position earlier she reminds him, in the first of their great confrontations:

> O, it is excellent
> To have a giant's strength; but it is tryannous
> To use it like a giant.

Seven lines later, she generalises the issue of this play into the sentiment that is the corner-stone of so much of Shakespeare's dramatic construction: that man, when 'dress'd in a little brief authority', will deny his individual personality and act stupidly or badly.

To call attention to this familiar theme of Shakespeare's is not to deny the overtone of Christian allegory in the play, which its title indeed suggests. But the use and abuse of power and the natures of justice and mercy are not contradictory but complementary themes. F. Fergusson puts the parable aspect of the play firmly within the Elizabethan preoccupation with the microcosm and the macrocosm in the state:

> St. Paul's distinction between Mosaic Law, with its rational and literal justice, and the new rule of Charity (or Mercy, as the Hebrew prophets put it) pervades the play. But so, I think, does the Platonic and Aristotelian philosophy of society, which is based upon the analogy between the body politic and the individual.[24]

Shakespeare, however, is concerned with a particular set of individuals, whom he succeeds for the first half of his play at least in making very believable, whether we approve of their actions or not.

For the play changes its nature in the last two acts. The distinction is stated most boldly by Tillyard:

The simple and ineluctable fact is that the tone in the first half of the play is frankly, acutely human and quite hostile to the tone of allegory, or symbol. And, however much the tone changes in the second half, nothing in the world can make an allegorical interpretation poetically valid throughout.[25]

Certainly the atmosphere is very different in the second half of the play, with the Duke becoming an ever more omnipotent controller of the action rather than a conventional character, and the predominant medium switching from a sinuous, flexible verse to prose.

At the beginning of the play, however, we are plunged straight into the familiar theme of the impact of power upon an individual personality. Angelo is not a villain who disguises his motives until he has the power to achieve his ends; there are no swift asides to the audience as we get from Richard of Gloucester or Iago. He does not yet know the preposterous genie which lurks within him, waiting to spring forth when the lamp of office is burnished. His name is a play not only upon the obvious meaning of angel but on the gold coin circulating in Shakespeare's day. His punning response to the Duke's making him his deputy indicates a premonition of the dangers power may bring to him:

> Now, good my lord,
> Let there be some more test made of my mettle
> Before so noble and so great a figure
> Be stamp'd upon it.

The brisk little opening scene closes with the Duke clasping Angelo's hand and discoursing upon his distaste for adulation and the trappings of power:

> I'll privily away; I love the people,
> But do not like to stage me to their eyes.
> Though it do well, I do not relish well
> Their loud applause and aves vehement.
> Nor do I think the man of safe discretion
> That does affect it.

Claudio in the next scene is aware of 'the demigod, Authority' and acknowledges his fault in the unpleasant terms characteristic of Shakespeare's writing at this time:

> Our natures do pursue,
> Like rats that ravin down their proper bane,
> A thirsty evil, and when we drink, we die.

Claudio puts the old dilemma of office and the individual personality before us, for he is uncertain whether it is Angelo's severe character or his newly acquired power which makes him harsh:

> Whether the tyranny be in his place,
> Or in his eminence that fills it up,
> I stagger in — but this new governor
> Awakes me all the enrolled penalties
> Which have, like unscour'd armour, hung by the wall.

In the next scene, the multifarious and often confusing functions of the Duke in the play begin to develop. The starting-point is the old folk-motive of the sovereign in disguise mingling with his people, which Shakespeare has already used a little in *Henry VI* and *Henry V*. But we find him at different times a formal commentator upon the action; the conventional stage character of the plot-promoting priest; the supreme ruler who dispenses justice and rules on disputes; the stage figure who rules Prospero-like over the action. As the play develops, he becomes steadily less a realistic character, an evolution signalled by his use of rhymed speech. Possibly he was intended as a flattering portrait of the new monarch, James I.[26] Always he is a key figure in guiding the audience, and thus crucial in indicating Shakespeare's intentions in this often puzzling play. At the end of Act I Scene iv he is quite unequivocal in stating that the impact of power upon personality is to be the lever of the forthcoming action:

> Lord Angelo is precise,
> Stands at a guard with envy, scarce confesses
> That his blood flows, or that his appetite
> Is more to bread than stone. Hence shall we see,
> If power change purpose, what our seemers be.

Already our appetite is whetted to see this marble figure under the stress of office, but Shakespeare first introduces the other and equally uncompromising player in this remorseless contest of good and evil. Isabella is immediately linked with Angelo by her extremism. The Duke has just told us that Angelo 'scarce confesses that his blood flows' and in a moment Lucio will warn Isabella as he sends her to plead with him that he is 'a man whose blood is very snow-broth'. Isabella's first words in the play are equally uncompromising: she begins by wishing for 'a more strict restraint upon the sisterhood' which she is about to join: Isabella is the object of some of the most antithetical views in the literature of criticism and there is not room even to summarise them here.[27] My concern is with her part in the dramatic construction of the play. In that she is allied with Angelo in important respects, so that she can provide a proper counterpoise and ensure dramatic tension. Her view of the law is as narrowly legalistic as Angelo's; she is as unswerving and reckless in her pursuit of virtue as Angelo is remorseless in his lust for her. There is no doubt that chastity was seen by Shakespeare's contemporaries as an absolute virtue; this makes even more remarkable his achievement in showing that even the most simple and unwavering of moral attitudes may be very complex in operation. And with a typical Shakespearian irony, he sets her through the location of power to sue to the man least proof against her charms. So the two principals in this drama of extremes embark upon their voyages of self-discovery.

They confront each other in two great scenes. In the first of these Shakespeare draws expertly Isabella's reluctant return to the more public role she thought to have forsaken. Tillyard points out how 'she gradually discards the drawing-in of herself into a cloistral concentration and reaches out again to a worldly observation she has newly renounced'.[28] The scene is built around the interplay of two characters struggling with different aspects of the conflict between public and private faces, for as it proceeds Angelo finds himself struggling to preserve his façade of cold justice against the conflagration Isabella has lit within him.

The effect office has had upon Angelo is suggested before Isabella enters; instead of the balanced, modest figure we saw accepting the Duke's directive in the play's first scene, he is now harsh and threatening even with the gentle and responsible Provost:

Do you your office, or give up your place,
And you shall well be spared.

As Isabella is ushered in, he disposes of Juliet in words which show his puritan's distaste for her sin, 'See you the fornicatress be remov'd.' Isabella's opening plea, couched in negatives, is cold with the same repugnance:

> There is a vice that most I do abhor,
> And most desire should meet the blow of justice,
> For which I would not plead, but that I must,
> For which I must not plead, but that I am
> At war 'twixt will and will not.

Without Lucio's repeated insistence 'You are too cold' she would give up at the outset:

> O just but severe law!
> I had a brother, then. Heaven keep your honour.

When she asks that he exercise his authority to grant mercy, the familiar brutal impact of power upon personality flashes out from Angelo:

> Look, what I will not, that I cannot do.

In a key passage, Isabella asserts the pre-eminence of Christian mercy over the letter of man-made law, and Agnelo makes the ruler's age-old retreat to a generalised authority to deny a personal appeal:

> How would you be,
> If he, which is the top of judgment, should
> But judge you as you are? O, think on that,
> And mercy then will breathe within your lips,
> Like man new made.
> *Angelo*:            Be you content, fair maid:
> It is the law, not I, condemn your brother.
> Were it my kinsman, brother, or my son,
> It should be thus with him; he must die tomorrow.

Isabella provides the comment on this attitude, that to use a 'giant's strength' without discretion is tyranny. This is what Lear has to learn about power, and Isabella follows it immediately with a great speech on power and authority which foreshadows the more coherent examination of the issues in the later play:

> Could great men thunder
> As Jove himself does, Jove would ne'er be quiet,
> For every pelting, petty officer
> Would use his heaven for thunder.

Nothing but thunder. Merciful heaven,
Thou rather with thy sharp and sulfurous bolt
Splits the unwedgeable and gnarled oak
Than the soft myrtle. But man, proud man,
Dressed in a little brief authority,
Most ignorant of what he's most assured,
His glassy essence, like an angry ape,
Plays such fantastic tricks before high heaven
As makes the angels weep.

She concludes her devastating attack on the dangers of public man with a direct appeal to the individual man behind Angelo's civic façade:

Go to your bosom,
Knock there, and ask your heart what it doth know
That's like my brother's fault; if it confess
A natural guiltiness such as is his,
Let it not sound a thought upon your tongue
Against my brother's life.

Ironically, this inner man to whom she appeals, and which Angelo has struggled to conceal, is now in turmoil. Angelo is not a hypocrite but a man who knows himself so slightly that the sudden dazzling entry in his life of the chaste and vulnerable Isabella finds him totally unprepared. Many commentators forget how effective a dramatic stroke Shakespeare contrives at this point with out startling first view of the private man in Angelo. So far in the play we have had every reason to believe the reports that he is a man of severe and unflinching rectitude: his conduct as a ruler has endorsed them. Shakespeare carefully withholds all mention of Mariana until Act III. Angelo has begun the scene with Isabella with the bearing of an ascetic monk, balancing her entry as a nun. He ends it by revealing in soliloquy the inner man, torn by dark unsuspected drives which horrify him, and which will topple his exercise of power. It is a thrilling and disturbing stage moment, with his perturbation caught in the broken syntax and verse:

What's this? What's this? Is this her fault or mine?
The tempter or the tempted, who sins most?
Ha, not she. Nor doth she tempt; but it is I
That, lying by the violet in the sun,
Do as the carrion does, not as the flow'r,

Corrupt with virtuous season. Can it be
That modesty may more betray our sense
Than woman's lightness? Having waste ground enough,
Shall we desire to raze the sanctuary,
And pitch our evils there? O fie, fie, fie!
What dost thou, or what art thou, Angelo?
Dost thou desire her foully for those things
That make her good? O, let her brother live:
Thieves for their robbery have authority
When judges steal themselves. What, do I love her,
Then I desire to hear her speak again,
And feast upon her eyes? What is't I dream on?
O cunning enemy, that, to catch a saint,
With saints dost bait thy hook! Most dangerous
Is that temptation that doth goad us on
To sin in loving virtue. Never could the strumpet,
With all her double vigor, art and nature,
Once stir my temper; but this virtuous maid
Subdues me quite. Ever till now,
When men were fond, I smiled, and wond'red how.

I quote the speech in full because it is impossible to break down this
great whirlpool of distress. There is no speech in Shakespeare that better
catches a mind and a soul in turmoil, no scene which is built more
effectively around the clash between public face and private feeling.

The second great scene between the two principals is separated only
by the low-key scene with the pathetic Juliet, which does scarcely more
than mark the passage of time. When Act II Scene iv opens, Angelo is
no more composed for the passing of a night; the contrast between
'place' and 'blood', between the dignified public appearance and the
corrupt individual soul, is torturing him as when we left him:

                    O place, O form,
How often dost thou with thy case, thy habit,
Wrench awe from fools, and tie the wiser souls
To thy false seeming! Blood, thou art blood.
Let's write 'good angel' on the devil's horn,
'Tis not the devil's crest.

Angelo's puritan exterior (he called himself a 'saint' in his
soliloquy, accepting the label the Duke had put upon him wit'

word 'precise', the normal adjective of the day for Puritans) is discarded in the language of a Victorian villain: 'You must lay down the treasure of your body.' This of course is the expression of a frustrated sensualist, who has known little of women. Isabella's reaction shows an even more remarkable psychological insight in her creator. The resolution she has shown throughout becomes ferocious; her contempt for life makes her seize upon the idea of death as eagerly as an early Christian martyr. She shows also what F. R. Leavis calls 'a kind of sensuality in martyrdom'[29] when she considers death;

> were I under the terms of death,
> Th'impression of keen whips I'd wear as rubies,
> And strip myself to death as to a bed
> That longing have been sick for, ere I'd yield
> My body up to shame.

As in all the problem plays, the action of *Measure for Measure* is built around a series of strippings away of public fronts to reveal the essentials beneath. Angelo's rectitude and Claudio's resolution in the face of death both prove inadequate. In this scene and her painful meeting with Claudio, we see the inflexibility of Isabella's martyr's stance. Her convictions are not mocked, but Shakespeare surrounds her with circumstances which show that life is too complicated for any dogma to control it completely, however worthy the creed employed. Isabella has aroused much distaste among critics. Shakespeare does not ask us to applaud her: he is investigating the martyr's make-up as thoroughly as he investigates Angelo's seeming virtue. Because the framework is experimental and not fully worked out, the work as a whole lacks the coherence which make *King Lear* or *The Winter's Tale* more satisfying experiences, but the behaviour of the characters in the first three acts of the play is totally convincing.

By the end of this scene, power and public position are being marshalled to the purposes of the corrupt individual as Angelo threatens his victim:

> My unsoil'd name, th' austereness of my life,
> My vouch against you, amd my place i' th' state,
> Will so your accusation overweigh,
> That you shall stifle in your own report,
> And smell of calumny. I have begun,
> And now I give my sensual race the rein.

Even at this moment of anguish Isabella is linked with her tormentor, for the soliloquy with which she follows Angelo's exit shows that her knowledge of life is as limited as was Angelo's of himself. Her martyr's strain shows strong again, driving out all thought that her brother might not react in her way to the thought of death:

> Yet hath he in him such a mind of honour,
> That, had he twenty heads to tender down
> On twenty bloody blocks, he'd yield them up,
> Before his sister should her body stoop
> To such abhorred pollution.
> Then, Isabel, live chaste, and, brother, die:
> More than our brother is our chastity.

This famous cry sets up the scene which follows, one of the most painful in Shakespeare. Isabella brings Claudio the news of his doom with the elaborate circumlocution of the insensitive and self-absorbed:

> Lord Angelo, having affairs to heaven,
> Intends you for his swift ambassador,
> Where you shall be an everlasting leiger:
> Therefore your best appointment make with speed;
> Tomorrow you set on.

Shakespeare knows that the insensitive are always unimaginative: Claudio now shows a more vivid apprehension of death than Isabella's vague vision of sacrificial glory:

> Ay, but to die, and go we know not where,
> To lie in cold obstruction and to rot,
> This sensible warm motion to become
> A kneaded clod; and the delighted spirit
> To bathe in fiery floods, or to reside
> In thrilling region of thick-ribbed ice;
> To be imprisoned in the viewless winds,
> And blown with restless violence round about
> The pendant world; or to be worse than worst
> Of those that lawless and incertain thought
> Imagine howling — 'tis too horrible!

Isabella has no reply to this, and when Claudio begs 'Sweet sister let me live,' there comes the most astonishing of all her outbursts:

> O you beast,
> O faithless coward, O dishonest wretch!
> Wilt thou be made a man out of my vice? . . .
> Take my defiance,
> Die, perish! Might but my bending down
> Reprieve thee from thy fate, it should proceed.
> I'll pray a thousand prayers for thy death,
> No word to save thee.

Angelo's disillusion is with himself. Isabella's is with Claudio. With the thought of the violation of her chastity, of having to undertake herself the vice she has said she most abhors at the beginning of the play, she becomes almost hysterical with fear, and Claudio cannot get her to listen to him. The Duke has to come forward to resolve the impasse, very much as the Ghost has to reappear to Hamlet to save Gertrude from physical violence and whet his almost-blunted purpose.

The Duke addresses her as 'young sister' when he comes forward, and Isabella's panic at the threat to her chastity is wholly believable in an intending nun. It is not her ethical stance which shocks us, but the intensity and self-righteousness of her revulsion. As with the rejection of Falstaff, it is the manner, not the fact, of her attitude towards Claudio which offends. It is, of course, strikingly effective on stage, precisely because it is at once so extreme and so convincing.

With the Duke's intervention at this point in Act III, the second half of the play begins. The predominant medium switches from verse to prose, the Duke emerges from the shadows to direct the action, and the allegorical and symbolic elements in the play loom ever larger. Angelo, who is so important thus far, drops out of the play for almost two acts and even Isabella, so resolute and energetic earlier, becomes entirely subservient to the Duke's instruction in the second half of the play.

The inconsistencies in the play derive from the switch in tone from an intensely realistic and dramatic first half to a deliberately unrealistic second half. There are flashes of the earlier style and construction, as when Angelo emerges to show, significantly in verse, how power is compounding the moral decline of the individual in him. Mere might will now serve to cloak his crime:

> For my authority bears of a credent bulk
> That no particular scandal once can touch
> But it confounds the breather.

But, for the most part, the temper of the play is changed. Nothing illustrates this better than Isabella's sanctioning of the bed-trick. We can accept, as I said of *All's Well*, that this is a conventional device of folklore, but it is even more impossible to reconcile its use with the Isabella of the first part of the play than with the Helena of *All's Well*. In the long and artificial last scene, Isabella is pushed forward before the Duke to foreshadow, in speech as well as situation now, the wronged Victorian heroine:

> Justice, O royal Duke! Vail your regard
> Upon a wronged — I would fain have said, a maid.
> O worthy prince, dishonor not your eye
> By throwing it on any other object
> Till you have heard me in my true complaint,
> And given me justice, justice, justice, justice!

When she kneels to pray for Angelo, her argument is mere casuistry, and all her earlier intensity is gone.

What happens in this last scene is that the earlier realities are sacrificed to the allegory, with its direct echoes of the Christian message of the Sermon on the Mount. The overall effect of the play is pessimistic, perhaps because its investigation of the use and abuse of power produces findings which are wholly negative. The prolonged reconciliations of the last act are inconsistent with the earlier treatment — even that notable hedonist Swinburne felt that with Angelo's pardon we have been 'defrauded and derided and sent empty away'![30]

*Measure for Measure* is a more successful work than either of the other works I have characterised as problem plays. Considered against Shakespeare's best work, however, it fails as do *Troilus and Cressida* and *All's Well that Ends Well* through the lack of coherence in its construction. There is much in the construction and language of these plays that is experimental, even tentative. As they are Shakespeare's experiments, they are often more instructive and satisfying than the successes of lesser writers, especially as he was at or near the height of his powers when he wrote them. In each play there are one or two scenes which are highly effective in the theatre. But he does not solve the problems of combining realistic, satirical and allegorical strains into a logically developed theatrical experience. This accomplishment he will achieve only in the late romances of his last writing years.

# Notes

1. *Shakespeare: a Survey*, pp. 163–4.
2. *An Approach to Shakespeare*, pp. 61–2.
3. Ibid., p. 63.
4. See *Shakespeare's Problem Plays*, pp. 54–8.
5. Ibid., p. 70.
6. Ibid., p. 60.
7. *Shakespeare's Comedies*, pp. 184–5.
8. *Satiric Catharsis in Shakespeare*, Chapter 5.
9. See *Some Shakespearean Themes*, pp. 65–83.
10. *An Approach to Shakespeare*, p. 82.
11. *Shakespeare's Problem Plays*, pp. 54–8.
12. G. K. Hunter, Introduction to Arden edition, p. xxix.
13. Ibid., p. xxi.
14. Ibid., p. xlvii.
15. Jonson's 'Humours' comedies were written three or four years earlier.
16. *Shakespeare: the Problem Plays*, p. 18.
17. In *Shakespeare's Problem Comedies*.
18. Introduction to Arden edition, p. xliv.
19. *Characters of Shakespeare's Plays* (Everyman edn, Dent, London), p. 245.
20. *Coleridge: Critic of Shakespeare* (Cambridge University Press, Cambridge, 1973), vol. 2, p. 352.
21. See *The Wheel of Fire*, pp. 73–96.
22. *The Jacobean Drama*, p. 260.
23. *An Approach to Shakespeare*, pp. 124–5.
24. *The Human Image in Dramatic Literature*, p. 129.
25. *Shakespeare's Problem Plays*, p. 123.
26. Some interesting arguments for this view are given in E. Schanzer, *The Problem Plays of Shakespeare* (Routledge and Kegan Paul, London, 1965), pp. 122–5, and in P. Alexander, *Measure for Measure* (TV Shakespeare Series, BBC Publications, London, 1979), pp. 13–15.
27. There is, however, an excellent sample in Schanzer, *The Problem Plays of Shakespeare*, pp. 96–112.
28. *Shakespeare's Problem Plays*, p. 236.
29. 'The Greatness of *Measure for Measure*' in *Scrutiny*, vol. 10 (January, 1942), p. 234.
30. *A Study of Shakespeare* (1879), p. 203.

*Hamlet* has many of the characteristics of the problem plays considered in the last chapter. It has the imagery of food, drink and disease, the apparent disillusionment with sexual attachments, which are prominent in *Troilus and Cressida.* It has the variety of verse-styles characteristic of these plays written in the first years of the new century, as T. S. Eliot pointed out many years ago.[1] Yet it has a coherence which the other plays lack. Amongst the libraries of criticism of the play, very few writers accuse the play of failing to work in the playhouse.

The play has survived a vast series of eccentric theatrical approaches over the centuries; through all of them it has continued to work, often thrillingly, for a huge range of audiences. Ironically, in a play that has produced more writing than any other work of art, it is above all an actor's play, with almost every actor's effect set carefully in a context which will enable the player to make the most of it. It is full of paradoxes, of course. It is a play which begins by committing a man to violent action, and then is built for the most part around his inaction; it takes one of the crudest of Elizabethan conventions, the revenge play, and makes of it one of the profoundest commentaries upon the mind of men and the complexity of life. It makes the most reflective of Shakespearian heroes the instrument of a final bloodbath which has become proverbial. Yet never does it fail to convince: critics will go on arguing into infinity about Hamlet's motives and psyche, but they will never find him unreal or disappointing dramatically.

For the dramatic structure of the play, which underpins its chameleon changes of tone, is surprisingly simple. Just as much as *Richard II,* with whose eponymous hero Hamlet has often been thought to have much in common, this play is the contest between the individual mind of wide-ranging imagination and the public man who subjugates private thought to the demands of political action. In the interests of dramatic balance and the fullest arousal of our sympathies, Shakespeare has qualified his treatment of the parties on each side of the scale, so that the issues are incomparably more complex and wide-ranging than in the earlier play. The individual is made more profound and less irritating than Richard (or Brutus, the other character whom critics have often detected in the evolution of Hamlet); the public man is guilty from the start, but he is a competent ruler, clinging to his ill-gotten gains by a series of political manoeuvres and a shrewd assessment of what is possible in the world in which he moves.

It was Marlowe who wrote in *Dr. Faustus* of potential which 'stretcheth as far as doth the mind of man', but it took Shakespeare to give the fullest account of that infinite capacity. J. Dover Wilson said that after years of work on the play, the quality of Hamlet's character remained the key factor and was still elusive.[2] Shakespeare would have been well satisfied to hear this, for Hamlet's unpredictability is his most effective stage characteristic: the author's skill was to ensure that this unpredictability would never be unconvincing. Indeed, Hamlet's conduct is for the most part immediately recognisable, because the hero strikes a series of notes in our own experience. Hazlitt wrote in 1818:

> It is *we* who are Hamlet. This play has a prophetic truth, which is above that of history. Whoever has become thoughtful and melancholy through his own mishaps or those of others . . . and could find in the world before him only a dull blank with nothing remarkable in it; whoever has known 'the pangs of despised love, the insolence of office, or the spurns which patient merit of the unworthy takes' . . . whose powers of action have been eaten up by thought, he to whom the universe seems infinite, and himself nothing; whose bitterness of soul makes him careless of consequences, and who goes to a play as his best resource to shove off, to a second remove, the evils of life by a mock representation of them — this is the true Hamlet.

Hamlet is Shakespeare's most comprehensive study of the individual. He is a student as well as a prince. At the age of thirty (though this information is given late in the play and for much of the time he seems much younger, a contemporary of Guildenstern, Rosencrantz and Laertes, all presumably of a more conventional student age) we see him anxious to excape a carousing, Philistine court and go 'back to school in Wittenberg'. In an alien society, although he can count on the support of the 'general gender', his preference is not for the immediate activity of reform but for the seclusion of contemplation. Coleridge noted in him 'that aversion to action which prevails among such as have a world in themselves' and it is this individual world which he displays so amply to us in the play. Hamlet's world is the limitless one of the imagination; his opponent is shown from the start as competent and at ease in the clearly defined political world in which he operates. Morally, of course, Claudius is wrong and seen to be so from the start, but this play is not a study of the processes of evil, as *Macbeth* will be:

Shakespeare sets the moral supremacy and imaginative suggestion of Hamlet's individual world against the practical skills of a clear-sighted and ruthless public man, operating in the amoral world he has created for himself. It is a dramatic equation which is splendidly balanced, and the playwright exploits its possibilities with all the resources of his maturity.

Hamlet is an individual who is increasingly alone in an alien political world as the play proceeds. Ophelia he rejects; Horatio disappears for a long section of the play; Rosencrantz and Guildenstern, whom he welcomes as student-companions, turn out to be spies, explicitly summoned by the King to act as unofficial gaolers in the prison which is in Denmark. His reaction helps to explain why this is supremely an actor's play. For Hamlet plays out his opposition in a series of roles. His eager welcome of the players and his subsequent advice to them show him an actor manqué; the players are 'the abstract and brief chronicles of the time'. His response to a time which is out of joint is the adoption of a series of roles, which he plays out before audiences large and small. He appears for the first time in one of the most outrageous of these: that of obstinate mourner and challenge to the King in a glittering court, newly released from mourning and still self-conscious in its new finery. His reaction to the Ghost's revelation is the scheme of assumed madness, the actor's ideal device, for it will enable him to indulge a variety of subsidiary roles — and if he pleases to go 'over the top' in some of them! For who can define the rules which govern a lunatic's conduct? He will mime the distraught lover to Ophelia, and then exhibit a different and more sinister lover when he plays a scene with her for his enemy audience behind the arras. For Polonius, he will turn on for a few moments a brilliant and bitter Fool, a Feste who has no need to fear for his position. When the opportunity falls into his lap, he will turn director of a vagabond professional troupe to release his histrionics directly upon the King, though he will not be able to resist the chance to bespatter Ophelia with obscenities before a bewildered court audience. Faced with the reality of the revenger's role that was put upon him — and without an audience — he will sheath his dagger with an ingenious excuse, forsaking in the awful moment of truth the bloodlust he has conjured in himself while role-playing a moment earlier. When he sees Laertes striking a pose in Ophelia's grave, he will leap in beside him and appropriate the star-role in this macabre cameo. Summoned to the duel which he feels obscurely may be his final performance ('thou woulds't not think how ill all's here about my heart'), he will be unable to resist the final theatrical setting of the assembled court. Presented at last with the occasion of revenge he has so conspicuously failed to organise for himself, he will seize it, dying valiantly before the court audience he has played upon so effectively earlier in the play.

If this sounds cynical, or uncomplimentary to the character who has been thought the brightest of Renaissance men, it should be remembered that no man acts all the time, though some actors have difficulty in deciding when to stop. Hamlet's roles never deny or subjugate his individual feelings; they channel them. Like most good modern actors, he projects into his roles those elements of himself which he thinks it appropriate to display. He is constantly improvising, but not showing what he believes to be false. And alongside his indulgence of his actor's temperament, we are given his own wide-ranging emotions, usually of course when he is without an audience, and most prominently of all in the great soliloquies which characterise the play. If Hamlet strikes continual notes of recognition in us, it is because Shakespeare has distilled into the character so much of what his alert and receptive mind has learned over the years. His hero, meditative or histrionic, embodies these perceptions in the fresh and economical language which makes *Hamlet* for us a play full of quotations.

I have stressed how successful a play *Hamlet* is in the theatre partly because some of the writings about it seem to have extracted it almost completely from that context. We suffer as usual from familiarity with what happens: it was only when I watched the play a year or so ago with two young people who knew nothing of the story that I realised again how exciting and unpredictable are the turns of the plot for those blissfully uninitiated. It begins, for instance, with an unusually long first scene for Shakespeare, carefully plotted to make the maximum impact for the martial figure upon the battlements which will not speak to the affrighted sentries. The general scene is set for the appearance of the mighty principals; we learn that young Fortinbras has 'sharked up a list of lawless resolutes' to threaten the lands old Hamlet won; we are told of the 'post-haste and romage' in a disturbed Denmark.

This opening serves as an extended prologue to the second scene, with which it so superbly contrasts. Amidst the brilliantly clad courtiers who enter in splendid procession as we move indoors and into the light, one dark figure has clad himself carefully for the first of his roles, and Shakespeare leaves him to intrigue us by this visual impact for sixty-five lines before he speaks. I have seen four productions of this play in the last six years, and all of them have ignored this telling stroke with which the author presents them. Yet the evidence of Hamlet's obstinate continuance of mourning garb is plain in the text: the Queen asks Hamlet to cast off his 'nighted colour' and Hamlet acknowledges in reply his 'inky cloak', even if we choose to cast away his brilliant double pun to Claudius about being 'too much i' the sun'.

Whilst we speculate about the identity of this black-suited observer, there is plenty of action around the thrones up-stage. The first sixteen lines of the scene, avuncular, emollient, built round a series of carefully prepared antitheses, are superbly crafted. The polished and experienced politician tries to disguise the jarring antipathy of his incestuous marriage in a half-humorous account of the situation which is the play's starting-point, though in the end the brutal fact leaps out:

> Therefore our sometime sister, now our queen,
> Th' imperial jointress of this warlike state,
> Have we, as 'twere with a defeated joy —
> With one auspicious, and one dropping eye,
> With mirth in funeral, and with dirge in marriage,
> In equal scale weighing delight and dole —
> Taken to wife.

But this smooth and sensual apologist is no fool: he reminds the court that they have 'freely gone with this affair along' to implicate those around him in the situation. Then he turns with relief to the business of state, and disposes of two items with commendable expedition. The ambassadors are briskly despatched to Norway to check the ambitions of young Fortinbras. Laertes is courteously granted permission to return to France.

When Claudius turns to the third item on his unwritten agenda, he is less successful. He meets not the courtly, impersonal language in which Polonius and Laertes have conducted their parallel request for permission to leave court, but the bitter barbs of a razor-sharp individual mind, scoring its first verbal hits before an audience thrilling with an excited horror at the daring jibes of this audacious prince:

> *King*:            But now my cousin Hamlet, and my son —
> *Hamlet* (aside): A little more than kin, and less than kind.
> *King*:            How is it that the clouds still hang on you?
> *Hamlet*:          Not so, my lord; I am too much i' th' sun.

Two stinging puns in his first lines, the second one a double one on 'sun' and 'son', set Hamlet upon his way as Shakespeare's most scintillating and resourceful wordsmith, more varied than Richard, more flexible than Macbeth. T. S. Eliot thought that: 'The levity of Hamlet, his repetition of phrase, his puns, are not part of a deliberate piece of dissimulation, but a form of emotional relief' and certainly here they are spat at Claudius in a sudden release of hatred and frustration.

The roles Hamlet assumes are effective channels for his feelings rather than means of disguising them: although he has dressed carefully to provoke this opening exchange with Claudius, and secured his effect as publicly as possible, he asserts to his mother that his grief is genuine, unlike that represented by the mourning the court has so easily cast off:

> These, indeed, *seem,*
> For they are actions that a man might play.
> But I have that within which passeth show;
> These but the trappings and the suits of woe.

Claudius makes the best of a difficult situation, as that other usurper and politician Bolingbroke did with Richard. He is more at home with words than Bolingbroke, responding to this defiant mourning which Hamlet is making a challenge to his authority with practised emollience:

> 'Tis sweet and commendable in your nature, Hamlet,
> To give these mourning duties to your father.
> But you must know your father lost a father;
> That father lost, lost his.

He is able enough to throw in a bribe after this elaborate and gentle rebuke, reminding the Prince that he is 'the most immediate to our throne' and clothing his refusal of Hamlet's request to leave Denmark with the appearance of appeasement:

> And we beseech you, bend you to remain
> Here, in the cheer and comfort of our eye,
> Our chiefest courtier, cousin and our son.

This is the climax of a thirty-line speech which bends every sinew to a reconciliation of this embarrasing breach in the royal household. As the court waits expectantly for the Prince to accept this carefully weighted olive branch, Hamlet takes his chance for his most theatrical insult, turning with elaborate contempt from the waiting King to tell the Queen, 'I shall in all my best obey you, madam.'

Claudius cuts his losses: Hamlet is left with his victory in the contest of words and the refusal of his request to leave court, as the King accepts the affront as 'a loving and a fair reply'. He diverts the court from Hamlet's bitter opposition with a promise of the pomp and circumstance of power, and sweeps out before he can be ruffled further:

> This gentle and unforc'd accord of Hamlet
> Sits smiling to my heart, in grace whereof,
> No jocund health that Denmark drinks today,
> But the great cannon to the clouds shall tell,
> And the king's rouse the heaven shall bruit again,
> Re-speaking earthly thunder. Come, away.

The public man leaves amidst the elaborate panoply of power; Hamlet looks after his train of followers and, as the braying of trumpets fades, individual man erupts into his first great outburst of melancholia:

> O, that this too too solid flesh would melt,
> Thaw, and resolve itself into a dew!
> Or that the Everlasting had not fix'd
> His canon 'gainst self-slaughter! O God! God!
> How weary, stale, flat, and unprofitable
> Seem to me all the uses of this world!
> Fie on't! O, fie! 'Tis an unweeded garden
> That grows to seed; things rank and gross in nature
> Possess it merely.

Through the convention of the soliloquy, we get to know Hamlet more fully than any other character in Shakespeare, probably because he assumes so many roles elsewhere. After the slow tempo and heavy syllables of these opening lines, the verse and syntax break as his emotions rise to a significant climax, 'Frailty, thy name is woman!', the sentiment which will dominate his conduct in the play. His mother's sin, as always, comes before his loathing of his uncle. When he considers Claudius, he produces in looking for an extreme contrast a most significant assessment of himself:

>                   married with mine uncle,
> My father's brother, but no more like my father
> Than I to Hercules!

Looking for the figure most unlike himself, this most acute of princes fixes upon the legendary man of action.

So Shakespeare's daring experiment is becoming clear: within the melodramatic framework of the revenge-play convention, he will set as his revenger the most acute of thinkers, beset with the agonising self-knowledge that he is totally unfitted by nature for the violent deeds which will shortly be demanded of him.

Shakespeare makes his audience wait for the high drama of the Ghost's re-appearance to his intriguing son, through the pleasant little scene in which Ophelia and Polonius bid farewell to Laertes: an affectionate family who will meet their several deaths through the mightier events already in train around them. There is a hint in Ophelia particularly of the redemption of old age and the abuse of power through innocence and youth, a strain developed through Cordelia into the mellow notes of the last plays: but here Polonius crushes the strain when he dismisses her talk of Hamlet's tenderness: 'Affection! Pooh! You speak like a green girl.' It is not until Ophelia's body is being interred in the final section of the play that we learn that Hamlet's approaches to Ophelia would have been royally approved.

When the scene switches to the bitter night of the battlements, Shakespeare ensures that the Ghost's expected re-appearance will still surprise us by making it interrupt one of the play's most complex sections of thought and syntax. As always in this play, it is wholly in character that Hamlet should indulge his penchant to philosophise even while his companions peer nervously into the darkness for the supernatural martial figure. He moves from the noise of drunken carousing off stage to the case of individual man in the passage beginning, 'So oft it chances in particular men'.

His excitement at the Ghost's revelation of murder prompts him to a reaction which will acquire irony in the months to come:

> Haste me to know't, that I, with wings as swift
> As meditation or the thought of love,
> May sweep to my revenge.

The Ghost freezes him with one of the play's most typical and memorable expressions of distaste:

> And duller shouldst thou be than the fat weed
> That roots itself in ease on Lethe wharf,
> Wouldst thou not stir in this.

As his brain reels after the Ghost's exit, Hamlet's resolution turns significantly first against the mother whom the Ghost has warned him not to harm:

O most pernicious woman!
O villain, villain; smiling, damned villain!

When he finally turns to the strategy of revenge, there are two significant moments. The first is his determination 'to put an antic disposition on'. This is a typically indirect manoeuvre. More important, it is an indulgence of his actor's temperament, for what better excuse for histrionics can a player have than the cloak of madness? It gives the excuse for a full range of bravura effects, and opportunities for a whole series of secondary roles which may be occasioned by the rapidly changing moods of madness.

The second key point closes the scene. Hamlet, prepared a few moments earlier to sweep to his revenge, is back to the self-knowledge which made him contrast himself with Hercules. Emotionally exhausted after the Ghost's revelations, realising at last the brutal nature of the mandate set upon him, he faces the reality of his situation:

The time is out of joint, O cursed spite
That ever I was born to set it right.

After the occult melodrama of the Ghost, we are given relief in another of the play's sharp contrasts, the scene in which Polonius instructs Reynaldo at great length in the techniques of petty espionage. The politician gets a bad press from Shakespeare again, as Polonius, enjoying a tawdry game for its own sake, sets a spy upon his son and sullies his reputation: 'put on him / what forgeries you please'.

Ophelia then gives an account of Hamlet's first feigned lunatic role, that of distraught lover:

My lord, as I was sewing in my closet,
Lord Hamlet, with his doublet all unbrac'd,
No hat upon his head, his stockings foul'd,
Ungarter'd and down-gyved to his ankle;
Pale as his shirt, his knees knocking each other,
And with a look so piteous in purport
As if he had been loosed out of hell
To speak of horrors — he comes before me.

It is a cruel mime, both in its theme and its choice of audience. It has a ruthless logic with what has gone before, for before the Ghost's revelations Hamlet was generalising his mother's incest into the frailty of all women, and his first thought of revenge was for 'pernicious woman'. Polonius' earlier command to Ophelia to repel Hamlet's letters and deny him access to her has given him whatever excuse he needed to manifest his madness in this way. It is, of course, a very oblique way to set about revenge on Claudius, but the excitement of acting games and setting false scents turn the intellectual away from his quarry.

As if to emphasise Hamlet's ineffectiveness, we see his quarry making brisk practical moves against him amidst his effective conduct of the other business of state. The ambassadors return to announce the successful conclusion of their mission; the smiling public man thanks them briefly but expertly. Already he has set Rosencrantz and Guildenstern to work with gracious words which disguise the fact that they are to be spies under the cloak of an assumed concern for his stepson. Then he accepts the busy Polonius' plan to set Ophelia before Hamlet whilst they mark the encounter. It is all a notable contrast: the practised man of state proceeding bland and inexorable with a series of actions whilst the individual postures in soundless parody before his bewildered girl.

Though the public men may move more effectively, their morality is coarsened by the game: Polonius uses the language of stable couplings as he throws his fair and innocent daughter into this dangerous game: 'At such a time I'll loose my daughter to him.' And if the individual man's action is too oblique, his mind is acute, though to no political purpose: within a hundred lines of his entry, Hamlet taunts Polonius, exchanges bawdy figures with his contemporaries, and spots them as spies. Yet this apprehension of his danger leads only to one of his most famous pieces of philosophical melancholia:

What a piece of work is man! How noble in reason! How infinite in faculty! In form and moving how express and admirable! In action how like an angel! In apprehension how like a god! The beauty of the world! The paragon of animals! And yet, to me, what is this quintessence of dust? Man delights not me.

For this long section of the play, extending to the closest scene with his mother, we are in the Danish court, the 'prison' in which Hamlet is hedged about with enemies and spies whilst he plays his absorbing duel with the King. This speech is a sudden searing recollection of the brighter world outside. 'Hamlet is sickened by what some men are for the very reason that he is so acutely aware of what all men should and could be.'[3] With the news of the arrival of the players, he is animated again; though he begins for Rosencrantz's sake 'He that plays the king shall be welcome,' his busy mind already at work, he goes on to enumerate a number of stock parts, becoming the enthusiastic amateur with whom all professional actors are familiar. He knows the actors personally and greets the company as old friends. But first he has to despatch the spies; living dangerously as always, he sends a message to his 'uncle-father and aunt-mother' that he is 'but mad north-north-west'.

After the strange section of the Player's Hecuba speech, we have the second of Hamlet's great soliloquies: significantly, it is the players who excite him to this great outburst of self-denigration, a virtuoso display of various moods. It is one of Shakespeare's most audacious parallels: Hamlet re-enacts for us the details of the Player's performance – the visage wann'd, the tears in his eyes, the distraction in his aspect, the broken voice – and pricks the bubble of this inflated passion: 'And all for nothing!' When Hamlet goes on in turn to drown the stage with tears, down on the apron stage amidst his audience, the actor has to convince us that this is real and the Hecuba speech was mere play-acting. Shakespeare succeeds because of the immense flexibility of the verse-medium he has by now evolved, with its apparent closeness to ordinary speech:

> Yet I,
> A dull and muddy-mettled rascal, peak,
> Like John-a-dreams, unpregnant of my cause,
> And can say nothing – no, not for a king
> Upon whose property and most dear life
> A damn'd defeat was made.

This is a quiet contrast to the Player's speech, but as he attempts to lash himself into the violent action which is so alien to his nature, he piles adjective upon adjective in a style which almost parallels the Player's extract:

> I should have fatted all the region kites
> With this slave's offal – bloody, bawdy villain!
> Remorseless, treacherous, lecherous, kindless villain!
> O, vengeance!

This clamorous abuse of Claudius, with its hammer-blows of repetitive assonance, strikes harshly upon his sensitive ear, so that he sees his own ridiculous state and puts it bitterly before us:

> Why, what an ass am I! This is most brave,
> That I, the son of a dear father murder'd,
> Prompted to my revenge by heaven and hell,
> Must, like a whore, unpack my heart with words,
> And fall a-cursing, like a very drab,
> A scullion!

The exploit Hamlet now proposes against the King is a play: this is the limit of his action. Instead of peaking like John-a-dreams in private and play-acting in public, he will for a while be director and stage-manager of his own company in his own adaptation of a drama. What more fitting weapon could there be for this congenital escapist into role-play? What better move in the intellectual cat-and-mouse game he plays with the King as a substitute for real action? The reason he gives for the proceeding he has already decided upon (he has already asked the Player to play *The Murder of Gonzago* and arranged to insert his own speech) is one of the more remarkable of his self-deceptions:

> I have heard
> That guilty creatures sitting at a play
> Have by the very cunning of the scene
> Been struck so to the soul that presently
> They have proclaimed'd their malefactions.

Claudius does in fact sweep out discomfited from the performance in due course, but that is very far from formally confessing his guilt in words: in his more rational moments Hamlet knows his uncle, the remorseless villain he has characterised only eight lines earlier, too well to hope for such abject admissions.

There are those, of whom the most notable is J. Dover Wilson,[4] who maintain that we are to take Hamlet at his word when he doubts the Ghost's credentials. The crucial factor is not what Elizabethans thought of ghosts (though we should note that no other ghost in Shakespeare deceives in this way) but the way things are ordered in the play. Hamlet is the most reflective and communicative of heroes: if he had doubts about the Ghost, we should surely have been told of them before now. The play plan has been forming since he first heard of the actors' arrival and rapped out menacingly 'He that plays the King shall be welcome.' Announcing the play, he savours delightedly the effect upon Claudius:

> I'll have these players
> Play something like the murder of my father
> Before mine uncle. I'll observe his looks;
> I'll tent him to the quick. If he but blench,
> I know my course.

Only then does he introduce the idea that 'The spirit that I have seen / May be the devil.' Coming when it does, the idea has every stamp of an afterthought, a rationalisation of the latest evasion to spring to his fertile brain.

Of course, in the theatre, it makes little difference what view we take. The play-scene is a marvellous dramatic invention, one of those scenes which should never fail in performance, and Hamlet's motivation is of little importance. It may well be that Shakespeare, writing for the widest cross-section of society any playwright in English has encompassed, was content that the groundlings should take the straight-forward explanation and the more educated among his audience another. But certainly when we study the play and weigh the very belated intervention of the doubts about the Ghost, it reads like the extenuation of a plan which has elated Hamlet for its own sake.

Again we move, in the first scene of Act III, to the spectacle of the public man, anxious perhaps but clear-sighted, steadily closing the net around the obstinate individual mind which opposes him. Claudius questions his spies, despatches his Queen from the indelicate business at hand, and slips behind the arras with the busy Polonius to observe Hamlet with Ophelia. To increase the tension and show some of the strain which lies behind the smiling urbanity he presents to the world, Shakespeare gives us the first brief glance of the private man Claudius has subjugated:

> How smart a lash that speech doth give my conscience!
> The harlot's cheek, beautied with plastering art,
> Is not more ugly to the thing that helps it
> Than is my deed to my most painted word.

Immediately Shakespeare plunges us into the opposite dilemma, that of the private, reclusive man meditating about the sea of troubles which the demands of action have brought to him. It is only 55 lines since we saw Hamlet yelling himself into a fury about his alleged cowardice; now we see him musing quietly, in the soliloquy which is distinguished by its unvarying subdued tone and deliberate rhythm:

To be, or not to be — that is the question.
Whether 'tis nobler in the mind to suffer
The slings and arrows of outrageous fortune,
Or to take arms against a sea of troubles,
And by opposing end them? — To die — to sleep —
No more; and by a sleep to say we end
The heart-ache, and the thousand natural shocks
That flesh is heir to; 'tis a consummation
Devoutly to be wished.

The soliloquy is often regarded as a great humanist tract, instinct with Renaissance questioning. What is certain is that it is full of the dilemmas of the individual, with none of the accustomed pragmatism of the public man who deals with day-to-day decisions. Hamlet's discernment of how

the native hue of resolution
Is sicklied o'er with the pale cast of thought

is a recognition of his own situation and a statement of the central antithesis of the play, the stateman's necessity to act and the individual's wish to contemplate life and be sure of the moral basis of that action.

Nevil Coghill points out how this soliloquy 'creates the stillness and intimacy that are needed to prelude his only scene with a girl he once loved'.[5] Certainly it is effective, but effective as a contrast to the violence of Hamlet's language in the searing exchanges with Ophelia which follow it. There is no stage direction to indicate when the Prince realises that Ophelia is a decoy. Often Hamlet is made to detect a movement of the watchers behind the arras which prompts his 'Are you honest?' to Ophelia at line 104. It is up to the director, for the line is immediately preceded by Ophelia's return of Hamlet's presents with a rhyming couplet, so often a symbol of falseness or artificiality in the mature Shakespeare:

Take these again; for to the noble mind
Rich gifts wax poor when givers prove unkind.

From this point on, Shakespeare uses, to thrilling effect, one of his most effective dramatic ploys, that of the double audience. Hamlet acts out his Oedipus complex[6] not only to relieve his hatred of Gertrude and womankind on Ophelia, but for the benefit of his listening enemies. He spits his poison at the hapless girl before him, consigning her to the nunnery which is fit for her seeming innocence and, in its other Elizabethan sense of 'brothel', a fit repository for Gertrude and all her kind. But he warns Polonius that he should 'play the fool nowhere but in's own house', throws in words to confuse the listening King, 'I am very proud, revengeful, ambitious,' and reserves his most chilling threat — and the scene's finest moment — for the man who sits cold with fear in hiding, waiting for him to go: 'Those that are married already, all but one, shall live.'

But the royal usurper has not come so far without nerve and resilience. Hamlet has scored all the best hits in the macabre spectacle he has just staged, but in reality Claudius is the one who moves. Ignoring completely Ophelia's anguished eulogy for the Hamlet she once knew, Claudius moves swiftly into practical measures:

> I have in quick determination
> Thus set it down: he shall with speed for England.

Polonius is so busy with his next suggestion for the politician's world which so intrigues him that he has no time to comfort this near-hysterical pawn in this deathly game, though she be his daughter:

> How now, Ophelia!
> You need not tell us what Lord Hamlet said;
> We heard it all. *(To the King)* My Lord, do as you please;
> But, if you hold't fit, after the play
> Let his queen mother all alone entreat him
> To show his griefs. Let her be round with him.
> And I'll be plac'd, so please you, in the ear
> Of all their conference.

Many recent productions have attempted to show Polonius as a wise and trusted senior minister, probably in reaction against the Dickensian caricature which always threatens such parts. The text does not support this view: there are frequent indications of his verbosity and his impenetrable insensitivity. Granville-Barker's description of him as a 'tedious old wiseacre who meddles his way to his doom'[7] is the best summary of the way the role should be played.

We are left at this point with three distinct developments to look forward to in this play which centres upon a man's inaction: the play, the meeting of mother and son, and the shipping of Hamlet away from the scene of his revenge to England. Shakespeare makes us wait for all of these whilst Hamlet indulges himself with advice to the players: perhaps his creator indulges himself too, but the section is wholly in character for Hamlet. How well Shakespeare knows the eager escapism of the creative mind!

Whilst he waits for his players and their regal audience, Hamlet, permitted a rare moment of intimacy with his only confidant, shows his distrust of the power and position which could be his:

> Nay, do not think I flatter;
> For what advancement may I hope from thee,
> That no revenue has but thy good spirits
> To feed and clothe thee? Why should the poor be flatter'd?
> No, let the candied tongue lick absurd pomp,
> And crook the pregnant hinges of the knee
> Where thrift may follow fawning.

The ceremonial entry of the court gives us the last sight of the ordered world Claudius has striven so hard to preserve: by the end of this scene it will be shattered for ever. At the sight of his mother in her richest robes and her attempt at affectionate reconciliation, 'Come hither, my dear Hamlet, sit by me,' Hamlet rounds upon Ophelia. With the audience of courtiers waiting for him to sit, he cannot resist the opportunity to play a public interlude, besmirching her with indecent jests which strike more harshly because she is not light-tongued enough to turn aside his bawdry.

Hamlet has told us with Horatio to watch the King: *The Murder of Gonzago,* with its dumb-show and deliberate, repetitive style, enables us to focus upon the real drama being played out among the stage audience. Even here, at the play's supreme moment of suspense, Hamlet cannot concentrate upon the King but yields to his old obsession with his mother's guilt, as he asks her, 'Madam, how like you this play?' Perhaps his name for the play, *The Mouse-Trap,* flashed at the King in their one tiny exchange in the scene, manifests the same fixation, for he implies later in the closet scene with his mother that this is one of Claudius' pet-names for her ('call you his mouse'). Though his play succeeds, this preoccupation with his mother is the seed of Hamlet's failure to exploit its success.

The play is another example of Hamlet turning the psychological screws when physical action is what is called for in a revenge-play. It is brilliantly devised, of course: the dumb-show shows the action, then the elaborate phrases and posturings of an older dramatic tradition string out the King's agony of mind. When Claudius is driven to intervene, Hamlet taunts him before his court, playing the part now of insolent jester:

> You shall see anon; 'tis a knavish piece of work: but what o'that?
> Your majesty, and we that have free souls, it touches us not.

When the King rises, for once publicly shaken, shouting for light and rushing out in a confusion which is a striking contrast to the formal entry of the court, Hamlet hurls after him contemptuously, 'What, frighted with false fire?'

But that is precisely what this actor-prince deals in. In this triumph, he cries to Horatio not of the revenge the Ghost demanded so long ago but of his capacity to hold 'a fellowship in a cry of players'. When he should move to capitalise on the King's discomfiture, he falls straight in with the next plan his enemies have devised for him, the meeting with his mother. Because he cannot bear to lose any intellectual duel, he reminds the King's spies who bring the directive that he knows them for what they are. His terms show how jealous he is of his private individual soul. 'You would pluck out the heart of my mystery,' he rebukes them bitterly.

Left alone, he behaves like an actor working hard upon himself in the dressing-room to summon emotions beyond his normal range, attempting in the language of a revenge-play to thrust himself into the role he now cannot escape:

> 'Tis now the very witching time of night,
> When churchyards yawn, and hell itself breathes out
> Contagion to this world. Now could I drink hot blood,
> And do such bitter business as the day
> Would quake to look on.

And, of course, as we should now expect, he turns in this mood of contrived blood-lust not to the King but to his mother, telling himself to 'speak daggers, but use none'.

As so often in this play, we are given an immediate contrast in the content and manner of the King's speech. While Hamlet parades his excitement in a torrent of words, Claudius shows that he is not so shaken as to be incapable of firm and ruthless reaction:

> I like him not; nor stands it safe with us
> To let his madness range. Therefore prepare you;
> I your commission will forthwith dispatch,
> And he to England shall along with you.

Polonius passes wordily on his way to his last, fatal eavesdropping and Claudius turns from his brisk public action to a sudden and startling revelation of the tumult in his private soul. He acknowledges the ability of power to outwit justice in the world of men:

> In the corrupted currents of this world
> Offence's gilded hand may shove by justice,
> And oft 'tis seen the wicked prize itself
> Buys out the law. But 'tis not so above.

The climax of the King's struggle is couched in lines which might come from Donne's religious verse:

> O limed soul, that, struggling to be free,
> Art more engag'd! Help, angels! Make assay.
> Bow, stubborn knees; and, heart with strings of steel,
> Be soft as sinews of the new-born babe!

Whilst the public man kneels in the struggle to regain his private integrity, individual man comes upon the opportunity to implement his crude revenge. Probably more words have been expended on this incident than any other in the play. Down the centuries eminent critics have disagreed fiercely over it: Coleridge and Bradley maintain that the wish to send Claudius to hell is an afterthought; Johnson and Dover Wilson assume that the reasons given are genuine.

Hamlet begins significantly in the weaker, subjunctive mood, 'Now might I do it pat'. The most characteristic phrase in his speech, and the one that by now is a signpost to tell us he will not act, is 'that would be scanned'. Throughout the play he shows himself capable of action upon impulse, but incapable once he lets loose 'the pale cast of thought' upon any decision. It would be totally out of character for Hamlet of all tragic heroes to kill a kneeling man in cold blood: it would take a Richard of Gloucester, at the other end of the psychological continuum, to act here. He is quick enough with a reason for inaction, but the other factor in his decision comes upon its heels, 'My mother stays'.

Hamlet's reason for sparing Claudius — that he would send him to heaven if he killed him at prayer — is impeccable in the terms of the revenge-play, although even an Elizabethan audience would have found an execution upon a helpless victim anticlimactic and unheroic. It is quite possible, as with his claim earlier to doubt the Ghost's word, that the groundlings took Hamlet at his word whilst the more educated section of his audience saw his reasoning as a rationalisation. There is food for the first group in the relish of Hamlet's phrasing as his quick intellect is excited to the defence of his conduct:

> Up, sword, and know thou a more horrid hent.
> When he is drunk asleep, or in his rage,
> Or in th' incestuous pleasure of his bed;
> At gaming, swearing; or about some act
> That has no relish of salvation in't —
> Then trip him, that his heels may kick at heaven,
> And that his soul may be as damned and black
> As hell, whereto it goes.

Those who think as I do that Hamlet strains to explain away an act his mind cannot contemplate are left to savour the immediate irony of the King's couplet:

> My words fly up, my thoughts remain below;
> Words without thoughts never to heaven go.

There is no time for reflection as we watch this crowded play, for we plunge straight into the high drama of the Queen's closet scene. For once, Hamlet is not playing a part, though his mind and his tongue are as sinuous as ever. His answer to the Queen's first line contains both a play upon the word 'father' and a response to her 'thou' with the insultingly distanced 'you':

> *Queen*:  Hamlet, thou hast thy father much offended.
> *Hamlet*: Mother, you have my father much offended.

The killing of Polonius emphasises that he can act, on impulse, and contrasts with his sparing of the King a moment earlier. There is a ruthless, clear-sighted accuracy about his epitaph upon Polonius and his disappointment that it is not the King:

Thou wretched, rash, intruding fool, farewell!
I took thee for thy better. Take thy fortune;
Thou find'st to be too busy is some danger.

This even, chilling authority lasts only until he turns back to his mother's
sin, which extends beyond Gertrude to Ophelia, since it

takes off the rose
From the fair forehead of an innocent love
And sets a blister there.

Hamlet releases upon his wretched, shallow mother his long-frustrated
resentment, until she acknowledges the 'black and grained spots' upon
her soul. But by this time he cannot stop to direct her penitence: her
sexual sin has for him a morbid fascination:

Nay, but to live
In the rank sweat of an enseamed bed,
Stewed in corruption, honeying and making love
Over the nasty sty.

Even after the Ghost has appeared to protect his mother, he returns
in disease-imagery to his revulsion:

Lay not that flattering unction to your soul,
That not your trespass but my madness speaks.
It will but skin and film the ulcerous place.
Whilst rank corruption, mining all within,
Infects unseen.

His parting injunction to her concerns her incest, not the King's murder:
'Good night. But go not to my uncle's bed.' Even then, he returns from
dragging away Polonius' body to the picture which so hideously enthralls
his mind, warning her not to

Let the bloat king tempt you again to bed;
Pinch wanton on your cheek; call you his mouse;
And let him, for a pair of reechy kisses,
Or paddling in your neck with his damned fingers,
Make you to ravel all this matter out.

When he can think about other things than his mother's sin, he is
brutally clear-sighted again about Rosencrantz and Guildenstern:

> There's letters sealed. And my two school-fellows—
> Whom I will trust as I will adders fanged —
> They bear the mandate; they must sweep my way,
> And marshal me to knavery. Let it work;
> For 'tis the sport to have the engineer
> Hoist with his own petar.

As usual, though, he is moved by the thought of indirect rather than
direct action: it is the notion of outwitting them through their own
treachery that really excites him. His mordant epitaph on Polonius
shows that intricate brain racing as fast as ever:

> Indeed, this counsellor
> Is now most still, most secret, and most grave,
> Who was in life a foolish prating knave.

The King, hearing of the death of Polonius, and realising that 'It
had been so with us had we been there,' moves more directly and
consistently against his enemy:

> The sun no sooner shall the mountains touch,
> But we will ship him hence.

In the next scene (**IV ii**) Hamlet warns Rosencrantz and Guildenstern
again of their danger, as if his conscience has to be clear before he acts
against them, however perilous he makes his own situation.
  Whilst he indulges his subtle individual mind in this way, power
slips steadily through his fingers; Claudius sends him, virtually under
guard, away from the court and to his intended death. Soon Hamlet is
commenting himself on the fact as he passes a section of Fortinbras'
army in full battle array, analysing with cold detachment his

> craven scruple
> Of thinking too precisely on the event.

We may speculate how genuine is his declared admiration of the 'delicate
and tender prince' who puts the lives of twenty thousand men into
hazard over a worthless plot of land. Perhaps it is a genuine piece of

self-deception to spur his dull revenge, perhaps it is an echo of the satire of deeds of arms indulged at such length in *Troilus and Cressida*. At the end of the speech, Hamlet strides out purposefully with a sentiment in the best revenge-play tradition:

> O from this time forth
> My thoughts be bloody or be nothing worth!

Ironically, he is full of resolution as he is conveyed under armed guard away from the scene of action, exhibiting still the lack of realism which marks him as a private man unable to come to terms with a situation framed for public, political man.

In Hamlet's absence, Claudius becomes for a time the mainspring of the action, and even as the tragic impetus gathers speed and his situation becomes more perilous, we see his political qualities. With Polonius buried and Ophelia mad, Laertes bursts in with an armed following at his back, a reminder of how easily Hamlet, beloved of the 'general gender', might have rallied support. He forces the emotion which rules his brain into words which recall a metaphor of Hamlet's:

> That drop of blood that's calm proclaims me bastard;
> Cries cuckold to my father; brands the harlot
> Even here, between the chaste unsmirched brow
> Of my true mother.

Claudius responds with coolness, courage and tactical acumen, and throws in for good measure a piece of philosophical humbug outrageous enough for Richard III:

> What is the cause, Laertes,
> That your rebellion looks so giant-like? —
> Let him go, Gertrude; do not fear our person.
> There's such divinity doth hedge a king
> That treason can but peep to what it would,
> Acts little of his will.

Laertes strikes the attitude appropriate to a Revenger:

> To hell, allegiance! Vows, to the blackest devil!
> Conscience and grace, to the profoundest pit!
> I dare damnation. To this point I stand,

That both the worlds I give to negligence,
Let come what comes; only I'll be reveng'd
Most throughly for my father.

But Claudius becomes more confident as Laertes' posture becomes more vague and unrealistic: the King becomes the urbane public man, expert in handling those who adopt stances less subtle than his own. While Laertes' mind reels still from the impact of the mad Ophelia, Claudius moves smoothly forward to consolidate his advantage and turn rebellion into compromise:

Laertes, I must commune with your grief,
Or you deny me right. Go but apart,
Make choice of whom your wisest friends you will,
And they shall hear and judge 'twixt you and me.

After the brief scene in which Horatio receives Hamlet's letter, the contrast in political acumen between Claudius and Hamlet continues. Whilst the King continues his skilled conversion of Laertes from insurgent to protégé, Hamlet by sending word that he is back in Denmark again casts away the precious political card of surprise for the actor's ploy of frightening his opponent. If Claudius is shaken for a moment, by the end of the scene he has pressed forward with the practice which will secure Hamlet's death, a practice which depends on his shrewd estimate of his opponent as 'most generous and free from all contriving'. With Laertes' blood so in command of his judgement that he is ready 'To cut his throat in the church,' Claudius, avuncular and secure in his man, puts forward one of his most flagrant pieces of ironic humbug:

No place, indeed, should murder sanctuarize;
Revenge should know no bounds.

Laertes, in raising a rebellion and storming the palace, shows how easily Hamlet might have acted; yet Claudius in turn shows how adept he is in handling the young man who strikes a series of conventional attitudes but is devoid of real political skills.

Whilst the King concludes his deadly preparations, Hamlet observes and converses with the gravediggers, musing upon the transience of rank and authority, considering as Claudius re-enters his world how imperious Caesar might be reduced to a draught-excluder. His old preoccupation with his mother is with him still, flashing out harshly to conclude his meditations upon Yorick's skull:

Now get you to my lady's chamber, and tell her, let her paint an inch thick, to this favour she must come.

Laertes leaps into Ophelia's grave with a ranting speech which marks the intellectual fatuity of the man who falls easily into conventional attitudes. Hamlet, no doubt genuinely outraged by the inflation of Laertes' style, seizes his opportunity to parody the attitude and make the most dramatic re-entry into the play's main action:

What is he whose grief
Bears such an emphasis; whose phrase of sorrow
Conjures the wandering stars, and makes them stand
Like wonder-wounded hearers? This is I,
Hamlet the Dane.

It is a superb dramatic moment, and immediately Hamlet, the centre of attention on stage once again, can state his real feelings with stunning Shakespearian simplicity:

I loved Ophelia. Forty thousand brothers
Could not, with all their quantity of love,
Make up my sum.

Hamlet's actions, as usual, are diversions from his revenge mission. Though he is at his most vigorous and winning in this scene — and steals it hands down as an actor — it is Claudius at the end who takes Laertes by the arm and consoles him that their plot will now be put 'to the present push'.

Hamlet's recognition at the beginning of the play's last scene that

There's a divinity which shapes our ends,
Rough-hew them how we will

has often been taken as marking a new resolution on his return to Denmark. It is in fact a comforting fatalism, for it allows him to relinquish the initiative in continuing his revenge to an all-embracing Providence, which will absorb also his prevailing melancholia. Although his acute mind suspects trickery in the fencing-bout ('thou wouldst not think how ill all's here about my heart') he welcomes one more piece of action which seems a diversion from the heavy burden of his revenge mission.

Osric is more than a diverting piece of comic relief before the climax of the play's action; he is the last demonstration of the King's shrewdness in political contrivance and Hamlet's indulgence of his private inclinations. There could be no better messenger to disguise a treacherous purpose, and Hamlet is soon sidetracked into baiting him. The Prince is seen at his most attractive in this last scene; witty and dismissive with Osric, reflective in the quiet interlude with Horatio as he goes towards death with his eyes open, generous in his desire for reconciliation with Laertes even as that political *ingénu* looks nervously for the poisoned foil. When the plot is revealed and death is upon him, he rises at last with his mother dead to the role he has thrust aside so often, that of violent revenger. He knows the words for this role as all his others: significantly, his mother figures even in his belated achievement of the Ghost's commission:

> Here, thou incestuous, murderous, damned Dane,
> Drink off this potion. Is thy union here?
> Follow my mother.

Hamlet, the Renaissance individual with his contempt for rank and his mind so conscious of the possibilities of man, has achieved at the last the one sordid deed of state which has so perplexed him. But only when events left him no escape: to the last he has scorned to force circumstances to his own purposes.

Hamlet fails for so long because his individualism is at once too narrow and too wide-ranging to allow him to succeed in the particular political situation in which his creator places him. He is, as Turgenev saw, 'preoccupied with his own personality',[8] which predisposes him always towards reflection rather than action. But it is his concern also with the universal problems of man, with universal codes of conduct, which drives him to look always beyond the squalid confines of his contemporary Denmark to a larger, more exciting world beyond it. Public man, with his concern always for immediate political problems, outwits him in day-to-day action, but is left outside the larger imaginative world which concerns all men.

## Notes

1. *Selected Essays* (Faber, London, 1951), pp. 143-4.
2. See his introduction to New Cambridge Shakespeare edition (1934) and *What Happens in Hamlet?*
3. Prosser, *Hamlet and Revenge*, pp. 98 ff.
4. See particularly *What Happens in Hamlet?*

5. *Shakespeare's Professional Skills,* p. 158.

6. The most famous, or infamous, analysis of the character on these lines is Ernest Jones's *Hamlet and Oedipus* (1949), a revised and expanded version of material published as long ago as 1910.

7. *Prefaces to Shakespeare* (Batsford, London, 1969).

8. Quoted by L. C. Knights in *Approach to Hamlet* (Chatto and Windus, London, 1960), p. 56.

# 5 OTHELLO

The tragic hero Shakespeare conceived in *Othello* is in many respects a mirror image of the one around whom he built *Hamlet*. Hamlet is the most intelligent of all his heroes, Othello the least: the plot depends on his lack of intellectual power, psychological insight and even common sense. Most important, where Hamlet is an essentially private man who finds himself in a situation which demands a politcal act, Othello is an essentially public man who is placed within the framework of a domestic tragedy. Beneath his delight and success as the public leader amidst the 'pride, pomp and circumstance of glorious war', the private man has been almost wholly concealed, even from himself, for he has had little need to explore it. When this inner man emerges under pressure, we see

the savage Othello, the barbarian stripped of his wishful thinking, who gives himself up to jealousy, black magic and cruelty, the man who coarsely announces of his wife that he will 'chop her into messes', the man who debases his magnificent oratory by borrowing shamelessly from Iago's lecherous vocabulary.[1]

Once we accept this key to the dramatic construction of the play, most of the critical arguments fall into place. There are three schools of criticism on *Othello*. The first is that which takes Othello at his own valuation, or in Johnson's words, 'magnanimous, artless and credulous, boundless in his confidence, ardent in his affection, inflexible in his resolution, and obdurate in his revenge'. The second school, which may be dated largely from T. S. Eliot's 1927 essay onwards, stresses the Moor's pride, egoism, lack of self-knowledge, inflated rhetoric, and alacrity in responding to Iago's prompting. The third school is that which sees larger theological issues in the contest which dominates the play, making Othello and Iago the representatives of Good and Evil and denying the apparently narrow context of this, the most claustrophobic of the great tragedies. The most illustrious proponent of this school is still Wilson Knight, whose contribution in *The Wheel of Fire* dates from 1930.

Once we accept that the play is constructed around the struggles of an essentially public man in a private situation for which he is totally unprepared by temperament and experience, the argument over whether

Othello is 'innocent', wholly a victim of Iago, or 'guilty' is irrelevant, except that if he is seen as wholly either one or the other we shall hardly have the stuff of tragedy. The three schools of criticism outlined above will then be seen as not mutually exclusive. Othello's public quality, his military ethic of magnificence, pride and bravery, does not equip him for more private problems. When he meets these, 'Othello's inner timbers begin to part at once, the stuff of which he is made begins at once to deteriorate and show itself unfit',[2] writes F. R. Leavis, one of the most prominent debunkers of Bradley's noble Moor. But there is no contradiction in this: what it means is that the private, inner man is unable to reproduce the confidence and success of the public figure when called upon to react to more intimate struggles. If we choose to see larger and more allegorical issues grafted on to these struggles, as does the third school of criticism, it is open to us to do so while still recognising the simple dramatic construction of the play, though *Othello* seems to me to lend itself less easily to such theological inter-pretations than any other of the great plays.

As always, there is far more involved in Shakespearian greatness than an effective dramatic composition. The author gives to his two protagonists their characteristic imagery, poles apart; as Othello sinks into his decline, his gradual adoption of Iago's type of language is one of the most chillingly effective graphs of his deterioration. And how confident the author is of his powers! Othello does not enter for 184 lines and is not named for another 130. Almost everything we hear of him before his entry is derogatory. He 'loves his own pride and purposes'; his speech is characterised by a 'bombast circumstance, / Horribly stuff'd with epithets of war'; he has apparently appointed an effete and inexperienced theoretician in preference to the blunt and effective soldier who tells the tale.

Yet as soon as he enters and what Wilson Knight called 'the Othello music' sounds forth, we are aware that he is a quite different and much nobler character than Iago, Roderigo and Brabantio would have us believe. Even before that, our ears do not have to be particularly acute to pick up the inference that the blunt soldier who so hates him is not to be trusted. The language in which he instructs his dupe suggests a diseased mind:

Rouse him, make after him, poison his delight,
Proclaim him in the street, incense her kinsmen,
And though he in a fertile climate dwell,
Plague him with flies.

The words in which he informs Brabantio of his daughter's actions are cruelly coarse not only to his master but to the confused old man he is seeking to rouse:

> Even now, very now, an old black ram
> Is tupping your white ewe

A man who can turn the knife in suffering with such relish may well be an expert in narrow, personal intrigue. When he emerges from the darkness with the master we already know he hates, he is daringly exploiting Othello's innocence of such black games, complaining sadly that

> I lack iniquity
> Sometimes to do me service.

When his master speaks, the verse takes on a broader flow and a more mellow ring, and we are reminded that even the jealous Ancient has conceded that the proud senate of Venice have no one else of this fathom to lead their business:

> Let him do his spite;
> My services, which I have done the signiory,
> Shall out-tongue his complaints; 'tis yet to know —
> Which, when I know that boasting is an honour,
> I shall provulgate — I fetch my life and being
> From men of royal siege, and my demerits
> May speak unbonneted to as proud a fortune
> As this that I have reach'd.

It is measured, confident, dignified. It is also self-conscious and even with a hint in the parenthesis of that overweening pride which Shakespeare's Caesar exhibited on his last, fatal journey to the forum. Most significantly, it is an egoistic speech, directed at Iago as if he were an admiring crowd rather than a close servant awaiting orders. Traversi writes: 'The dramatic construction of the play, in short, turns upon the close intricate analysis by which the two contrasted characters of the Moor and his Ancient are at every moment dovetailed, seen as opposed but related conceptions.'[3] Shakespeare establishes this dramatic relationship with unobtrusive skill from this first scene together, in which Othello, the self-centred public man, seems already dangerously vulnerable to the skills of the intense private intriguer and dissembler.

The one thing Othello has in common with Hamlet, his polar opposite in so many respects, is that he seems usually to be looking for an audience. When he has one, he responds in a very different manner, with all the eager alacrity of a natural man of action.

> Keep up your bright swords, for the dew will rust'em

he commands the warring factions, and reduces them to so many pygmies. When Brabantio pours out his insulting accusations of the 'foul charms' he has exercised to lure Desdemona to his 'sooty bosom', Shakespeare suggests in Othello's response both a superb command and a dignity that is just a little too self-conscious:

>                     Hold your hands,
> Both you of my inclining and the rest:
> Were it my cue to fight, I should have known it,
> Without a prompter.

In the third scene of the play, Shakespeare prepares carefully for the great organ peals of 'Othello music' which are to be its centre. He gives us 70 lines of troubled, broken verse-rhythms wherein the senators worry about the Turkish threat to Cyprus and Brabantio interposes his more personal grief. Othello, waiting patiently for his cue to speak for thirty lines after his entry, responds with magnificent amplitude, and the frenetic activity which has preceded the moment falls silent around him:

> Most potent, grave, and reverend signiors,
> My very noble and approv'd good masters:
> That I have ta'en away this old man's daughter,
> It is most true: true, I have married her,
> The very head and front of my offending
> Hath this extent, no more. Rude am I in my speech,
> And little blest with the set phrase of peace,
> For since these arms of mine had seven years' pith,
> Till now some nine moons wasted, they have us'd
> Their dearest action in the tented field,
> And little of this great world can I speak,
> More than pertains to feats of broil, and battle,
> And therefore little shall I grace my cause,
> In speaking for myself; yet, (by your gracious patience)

I will a round unvarnish'd tale deliver,
Of my whole course of love, what drugs, what charms,
What conjuration, and what mighty magic,
(For such proceedings am I charged withal)
I won his daughter.

The splendid, slow rhythms are full of the confidence which will be so roughly shattered later, the poetic note full of the detached effects possible only to an ordered mind. It is easy for the twentieth-century mind, heavy with the memory of holocausts, to value Othello's soldiership less highly than Shakespeare intended, but there is no doubt that it is meant to emphasise his heroic quality. Helen Gardner has an interesting view on this:

> As a great poetic dramatist, Shakespeare heightened all the elements in the story he dramatised. His subject being sexual love and marriage, he heightened in every way the contrast of masculine and feminine, to show love as the discovery of union in opposites. Othello's absolute soldiership is the symbol of his entire masculinity. It is a symbol that has lost much of its force today, as has the concept of distinctively masculine virtues.[4]

It is noticeable that Othello feels the need to stress his own image before he speaks of Desdemona. When he tells his tale, he is a self-conscious story-teller, confident of the power of the image of himself he conveys to move men, as it moved his bride:

Her father lov'd me, oft invited me,
Still question'd me the story of my life,
From year to year; the battles, sieges, fortunes,
That I have pass'd:
I ran it through, even from my boyish days,
To the very moment that he bade me tell it.
Wherein I spake of most disastrous chances,
Of moving accidents by flood and field;
Of hair-breadth scapes i'th'imminent deadly breach;
Of being taken by the insolent foe;
And sold to slavery, and my redemption hence,
And with it all my travel's history;
Wherein of antres vast, and deserts idle,
Rough quarries, rocks and hills, whose heads touch heaven,

It was my hint to speak, such was the process:
And of the Cannibals, that each other eat;
The Anthropophagi, and men whose heads
Do grow beneath their shoulders: this to hear
Would Desdemona seriously incline.

Othello's account has an impressive gravity, but it reveals also the Achilles' heel of his character. It is a speech which succeeds in making the public impression its speaker envisaged, but, as Traversi notes:

Othello is rarely able to get sufficiently far from himself fully to love Desdemona. His happiness in the opening scenes is, like everything else in his character, self-centred, naive, even egoistic; and his account of his wooing makes this clear. It was, in fact, by his passionate simple-minded delight in his own magnificent career that he won her; and — we may fairly add — it was in no small part because she ministered to his self-esteem that he valued her . . . Othello's estimate of his situation is nothing if not simple; but his simplicity is terribly, tragically vulnerable.[5]

Certainly his summary of the courtship shows his love as both indirect and self-centred, vulnerable to that dark delver into his psyche who ushers in Desdemona even as he delivers the lines

She lov'd me for the dangers I had pass'd
And I lov'd her that she did pity them.

The Duke, attempting to heal differences as the public man must, pronounces a series of platitudes in rhyming couplets, but Brabantio in a bitter parody emphasises the hollowness of this attempt to diminish fierce individual passions with bland diplomacy:

So let the Turk of Cyprus us beguile,
We lose it not so long as we can smile;
He bears the sentence well, that nothing bears
But the free comfort which from thence he hears

When the gathering turns again to the business of state, Othello, in accepting the commission, re-asserts his image with another superb piece of rhetorical bravura:

> The tyrant custom, most grave senators,
> Hath made the flinty and steel couch of war
> My thrice-driven bed of down: I do agnize
> A natural and prompt alacrity
> I find in hardness, and would undertake
> This present war against the Ottomites.

Desdemona asserts the vigorous independence which is typical of Shakespeare's best women:

> That I did love the Moor, to live with him,
> My downright violence, and scorn of fortunes,
> May trumpet to the world: my heart's subdued
> Even to the utmost pleasure of my lord.

A. P. Rossiter thinks Desdemona 'a pathetic girlish, nearly-blank sheet'.[6] She is certainly not so in this scene, and invariably in performances she makes a strong effect, despite her passiveness in the later sections of the play. The submission she declares here to 'the utmost pleasure of my lord' is carried through later; the dark, barbarian recesses of Othello's personality which Iago explores are unknown territory for her. Her absolute trust, the quality so lacking in her spouse, can hardly be made a defect.

Shakespeare ends this part of the scene with one of those ironies which so heighten his dramatic effects, as Othello, warned by Brabantio that a girl who has deceived her father may deceive a husband also, asserts his confidence in her extravagantly, and in the same line consigns her to the dark angel who will break them both:

> My life upon her faith! honest Iago,
> My Desdemona must I leave to thee

He has carried all before him through his magnificent military image, but already his ignorance of people in more personal contexts is manifest. It has been pointed out that Iago takes in others as well as his master, but Othello in the play misjudges Cassio, Desdemona and Emilia as well as Iago: everyone, in fact, with whom he comes into close contact. He is too concerned with himself and the public image he presents to give close individual attention to others. Othello's speech has its own distinctive exotic note. But, like Henry V and the Mark Antony of *Julius Caesar*, his language is at its most vigorous when the excitement of public performance stirs the adrenalin.

Iago's most vigorous language, in contrast, comes when he drops his more neutral public mask to reveal his private face and passions. In his first exchange with Roderigo, 'Were I the Moor, I would not be Iago' and 'I am not what I am' established him as a Machiavellian villain with the taut understatement of a manic hatred. In his first exchange with old Brabantio, his references to Othello's colour, 'an old black ram' and 'a Barbary horse' tell us more about the man who speaks them than the man they are applied to. Like many of Shakespeare's intriguers, he is an opportunist who moves stage by stage in his villainy; at the end of the first act, he plans merely to supplant Cassio, revenging himself upon Othello only as 'a double knavery'.

The lines of the drama have been established clearly in the first act, which is almost wholly given up to the delineation of the major characters involved in the subsequent action. M. R. Ridley points out in the Arden edition:

> If we may regard Act I as being structurally in the nature of a prologue, *Othello* comes much nearer than any of Shakespeare's other great plays except *The Tempest* to observing the unities. The action in Cyprus occupies something a little less than thirty-six hours, and since some eight of these hours are compressed into one scene (II iii) the audience's impression is of even shorter time.[7]

This adds to the intensity of the simplest and most claustrophobic of the great tragedies. We do not have the sense in *Othello* of the state's dependence on the central figure. We are constantly reminded that nations' fortunes rise and fall with such as Macbeth, Lear and Antony: Othello is a valiant general, but the employee of government rather than the government itself. Shakespeare does everything possible by means of the unity and rapidity of the action, its isolation in Cyprus, and the inclusion of a very small number of important characters, to concentrate our attention upon what is essentially a domestic tragedy. Othello's nobility of soul, his generosity, and his sense of a more glorious world outside his household only emphasise the danger he is in in this more personal setting.

If this is Shakespeare's simplest drama, it is also the one in which his language dovetails most exactly with his stagecraft. When Othello is re-united with his bride in Cyprus, his response is magnificent, but perhaps too grand in scale for what is essentially an intimate greeting:

> O my soul's joy,
> If after every tempest come such calmness,

May the winds blow, till they have waken'd death,
And let the labouring bark climb hills of seas,
Olympus-high, and duck again as low
As hell's from heaven. It if were now to die,
'Twere now to be most happy, for I fear
My soul hath her content so absolute,
That not another comfort, like to this
Succeeds in unknown fate.

Wilson Knight had reservations over the 'Othello music'. He found
the Moor's characteristic language 'over-decorated' and 'highly coloured'
and with 'something sentimental in it' so that 'at moments of great
tension, the Othello style fails of a supreme effect'.[8] This is too general
a judgement: at almost all moments of tension in the first act, and
perhaps in his final speech, Othello is superbly effective. What Knight
has not apparently recognised is Othello's application elsewhere of a
public style to situations which demand a different response. In such
moments, his inflation allows him to indulge his egoism and blinds
him to considerations which would be obvious to a less determinedly
public man. The greeting above reminds one of Queen Victoria's
complaint that Gladstone addressed her always as a public meeting.
That would be too harsh a judgement on Othello's heartfelt joy here,
but the object of it might well feel it is aimed more at the audience
around them than at her. Othello's delight in rhetoric makes him
oblivious of all questions of scale; this is a cathedral constructed to
house a pair of turtle-doves.

As Iago's plot proceeds, we see clearly the general's vices and virtues,
so skilfully embodied in the style his creator has given to him. When
Cassio disgraces himself and Othello enters to a confusion of drawn
swords, alarum bells and wounded men, he is the supremely effective
man of action, stilling the commotion instantly, but his failure in
character assessment is pointed immediately as he turns to the trusted
Iago for details:

He that stirs next, to carve for his own rage,
Holds his soul light, he dies upon his motion;
Silence that dreadful bell, it frights the isle
From her propriety: what's the matter, masters?
Honest Iago, that looks dead with grieving,
Speak, who began this?

He has the deficiencies as well as the virtues of the natural man of action; when his drive for immediate remedies is frustrated, his judgement is immediately insecure:

> Now by heaven
> My blood begins my safer guides to rule,
> And passion having my best judgement collied
> Assays to lead the way.

When he takes the action his temperament demands, his lack of knowledge of the personalities involved ensures that it will be mistaken:

> I know, Iago,
> Thy honesty and love doth mince this matter,
> Making it light to Cassio: Cassio, I love thee,
> But never more be officer of mine.

Iago's soliloquy at the end of the scene shows Shakespeare exploiting the Machiavellian villain as vigorously as he did in Richard of Gloucester; here, however, Iago's diabolical energy is directed not to the winning of a crown but to narrower ends in the tight little world in which he operates:

> I'll pour this pestilence into his ear,
> That she repeals him for her body's lust;
> And by how much she strives to do him good,
> She shall undo her credit with the Moor;
> So will I turn her virtue into pitch,
> And out of her own goodness make the net
> That shall enmesh 'em all.

The first scene of Act III shows Cassio being deceived by Iago as comprehensively as is Othello. Cassio is of no great intellect, though he is clearly of the Establishment; although he might philander shamelessly with the likes of Bianca, he knows his station far too well to think of inviting Desdemona to his bed. This gilded staff officer is easy meat for the intelligent practical soldier, and Iago devours him with some relish: the fact that both Cassio and Desdemona consider the seduction unthinkable is skilfully exploited by Iago.

Desdemona's absolute innocence makes her insistently importunate on Cassio's behalf. Our last view of them undisturbed shows Desdemona joyfully submissive — 'Whatever'er you be I am obedient' — and Othello characteristically beginning every thought of love from himself as he replies:

> Excellent wretch, perdition catch my soul,
> But I do love thee, and when I love thee not,
> Chaos is come again.

The exchange is a typical piece of Shakespearian dramatic irony, placed to heighten the tension as Iago moves forward with his first evil suggestion about Cassio's access to Desdemona during Othello's courtship.

Throughout the great temptation scene, Iago's technique is based upon Othello's naivety and inexperience in private dealings, on to which he grafts a thorough knowledge of Othello's temperament as a natural man of action. His first tactic is a refusal to be explicit, similar to that which so infuriated the Moor when Cassio was dismissed. Helen Gardner has a salutary thought for those who condemn Othello's need for decisions:

> It is difficult for those whose responsibilities for the lives of others do not demand of them the capacity for swift decision and action to appreciate the qualities of those who have to act on disciplined instinct and make decisions in a flash: the surgeon confronted with something his diagnosis had not led him to expect, the general when the unexpected irrupts into his planned campaign. This demands a certain simplicity which the subtle and introspective are only too ready to equate with stupidity.[9]

Iago exploits the self-confidence and decisiveness which have been prerequisites for Othello's public career: when he destroys the first the second is transformed from a virtue to a vice.

When Iago has played his fish expertly for some seventy lines, refusing still to make any explicit accusation, Othello is already losing control and judgement, so that Iago can venture a daring generalisation, playing in the see-saw rhythm of his last line on the very uncertainty he has planted in Othello's brain:

> O, beware jealousy;
> It is the green-ey'd monster, which doth mock
> That meat it feeds on. That cuckold lives in bliss,
> Who, certain of his fate, loves not his wronger:

But O, what damned minutes tells he o'er
Who dotes, yet doubts, suspects, yet strongly loves!

Soon Iago's imagery is beginning to seep into Othello's language. 'Exchange me for a goat' he says, assuring the Ancient he will not act without proof. Traversi notes Othello's 'continual tendency to protest rhetorically against the presence of the very weaknesses that are undoing him'.[10] His credulity is part of his lack of knowledge of private affairs; as he stumbles deeper into the marsh, he relies more and more on the man who has led him there, so that Iago's honesty becomes an obsession, a raft he offers himself and clings to as he flounders ever deeper. As William Empson writes: 'Everyone calls Iago honest once or twice, but with Othello it becomes an obsession; at the crucial moment just before Emilia exposes Iago he keeps howling the word out.'[11]

This ill-chosen counsellor offers him advice which seems simple to the point of bluntness, but which he knows it is quite impossible for one of Othello's temperament to implement:

I speak not yet of proof;
Look to your wife, observe her well with Cassio;
Wear your eye thus, not jealous, nor secure.

Then he turns the unlikely dagger of his master's social inexperience to deadly effect:

I know our country disposition well;
In Venice they do let God see the pranks
They dare not show their husbands: their best conscience
Is not to leave undone, but keep unknown,.
She did deceive her father, marrying you;
And when she seem'd to shake and fear your looks,
She lov'd them most.

Iago's shrewd intelligence is most acute as his intrigue takes fire and his opponent's senses begin to reel: when the unhappy Moor, struggling to regain control insists 'I do not think but Desdemona's honest,' Iago seizes upon the subconscious doubt in the word:

Long live she so, and long live you to think so!

Othello's need for violent action is now diverted into appalling

channels, his style of vivid poetry tarnished when he applies it to his
personal agony:

> If I do prove her haggard,
> Though that her jesses were my dear heart-strings,
> I'ld whistle her off, and let her down the wind,
> To prey at fortune.

The vast, vulnerable self-confidence he felt in public conduct has drained
away in this private situation, and the ample rhythms of his public verse
are replaced by a sickening uncertainty as he nurtures the seeds of doubt
planted by his tormentor:

> Haply, for I am black,
> And have not those soft parts of conversation
> That chamberers have, or for I am declin'd
> Into the vale of years, — yet that's not much —
> She's gone, I am abus'd, and my relief
> Must be to loathe her: O curse of marriage,
> That we can call these delicate creatures ours,
> And not their appetites!

But his private suffering is as self-centred as his earlier glory. Not
only has his love for Desdemona no element of trust in it, but he speaks
of her as no more than a brilliant and desirable piece of property.

The departure of his judgement is signalled by his adoption of Iago's
imagery:

> I had rather be a toad,
> And live upon the vapour in a dungeon,
> Than keep a corner in the thing I love,
> For others' uses.

When Iago is absent and Desdemona enters, her husband's acute senses
reel instantly before her beauty:

> If she be false, O, then heaven mocks itself!

But he has seen her throughout as an angelic symbol who is an adjunct
of his own glory. Given time, he could have learned to love and trust
the human being he has scarcely investigated during courtship, by his

own account. Iago has denied him that time by moving in to exploit his inexperience of intimate private relationships. One of the most ironic aspects of his fall is his failure to indulge his own best traits. For, as Ridley points out: 'Whenever Othello trusts his instinct his is almost invariably right; whenever he thinks, or fancies himself to be thinking, he is almost invariably and ruinously wrong.'[12]

Othello's love is now debased into 'a barbaric crazed fury of physical jealousy, the jealousy which is the counterpart of lust, not that which is the counterpart of love'.[13] He is by now the tormented voluptuary:

> What sense had I of her stol'n hours of lust?
> I saw't not, thought it not, it harm'd not me,
> I slept the next night well, was free and merry;
> I found not Cassio's kisses on her lips.

This vein leads him to one of the most outrageous of his images:

> I had been happy if the general camp,
> Pioners, and all, had tasted her sweet body,
> So I had nothing known.

This bitter degradation of his love contains no thought of his bride. It is his image, the tarnishing of the bright enamel of his generalship, which excites him to an echo of his earlier poetic breadth:

> O now for ever
> Farewell the tranquil mind, farewell content:
> Farewell the plumed troop, and the big wars,
> That makes ambition virtue: O farewell,
> Farewell the neighing steed, and the shrill trump,
> The spirit-stirring drum, the ear-piercing fife;
> The royal banner, and all quality,
> Pride, pomp, and circumstance of glorious war!

The thought of his public humiliation drives him to his most terrible lines in the play:

> Villain, be sure thou prove my love a whore,
> Be sure of it, give me the ocular proof.

Iago may be shaken by the strength of the Moor's passion, but he is ready to turn the wheel of the rack with a response as daring as it is gross:

Would you, the supervisor, grossly gape on,
Behold her topp'd?

With the success of this, it is plain that nothing is beyond him, and he ventures the monstrous suggestion of Cassio's dream-talk. Bradley said that we can feel that part of himself that Shakespeare put into Iago, the artist's delight in developing a plot, the success of which excites him and possesses him as it proceeds. Nowhere is the feeling stronger than in this section of the temptation, as Iago risks more and more and is each time successful. He has played each of the cards of a thin hand with consummate skill and timing; now, as Othello screams 'I'll tear her all to pieces,' he produces his only small trump card, the handkerchief, to add to his 'other proofs'. It is sometimes said that Othello's temptation is not convincing. Yet, beginning from a sensualist's nature that has hitherto spent its energy almost wholly in public affairs, each stage of his decline is totally plausible, and the stages make up a steady and convincing descent into the abyss.

Othello, reeling now under the cumulative impact of Iago's efforts and calling wildly for blood, can regain composure only by a determined reversion to his public manner of speaking. He tries to distance his personal crisis by investing his vow of vengeance with the trappings of prayer:

Like to the Pontic sea,
Whose icy current, and compulsive course,
Ne'er feels retiring ebb, but keeps due on
To the Propontic, and the Hellespont:
Even so my bloody thoughts, with violent pace
Shall ne'er look back, ne'er ebb to humble love,
Till that a capable and wide revenge
Swallow them up. Now by yond marble heaven,
In the due reverence of a sacred vow,
I here engage my words.

It has a superb width that moves us the more because it is misapplied to a personal wrong, in which Othello is in any case monstrously deceived. In a chilling dramatic moment, which Verdi among others recognised — he constructed at this point of his opera the most thrilling of all male duets — Iago kneels beside his master in a triumphant devil's parody:

> Do not rise yet.
> Witness, you ever-burning lights above,
> You elements that clip us round about,
> Witness that here Iago doth give up
> The excellency of his wit, hand, heart,
> To wrong'd Othello's service.

When Iago turns him relentlessly back from himself to the individuals involved in his revenge, Othello's control of his verse and himself departs and he is back to 'Damn her, lewd minx: O damn her!' After Othello has demanded the handkerchief and manifested his madness for the first time to Desdemona, Iago is back with the brutal visual suggestions which so inflame his sensualist master:

> Or to be naked with her friend abed,
> An hour, or more, not meaning any harm?

After a few moments of this and Iago's old technique of hesitant revelation, Othello loses all control and falls into a swoon, the moment being marked by the transformation of his earlier verbal music into an incoherence that is absurd and hideous:

> Pish! Noses, ears and lips. Is't possible? — Confess?
> — Handkerchief? — O devil!

Iago, with his suggestion that the worst thing of all is 'To lip a wanton in a secure couch, / And to suppose her chaste' ensures that Othello will stay on the rack even in his absence, and the Moor's disintegration is completed in the awful ironies which spring from him after Iago has stage-managed the little charade between Cassio and Bianca:

> the pity of it, Iago: O Iago, the pity of it Iago . . . I will chop her into messes . . . Good, good, the justice of it pleases.

When he strikes Desdemona, it is Lodovico, newly arrived from Venice with the memory of the Othello we saw there in the first act, who reminds us of the contrast between his previous public performance and his present private mania:

Is this the noble Moor, whom our full senate
Call all in all sufficient? This the noble nature,
Whom passion could not shake? Whose solid virtue
The shot of accident, nor dart of chance,
Could neither graze, nor pierce?

In the next scene, Emilia tries to reason with him; she is one of the line of transparently honest, tactless, lovable Shakespearian womenfolk which begins with Juliet's Nurse and culminates in Paulina in *The Winter's Tale*. But she appeals to his judgement, not to his senses as her husband has done, and her sturdy and logical assurance fails:

I durst, my lord, to wager she is honest,
Lay down my soul at stake: if you think other,
Remove your thought, it doth abuse your bosom;
If any wretch ha' put this in your head,
Let heaven requite it with the serpent's curse,
For if she be not honest, chaste and true,
There's no man happy, the purest of her sex
Is foul as slander.

It is an exact analysis of the process of Othello's madness, but he does not even consider it.

When Desdemona asks Othello a few lines later 'Why do you weep? Am I occasion of those tears my lord?' he looks over her head into the distance and there contemplates not her but himself:

but, alas, to make me
A fixed figure, for the time of scorn
To point his slow unmoving fingers at.

The poet's soul is tainted increasingly by Iago's imagery:

But there, where I have garner'd up my heart,
Where either I must live, or bear no life,
The fountain, from the which my current runs,
Or else dries up, to be discarded thence,
Or keep it as a cistern, for foul toads
To knot and gender in!

When finally he turns to the distressed and bewildered woman before him, compelled at last to do so as she protests in that key word of this

play that she is 'honest', the unpleasant imagery remains even as her
beauty has its familiar disturbing effect upon his senses:

> O, ay, as summer's flies, are in the shambles,
> That quicken even with blowing:
> O thou black weed, why are thou so lovely fair?
> Thou smell'st so sweet, that the sense aches at thee,
> Would thou hadst ne'er been born!

Lodovico and Emilia are voices of sanity which Othello, locked in his
nightmare world, now cannot hear. It is Emilia who reduces to reality
Othello's attempts to elevate himself amidst his suffering when she
tells her husband, 'A beggar in his drink could not have layed such
terms upon his callat.'

Othello's murder of Desdemona is the more horrific because of her
total innocence, emphasised with a master's touch in the searing pathos
of her willow song, simple music denoting a free and undiseased mind
whilst her killer reels through his lunacy outside her door. But a second
reason why it is one of the most painful deaths in drama is the way in
which Othello's intense visual sense is now perverted to pictures which
have an almost sacrilegious impact, as when Othello strikes a dramatic
attitude as he prepares for the deed:

> strumpet I come;
> Forth of my heart those charms, thine eyes, are blotted,
> Thy bed, lust-stain'd, shall with lust's blood be spotted.

The screw of our emotions is turned even tighter in Othello's
soliloquy over the sleeping Desdemona, one of Shakespeare's triumphs,
in which Othello's virtues and deficiencies are enshrined as he stands
on the brink of his ruin. The self-deception is there again: he attempts
to elevate his killing to the level of a sacrifice, persuading himself of
his logic even as his intense visual response threatens to take him over:

> It is the cause, it is the cause, my soul,
> Let me not name it to you, you chaste stars:
> It is the cause, yet I'll not shed her blood,
> Nor scar that whiter skin of hers than snow,
> And smooth as monumental alabaster;
> Yet she must die, else she'll betray more men.

There is the breadth and sensual response of great poetry as he considers the deed, so that for a moment we are allowed to hope that these qualities may yet redeem his soul:

> Put out the light, and then put out the light:
> If I quench thee, thou flaming minister,
> I can again thy former light restore,
> Should I repent me; but once put out thine,
> Thou cunning pattern of excelling nature,
> I know not where is that Promethean heat
> That can thy light relume: when I have pluck'd the rose,
> I cannot give it vital growth again,
> It must needs wither.

Traversi says of this speech that 'Othello's passion at this critical moment is as cold on the surface as it is intense just below: it combines a certain momumental frigidity in the expression with a tremendous impression of the activity of the senses.'[14] What Othello in fact does is to attempt to distance the deed by the adoption of his earlier successful public style. When he is faced with the reality of the private relationship, his control disintegrates. Thus when he kisses Desdemona and she wakes, his composure departs, so that in a moment he is hastening to strangle her before she can cloud his resolution with reason. Eventually he stifles her without allowing her to say the one prayer she requests, the poet transformed thus swiftly to barbarian.

There is a seed of truth in Emilia's bitter description of the Moor as 'murderous coxcomb', for the faint strain of poseur that is suggested in almost all his great speeches is that most dangerous of all such strains, that of the self-deceiver. When he looks down upon the evidence of his deed in the speech beginning 'Behold I have a weapon,' he attempts to re-establish his position, but the sight of Desdemona's face produces one of the most memorable of all his conceits:

> O ill-starr'd wench,
> Pale as thy smock, when we shall meet at count,
> This look of thine will hurl my soul from heaven,
> And friends will snatch at it: cold, cold my girl,
> Even like thy chastity.

Confronted again with a personal rather than a public disaster, he breaks down into raving. It is not until he has resolved upon action, the action of his suicide, that he can regain composure. His final speech is another magnificent piece of writing, in which the man is manifest. T. S. Eliot called it both a splendid piece of self-centred poetry and a dupe's attempt at self-justification.[15] It is both of these, and also an evasion of his present private tragedy as he looks back to his earlier public glories. But the speech manages to suggest also the breadth and nobility of soul of that public figure, to convey the massive human waste that we have witnessed, whatever his private insufficiencies:

Soft you, a word or two:
I have done the state some service, and they know't;
No more of that: I pray you in your letters,
When you shall these unlucky deeds relate,
Speak of them as they are; nothing extenuate,
Nor set down aught in malice; then must you speak
Of one that lov'd not wisely, but too well:
Of one not easily jealous, but being wrought,
Perplex'd in the extreme; of one whose hand,
Like the base Indian, threw a pearl away,
Richer than all his tribe: of one whose subdued eyes,
Albeit unused to the melting mood,
Drops tears as fast as the Arabian trees
Their medicinal gum.

So Othello dies as he has lived throughout the action of the play, a public man bewildered by the complexities of private conduct and private judgements, the simplest but not the least moving of all the great tragic heroes.

## Notes

1. 'Egregiously an Ass' by Albert Gerard, SS 10, reprinted in K. Muir and P. Edwards (eds.), *Aspects of Othello*, p. 17.
2. *The Common Pursuit* (Chatto and Windus, London, 1952), p. 144.
3. *An Approach to Shakespeare*, pp. 128–9.
4. '*Othello*: a Retrospect, 1900–67', reprinted in *Aspects of Othello*.
5. *An Approach to Shakespeare*, pp. 134–5.
6. Essay in *Angel with Horns*.
7. Arden edition, p. xlvii.
8. 'The *Othello* Music' in *The Wheel of Fire* (1930; 4th edn, 1949).
9. '*Othello*: a Retrospect', p. 5.
10. *An Approach to Shakespeare*, p. 141.

11.   'Honest in *Othello*' in *The Structure of Complex Words* (Chatto and Windus, London, 1951).

12.   Arden edition, p. lv.

13.   Ibid., p. lvi.

14.   *An Approach to Shakespeare*, p. 129.

15.   See 'Shakespeare and the Stoicism of Seneca' in *Selected Essays* (Faber, London, 1951), pp. 130-1.

# 6 KING LEAR

Much of the debate about *King Lear* centres around the effectiveness of the play on stage. It was doubts about the actability of the original that led to Tate's amended version, with Cordelia surviving to marry Edgar and the Fool omitted, which held sway for a century and a half. The twentieth century has seen some impressive refutations of the view that Shakespeare's text is too mighty for the stage, such as Paul Scofield's celebrated 1962 RSC *Lear*, but any prolonged exploration of ground that has already been extensively covered would be inappropriate here.

What must be stressed is that on this vast and sombre canvas Shakespeare constructs his most mighty parable upon the theme of public and private man. In *King Lear*, the favourite Elizabethan correspondences of the microcosm of the individual, the macrocosm of the state in which he operates, and the relation of both to the wider moral world which envelops them, are thoroughly explored. And within this dark world where humanity is stripped bare of its pretensions, Shakespeare's preoccupation with the paradoxes of individual morality and the exercise of political power runs strong and consistent. As the world of man reels towards the abyss, all the forces for good, Cordelia, Kent, Gloucester, Edgar, the Fool and eventually Lear himself, are stripped of power or strip themselves of it before their virtue is revealed at its most radiant and compelling. Most significantly, Lear's purging and moral reform come as power is taken from him and the scales drop from his eyes.

The play may indeed be read as a savage cautionary tale which anticipates Lord Acton's well known, though often misquoted, dictum that 'Power tends to corrupt, and absolute power corrupts absolutely.' But the message, as in all Shakespeare's work involving the theme of power, is not so negative. If he feels that all who exercise power should beware of passing power into the hands of those whose individual natures indicate that they may misuse it, he never shirks the issue that states must be governed and power must be exercised by someone. Lear suffers as much and more than Shakespeare's Richard of Bordeaux for his failure to show responsibility in office; it is Shakespeare's triumph to suggest in each qualities of soul which extend man beyond the facts of power and its uses.

The first scene of the play is a distillation of Shakespeare's favourite theme: how power and the irresponsible exercise of it cloud judgement and moral sensitivity. Lear stands at the centre of the scene, 'a massive fortress of pride', in Granville-Barker's memorable phrase. As a corollary which shows that the issues of power are complex, we may note that those who preserve their integrity and love Lear most, Cordelia and Kent, refuse to acknowledge political facts and the new repositories of power at all: in a world already full of political threats they do not serve Lear best by doing so.

Those who find the scene unbelievable should remember that it is planned by Lear as an elaborate formal charade: the preliminary exchange between Kent and Gloucester makes it clear that it is to be the ceremonial implementation of a plan already determined. Lear's sense of humiliation when Cordelia denies him his formal declaration of love before his court is then more understandable, though his over-reaction is absurd and meant to be seen as absurd. Wilson Knight best sums up the spirit of the scene: 'Lear has, so to speak, staged an interlude, in which he grasps expressions of love to his heart, and resigns his sceptre to a chorus of acclamations. It is childish, foolish — but very human.'[1]

A grasp of the scene's ceremonial aspects makes more credible the behaviour and language of its principals. Cordelia, young, shining with that integrity which has a strain of puritanism, stands at one extreme of the continuum of human behaviour. At that extreme, individual feeling is sacred and thus private. Forced to declare her love amidst the courtly flourishes of manner and language which she knows to be artificial, Cordelia reserves the privacy of her heart's emotions even as she wrenches out the words which seem so grudging:

> Unhappy that I am, I cannot heave
> My heart into my mouth: I love your Majesty
> According to my bond; no more nor less.

At the other extreme of public behaviour, conscious only of the ritual of his staged scene and angered by Cordelia's fracturing of its happy solemnity, Lear responds in the inflated public style which indicates pride at its disastrous work:

> Let it be so; thy truth then be thy dower:
> For, by the sacred radiance of the sun,
> The mysteries of Hecate and the night,
> By all the operations of the orbs
> From whom we do exist and cease to be,
> Here I disclaim all my paternal care,

Propinquity and property of blood,
And as a stranger to my heart and me
Hold thee from this for ever.

Wilson Knight thinks that in Lear 'A tremendous soul is, as it were, incongruously geared to a puerile intellect.'[2] But the progress of the scene shows that his ignorance of character and wilful disregard of sound advice are the adjuncts of the near-absolute powers which have attached to a great king for so long. It is pride and wrath which obscure his judgement: he becomes steadily more formidable and more angry as he becomes more wrong. He warns Kent before hearing him, 'Come not between the dragon and his wrath.' When the worthy earl recalls his past service to get a hearing, Lear tries to silence him with another line of thundering monosyllables: 'The bow is bent and drawn; make from the shaft.' Good counsel, which the blunt Kent finally insists on offering, leads only to his banishment.

Both Cordelia and Kent are so concerned with the holiness of their personal reactions that they refuse to recognise political realities, to observe the necessity in a dangerous public world to indulge in those courtly decorations of language which oil the wheels of political action.

Cordelia stands silent throughout the disastrous treatment of Kent, characteristically intervening only to assert her personal integrity before France, beseeching her father to make it known that she is deprived of his favour not for any crime,

But even for want of that for which I am richer,
A still-soliciting eye, and such a tongue
That I am glad I have not, though not to have it
Hath lost me in your liking.

When Burgundy asks that Cordelia be given the lands Lear originally proposed for her, the structure of Lear's taut reply suggests the power and resolution of a great king, but the attitude he strikes has the stubbornness in the face of reason of an embattled child:

Nothing: I have sworn: I am firm.

In a dramatic postscript at the end of the scene, the wolfish beneficiaries of Lear's blindness to individual character comment ominously upon his conduct. Goneril makes the 'poor judgement' he has shown in casting off Cordelia and Kent an argument for his further restriction, and Regan agrees balefully that 'he hath ever but slenderly known himself'. Lear, by obscuring private moralities beneath the treacherous panoply of public declarations, has bound himself to his wheel of fire. In the second scene of the play, Shakespeare begins the sub-plot which runs parallel to and eventually dovetails with the main tragic action of the play. For Gloucester's brutal physical blinding will echo the spiritual catastrophe of Lear's madness, and both will see better when power has been stripped from them. The parallel to Lear's wolfish daughters will be the ruthless Edmund, as predatory as they are, even more clear-sighted about the political world in which he operates, ready to exploit its corruptions like some amoral natural force. He announces himself in the impudent soliloquy which never fails on stage, and ends, 'Now, gods, stand up for bastards!' Danby writes:

> Edmund in his opening soliloquy is the compact image of everything that denies the orthodox view. Shakespeare thought of him simply and exclusively as the Bastard, and 'bastard' is the Elizabethan equivalent of 'outsider'. Edmund is a complete Outsider. He is outside Society, he is outside Nature, he is outside Reason. . . . There is tremendous gusto in the portrait of the Bastard: energy, emancipation, a right-minded scorn of humbug, clear-headedness; the speed, sureness and lissom courage of a tiger. . . . But in spite of the attractiveness of the portrait, Edmund still belongs with Goneril and Regan. He is a Shakespearian villain. And condemned with him in the apocalyptical judgement of the play is the corrupt society he represents.[3]

All this is true, but it is true of all Shakespeare's depictions of Machiavellian villainy. Almost every word of it could be applied to Richard of Gloucester and his progress to the crown. What these characters do is to recognise more clearly than those around them the possibilities of a corrupt political system in which might may declare its own right. By concealing their individual personalities from those blind enough to take public observances for reality, they exploit the system for their own swift gains. Shakespeare adds to their energy and daring a clear-headed apprehension of the realities of state that their more virtuous victims do not possess. Thus when Gloucester, having swallowed with depressing eagerness Edmund's poisonous bait, attributes the dire happenings around him to 'these late eclipses of the sun and moon', Edmund dismisses this contemptuously as 'the excellent foppery of the world'.

It is the same contempt for those who refuse to consider the real world before their eyes which Goneril soon shows in her description of Lear:

> Idle old man,
> That still would manage those authorities
> That he hath given away!

Kent in the next scene assesses Oswald the individual as the cur he is, but deliberately flouts the realities of political power: because Oswald is Goneril's steward, Kent is in the stocks by II ii. It is the Fool, who never forgives Lear for his treatment of Cordelia, who provides for Lear a cauterising commentary upon what is really happening around him. Granville-Barker complained that producers are faced with a Fool who has been 'all etherealized by the Higher Criticism'.[4] Certainly those who see the Fool as seeking to take Lear's mind off the stark facts of his misuse of power are quite wrong, for he constantly recalls them to him. When Lear sees with devastating clarity the enormity of his conduct and the realities of power, the Fool has no longer any function and Shakespeare dismisses him from the rest of the play. He is at his most insistent in the early scenes, when Lear is still half-deceived about his daughters. In I iv, he reminds the King openly of his foolish actions at least half a dozen times, culminating in his bitter:

> I had rather be any kind of a thing than a fool; and yet I would not be thee, Nuncle; thou has pared thy wit o' both sides, and left nothing i' th' middle.

He subsides only when the formidable Goneril arrives and proceeds to make his message superfluous by her treatment of his master. The issues of power become more naked as each moment passes and Goneril becomes ever more direct:

> Be then desired
> By her that else will take the thing she begs . . .

Lear has to turn away from immediate events to construct his famous curse; he is a formidable individual still, fearsome as well as piteous, but the curse is terrible because it is that of a betrayed parent, not a splenetic head of state:

> Hear, Nature, hear! dear Goddess, hear!
> Suspend thy purpose, if thou didst intend
> To make this creature fruitful!
> Into her womb convey sterility!
> Dry up in her the organs of increase,
> And from her derogate body never spring
> A babe to honour her! If she must teem,
> Create her child of spleen, that it may live
> And be a thwart disnatur'd torment to her!
> Let it stamp wrinkles in her brow of youth,
> With cadent tears fret channels in her cheeks,
> Turn all her mother's pains and benefits
> To laughter and contempt, that she may feel
> How sharper than a serpent's tooth it is
> To have a thankless child!

When he returns to threaten Goneril with Regan, the power of his language and delivery is awesome still, but the real chill of the lines comes from our knowledge of how mistaken he is about his second daughter:

> I have another daughter,
> Who, I am sure, is kind and comfortable:
> When she shall hear this of thee, with her nails
> She'll flay thy wolvish visage. Thou shalt find
> That I'll resume the shape which thou dost think
> I have cast off for ever.

Caroline Spurgeon distinguished the dominant image of the play as being of 'a human body in anguished movement, tugged, wrenched, beaten, pierced, stung, scourged, dislocated, flayed, gashed, scalded, tortured, and finally broken on the rack'.[5] Lear, ironically, uses such imagery here to threaten others, when he is the one who will be lacerated: his learning of the realities of power for rulers and ruled has only just begun. At the end of Act I, as Lear prays 'O let me not be mad, not mad, sweet heaven' his Fool reminds him mercilessly: 'Thou should'st not have been old till thou hadst been wise.'

No one is as clear-sighted as the Fool about the realities of power.

Lear's great spiritual buttress in his sufferings, Kent, makes his physical situation worse by his reckless determination to ignore such considerations.   By II ii he is telling an assembly which includes Cornwall, Regan and Edmund:

> Sir, 'tis my occupation to be plain:
> I have seen better faces in my time
> Than stands on any shoulder that I see
> Before me at this instant.

His wilful disregard for his own safety is an effective enough piece of stagecraft, for our hearts warm to his defiance of the wolfish pack around him, but his immediate imprisonment in the stocks only implements another stage of Lear's decline in II iv. It takes the Fool to offer to Kent his most daring generalisation yet upon a society which depends upon the temperaments of powerful men:

> Let go thy hold when a great wheel runs down a hill, lest it break thy neck with following; but the great one that goes upward, let him draw thee after.

In a moment, Regan is operating such rules in her brusque dismissal of Lear's complaints against her sister:

> O, Sir! you are old;
> Nature in you stands on the very verge
> Of her confine: you should be rul'd and led
> By some discretion that discerns your state
> Better than you yourself. Therefore I pray you
> That to our sister you do make return;
> Say you have wrong'd her.

This is a painful scene, with the sisters eventually joining forces to make the reality of Lear's helplessness brutally apparent to him. But it is also the scene in which the greatness of the play and the daring breadth of Shakespeare's conception becomes apparent: this is the point at which Lear begins to move us with more than the mere pathos of his suffering and the sight of greatness fallen upon ill times in old age. For in his response to the gradual reduction of the knights which are the symbol of his power and independence, he shows his first apprehension of suffering which is more general than his own, of mankind's need for more intangible things than property:

> O! reason not the need; our basest beggars
> Are in the poorest thing superfluous:
> Allow not nature more than nature needs,
> Man's life is cheap as beast's. Thou art a lady;
> If only to go warm were gorgeous,
> Why, nature needs not what thou gorgeous wear'st,
> Which scarcely keeps thee warm.

He breaks down into violent threats which become incoherent as he realises he has no power to implement them. He has had his first searing insight into what he has done and into the lot of ordinary man. He reels from the scene with his equally impotent supporters, Gloucester and the Fool, certain now of the spiritual catastrophe into which he is moving: 'O Fool! I shall go mad.' The new creatures of power shut the doors upon him and when we see him next he is crazed individual man, totally stripped now of temporal power and defying the wildest of nature's forces.

The storm scenes are seen by most critics as the core of the play, though on stage they rarely impress as this. Lear's two great scenes of disillusionment with his elder daughters and the magical one of his re-awakening in the arms of Cordelia usually terrify and move us more than anything else in the theatre. The storm scenes there appear a transitional stage, in which Lear retains his individual power of speech and bearing while struggling to accommodate the knowledge that power to influence the progress of events has passed from him for ever. He defies the elements in a last magnificent spending of the pride and anger that have hung about him for the decades of his autocracy. In his exhaustion and his madness, he comes at last to a clear vision of the condition of man, of the helpless men who depend upon the justice of rulers, and of the responsibilities of government.

Kenneth Muir thinks that: 'In the storm scenes there is a wild quartet of madness — Lear, Poor Tom, the Fool, and the elements themselves — in which the Fool seems almost to stand for sanity. He fades from the picture when his is no longer needed, since Lear can act as his own Fool.'[6] His own Fool in the sense that he acquires for himself the insights about the world that the Fool so pitilessly outlined for him in the first two acts of the play. Lear adds to those sceptical, negative insights a wider perception of what is necessary if rulers are to administer a better world.

At first his storm speeches, defying the elements with the majesty of a mighty soul, concentrate upon his own situation:

> Rumble thy bellyful! Spit, fire! spout, rain!
> Nor rain, wind, thunder, fire, are my daughters:
> I tax you not, you elements, with unkindness;
> I never gave you kingdom, call'd you children,
> You owe me no subscription: then let fall
> Your horrible pleasure; here I stand, your slave,
> A poor, infirm, weak, and despis'd old man.

But as his suffering deepens, Lear's comprehension of how hypocrisy may deceive the blind men of power becomes more generalised:

> Let the great Gods,
> That keep this dreadful pudder o'er our heads,
> Find out their enemies now. Tremble, thou wretch,
> That hast within thee undivulged crimes,
> Unwhipp'd of Justice; hide thee, thou bloody hand,
> Thou perjur'd, and thou simular of virtue
> That art incestuous; caitiff, to pieces shake,
> That under covert and convenient seeming
> Has practis'd on man's life; close pent-up guilts
> Rive your concealing continents, and cry
> These dreadful summoners grace.

Significantly, it is with the imminence of the madness he has feared that Lear considers for the first time the comfort of the shivering Fool who stands drenched beside him:

> My wits begin to turn.
> Come on, my boy. How dost, my boy? Art cold?
> I am cold myself.

By the second of his storm scenes, III iv, the King as Kent tries to shepherd him into the hovel can say, 'Prithee, go in thyself: seek thine own ease,' and then to the Fool 'In boy; go first.' And his prayer for the meanest of his subjects as he stands in the storm by the hovel is a triumph of the human spirit, showing the possibilities of the mind of man as much as any soaring ecstasies of more obvious rhetoric; for Lear, the supreme egoist and autocrat of the play's opening scene, has stripped

away the trappings of pampered power to discover within himself the
forgotten humanitarian:

> Poor naked wretches, whereso'er you are,
> That bide the pelting of this pitiless storm,
> How shall your houseless heads and unfed sides,
> Your loop'd and window'd raggedness, defend you
> From seasons such as these? O! I have ta'en
> Too little care of this. Take physic, Pomp;
> Expose thyself to feel what wretches feel,
> That thou mayst shake the superflux to them,
> And show the Heavens more just.

Soon he contemplates the naked Edgar and finds:

> thou are the thing itself; unaccommodated man is no more
> but such a poor, bare, forked animal as thou art.

Lear's meeting with the blinded Gloucester in IV vi brings from him his
ultimate dismissal of the pomp of state. 'A dog's obey'd in office' he
cries, and goes on to the play's most daring undermining of the concepts
of birth and rank so dear to Elizabethans:

> Thorough tatter'd clothes small vices do appear;
> Robes and fur gowns hide all. Plate sin with gold,
> And the strong lance of justice hurtless breaks;
> Arm it in rags, a pigmy's straw does pierce it.

This is remarkable writing in a man often depicted ridiculously as a
honeyed flatterer of the Establishment, with his eye on the main chance.
Maynard Mack writes: 'No one, I suspect, who had responded to the
role of the King in Shakespeare's history plays, of the King's role in contemporary drama generally, could miss the shock in these lines, coming
as they did from "the thing itself".'[7]

By this stage Lear, in the magical scene in which he wakes in the arms
of Cordelia, has stripped himself of all pretensions and sees himself
starkly as he is:

> I am a very foolish fond old man,
> Fourscore and upward, not an hour more or less;

And, to deal plainly,
I fear I am not in my perfect mind.

Yet, devoid of power, conscious with a mystic's clarity of the realities of
spiritual life, Lear speaks his greatest truths in the aftermath of his madness: he is the last and most impressive repository of that Shakespearian
fascination with the wisdom of madmen and Fools.

It is because Shakespeare wishes to concentrate upon such issues that
the battle is the most perfunctory in all his work. When Lear is captured
by Edmund, 'He accepts eagerly the prison which marks his withdrawal
from the world's values, for he has his own new values to sustain.'[8] As
he does so, the relaxed rhythms and soft consonants of his verse could
hardly be a greater contrast to the thundering diatribes of the formidable despot who began the play:

> Come, let's away to prison;
> We two alone will sing like birds i' th' cage:
> When thou dost ask me blessing, I'll kneel down,
> And ask of thee forgiveness: so we'll live,
> And pray, and sing, and tell old tales, and laugh
> At gilded butterflies, and hear poor rogues
> Talk of court news; and we'll talk with them too,
> Who loses and who wins; who's in, who's out;
> And take upon's the mystery of things,
> As if we were God's spies: and we'll wear out,
> In a wall'd prison, packs and sects of great ones
> That ebb and flow by th' moon.

Lear has now the innocence and moral freedom, the spiritual strength,
of one who has shaken off the last vestiges of power. His death is the
natural end of this spiritual development: 'the ripeness is all' as Edgar
told Gloucester a little while earlier, and Lear is ready now for that
better world which the meek shall inherit. The point of Lear's death
beside Cordelia is well made by Maynard Mack:

> Tragedy never tells us what to think; it shows us what we are and
> what we may be. And what we are and may be was never, I submit,
> more memorably fixed upon a stage than in this kneeling old man
> whose heartbreak is precisely the measure of what, in our world of
> relatedness, it is possible to lose and possible to win. The victory and
> the defeat are simultaneous and inseparable. . . . Suffering we all

recoil from; but we all know it is a greater thing to suffer than to lack the feelings and virtues that make it possible to suffer.[9]

Bradley, who thought *Lear* 'certainly the most terrible picture Shakespeare painted of the world', wrote that 'There is nothing more noble and beautiful in nature than Shakespeare's exposition of the effect of suffering in reviving the greatness and eliciting the sweetness of Lear's nature.' He might have added also that as Lear's suffering progresses his power drops away from him, and that this loss is at least as important an element as his suffering in the spiritual purgation which is the centre of the play. Lear has to lose power before he recaptures the vision of how it should be exercised.

## Notes

1. *The Wheel of Fire*, p. 160.
2. Ibid., p. 162.
3. 'Edmund and the Two Natures' in J. Adelman (ed.), Twentieth Century Interpretations of *King Lear* (Prentice-Hall, Englewood Cliffs, New Jersey, 1978), pp. 53–5.
4. *Prefaces to Shakespeare* (Batsford, London, 1969), vol. 1, p. 200.
5. *Shakespeare's Imagery*, p. 339.
6. Introduction to Arden edition, p. 1xiv.
7. 'The World of *King Lear*' in Adelman (ed.), Twentieth Century Interpretations of *King Lear*, pp. 62–3.
8. Ibid., p. 66.
9. Ibid., p. 69.

*Macbeth* is a clear and simple play upon which modern criticism has imposed an unwarranted complexity. To claim that it is simple is not to deny the play's magnificence: it is the most concise and moving account in our literature of a man's decline into evil. Once Macbeth has succumbed to the witches' siren song of power, it is Shakespeare's superb delineation of the forest of the night in which his soul wanders which sustains the tale at the level of tragedy.

Shakespearian criticism of the last forty years has concentrated heavily upon the nature and function of poetic imagery. Particularly when writers have sought an overriding symbolism, there has been a tendency to read the plays as elaborate poems, with all consideration of the author's dramatic intentions thrust firmly into the background. Passages thought by former centuries to be unimportant or off-key, such as the reference to royal healing powers or Macbeth's catalogue of dogs, have been invested by some writers with a new importance; unimportant characters like Lady Macduff have suddenly been discovered as key figures within an elaborate chess-game of poetic symbolism. More seriously, the reaction against the 'character' approach to the play, of which Bradley was the most distinguished exponent, has led to some remarkable views. Kenneth Muir, who has much to say that is interesting about the play, writes:

> It must be emphasised that because Shakespeare makes Macbeth talk as only a great poet could talk, we are not to assume that Macbeth is a great poet: he is merely part of a great poem . . . if we go further and pretend that his poetic imagery is a proof that Macbeth had a powerful imagination, that he was in fact, a poet, we are confusing real life with drama.[1]

Rather is it Professor Muir who confuses plays with poetry. As V. Y. Kantak says in an admirably concise reply to this school of criticism: 'The poetry that a character speaks, in an important sense, "belongs" to and is revelatory of that character. It cannot simply be regarded as though it "belonged" only to Shakespeare in the way lyric poetry belongs to an author.'[2]

The poetry is the centre of *Macbeth*, for it is the instrument through which Shakespeare sustains our attention and our emotional involvement with his hero after the key point of moral decision in the play. For that point is placed daringly and uniquely early, so that for four acts of the play our interest is dependent upon Shakespeare's unforgettably vivid exposition of the march of evil through the territory of a man's soul. Macbeth is the most clear-sighted of the great tragic heroes, more consistent in his apprehension of what he does even than Antony. He is also a man of vivid imagination, with a poetic capacity to express his situation which is unsurpassed even in Shakespeare. To deny this not only undermines the dramatic structure of the play but asks us to believe that, because the play is Shakespeare's and not Macbeth's, he cannot be distinguished from the very different poet that speaks in Othello or Lear or Antony. Of course the poetry is Shakespeare's, but he uses his different veins to distinguish figures of very different temperaments, each of them poets, just as certainly as he uses a different kind of language to show us a Henry IV who is *not* naturally a poet. Within this play, to deny Macbeth his imagination is to deny the chief characteristic by which his creator distinguishes him from his wife.

The shift of modern attention to the symbolic force of imagery has forced some critics to argue for a dichotomy between imagery and character which is surely false. Irving Ribner, for instance, believes that 'As Shakespeare became more and more absorbed in the religious and ethical dimensions of tragedy, he concentrated more and more on the development of the symbol, with a corollary unconcern for character consistency.'[3] Kantak, discussing Ribner's view, comes surely to a more sensible conclusion:

> Critics are now trying to show, for instance, that in the total design of *Macbeth* there is an assertion of a moral order and a complete acceptance of the Christian ethic. It is argued that Shakespeare is closer to medieval traditions than was hitherto supposed, and *Macbeth* is now being read simply as a 'Morality' in which the characters figure as symbols of moral entities all diagrammatically disposed to illustrate the Christian code. Macbeth, the evil man who makes the fatal choice, is poised between Lady Macbeth and Banquo, the bad and the good angels respectively. . . . There is surely something wrong in the approach which considers Shakespeare's realism of character as a sort of technical proficiency, valuable in its way but not at all essential to his tragic vision. It is true that the characters are not 'real' but part of Shakespeare's artistry lies in convincing us that they are and in getting us emotionally involved with them.[4]

The last is so nearly a definition of drama that it seems a truism: it needs stating only because of the recent excesses of the imagist approach. The greatest danger of an excessive concentration upon imagery is that it may lead to a critics' text rather than an author's, by which I mean that almost any thesis may be argued if one dwells at length upon passages of text, especially if one chooses to ignore other evidence from elsewhere in the play. Robert Grudin,[5] for instance, argues that the early passages about Macbeth's valour argue an anti-militarism, which comes more obviously from post-Vietnam America than Jacobean England, and spends most of the rest of his account of the play upon an analysis of the lightweight Malcolm.

The earliest and best of the imagist critics see the language of the play as illuminating and enlarging issues which have long been apparent. L. C. Knights, for instance, begins his essay on the play: '*Macbeth* defines a particular kind of evil — the evil that results from a lust for power'[6] and goes on to show how the poetry of the play intensifies this definition. Few would argue with Traversi's extension of the play's theme beyond narrow 'character' considerations: 'The play deals this time with the overthrow of harmony, not merely in an individual tragic hero (such as Othello) but in an ordered society; and the conflict is worked out in terms that are clearly and unequivocally moral.'[7]

These profound issues are explored within a dramatic framework that is very simple. There is little conflict between the private and public man in Macbeth: from the first the strengths and weaknesses of his private personality are played out largely upon the stage of public life. His only defect of personality, overweening political ambition, is one which is at its most damaging when the temptation of great office beckons. At the prospect, Macbeth commits the great crime which destroys his moral being; with his decline, the state of which he has made himself the unauthorised centre collapses also. We have glimpses, in the scenes before and after the murder of Duncan, in the scenes with Banquo, in the banquet scene, of Macbeth trying to play the bland, proficient usurper, as efficient and enigmatic in a world of blood as Henry Bolingbroke. The glimpses are used only to set off the agonised conscience, the raw nerves of guilt, which dominate the presentation everywhere else. Private, damned Macbeth is continually before us, his public performance only emphasising the dark night in which his soul wanders. This bringing together of public and private man is the chief reason for that intensity which has so often been remarked in this shortest of the great plays. As Knights remarks; 'In none of the tragedies is there anything superfluous, but it is perhaps *Macbeth* which gives the keenest impression of economy.'[8]

This economy is apparent from the first, as Macbeth's military glory is sketched by two vigorous eye-witness accounts before his temptation proceeds at headlong pace. Those who see an irony in the Sergeant's and Ross's full-blooded reportage of Macbeth's valour in battle should remember that earlier centuries, and indeed every generation down to 1914, saw the successful warrior without the ambivalence with which we have lately invested him. Macbeth's exploits against the merciless Macdonwald are described more specifically, but with exactly the same exultant note, as those of Tennyson's Light Brigade. The audience around the stage of the Globe accepted without ambiguity the valour and nobility of 'Bellona's bridegroom', and awaited his arrival among them with interest.

Many in that audience, so much more alert to word-play than a modern one, would remark also how the hero's first words, 'So foul and fair a day I have not seen,' connected him immediately with the supernatural evil they had seen hovering in the filthy air of the play's opening. And in the reactions of the two generals to the witches' prophecies, there is again that economy of treatment which thrusts the drama's main action before us. Banquo is immediately cautious, distrustful of good news from such a source:

> And oftentimes, to win us to our harm,
> The instruments of Darkness tell us truths;
> Win us with honest trifles, to betray's
> In deepest consequence.

In contrast, Macbeth's aside marks not only his temptation but the teeming imagination which is now his warning and will later become his scourge:

>       This supernatural soliciting
> Cannot be ill: cannot be good: —
> If ill, why hath it given me earnest of success,
> Commencing in a truth? I am Thane of Cawdor.
> If good, why do I yield to that suggestion
> Whose horrid image doth unfix my hair,
> And make my seated heart knock at my ribs,
> Against the use of nature? Present fears
> Are less than horrible imaginings.

My thought, whose murther yet is but fantastical,
Shakes so my single state of man,
That function is smother'd in surmise,
And nothing is, but what is not.

Knights' fine analysis of this masterly piece of verse[9] draws attention to the 'sickening see-saw rhythm' of its opening. Wilson Knight marks this as the moment of the birth of evil in Macbeth.[10]

The short scene which follows, in which Duncan graciously welcomes his victorious generals, suggests the natural order which will soon be violated. But in a play built on the mature Shakespeare's mastery of language, there is a contrast of another sort. The elaborate courtly language in which Duncan pays his tributes and Macbeth and Banquo respond to him is in the public style with which we are familiar in court scenes: it is the strain which Hamlet and Cordelia, in their different situations, shatter into discord in their first appearances. Here we have a brief thirty lines of it, and there could scarcely be a greater contrast than that with the tautness of Macbeth's tortured asides which bracket the scene. For with the news of Malcolm's establishment as Prince of Cumberland, there is a further step towards regicide as darkness enters Macbeth's imagery:

Stars, hide your fires!
Let not light see my black and deep desires;
The eye wink at the hand; yet let that be,
Which the eye fears, when it is done, to see.

This has the terrifying vagueness of an evil dream, with the compressed, elliptical style marking the confusion induced by suggestions which that part of the mind we call conscience tries to thrust aside. The instrument which will resolve that confusion and translate it into concrete action is at hand, as she will be until the first and crucial murder is effected. Maynard Mack says of Macbeth: 'Throughout, except in his earliest scenes with Lady Macbeth, he is spiritually a man apart.'[11] Certainly he sets himself apart by his first great crime, though this does not mean that his tortured mind is not full of recognisable human thoughts. Until that decision, however, he is balanced on the spiritual knife-edge which we have already witnessed. It is Lady Macbeth who summarises the spiritual resources which she sees as weakness in her amoral drive towards greatness:

> Yet do I fear thy nature:
> It is too full o' th' milk of human kindness,
> To catch the nearest way. Thou wouldst be great;
> Art not without ambition, but without
> The illness should attend it; what thou wouldst highly,
> That wouldst thou holily; wouldst not play false,
> And yet wouldst wrongly win.

Lady Macbeth's dedication of herself to evil is the most terrible thing in the play. We do not share the belief in demonology of Shakespeare's audience, so that the horror of the witches is diminished; but Lady Macbeth's identification of herself with supernatural wickedness comes leaping across the centuries, with its superb climax:

> Come, you Spirits
> That tend on mortal thoughts, unsex me here,
> And fill me, from the crown to the toe, top-full
> Of direct cruelty! make thick my blood,
> Stop up th' access and passage to remorse;
> That no compunctious visitings of Nature
> Shake my fell purpose, nor keep peace between
> Th' effect and it! Come to my woman's breasts,
> And take my milk for gall, you murth'ring ministers,
> Werever in your sightless substances,
> You wait on Nature's mischief! Come, thick Night,
> And pall thee in the dunnest smoke of Hell,
> That my keen knife see not the wound it makes,
> Nor Heaven peep through the blanket of the dark,
> To cry, 'Hold, hold!'

If Macbeth is Shakespeare's supreme man of imagination, thinking through it and suffering through it, Lady Macbeth has limited imagination and thus no fear of the consequences of her actions in this world and the next. The witches made Macbeth's seated heart knock at his ribs; for his wife as she greets him, they are simply and reliably 'the all-hail hereafter'. She even indulges herself with a grim enigmatic joke, 'He that's coming / Must be provided for'. In a play which may be read as a series of interlocking ironies, there is an obvious one here as Lady

Macbeth, at her most masterful, speaks of the deed which will plunge both of them into an endless series of nights full of bad dreams:

> And you shall put
> This night's great business into my dispatch;
> Which shall to all our nights and days to come
> Give solely sovereign sway and masterdom.

Between this scene and the one in which Lady Macbeth finally confirms Macbeth's resolve, Shakespeare inserts the brief thirty lines of Duncan's reception at Inverness; nowhere in his work is such a scene used so economically. It has the obvious dramatic purpose of marking the passage of time and acting as a foil for the taut scenes on either side of it. It gives us a glimpse of the outdoors and the natural world at its gentlest, which contrasts with the intense, near-claustrophobic atmosphere of the scenes which follow. It gives us a last glimpse of the grace and kindness which surround a natural order of power: both Duncan's and Banquo's speeches are full of images of beauty, fertility, love and procreation. The measured, courtly language in which these images are framed could scarcely be a greater contrast to the compressed, elliptical verse and tumbling rhythms of Macbeth's great soliloquy, which follows hard upon it.

As the play's key speech and one of the greatest in Shakespeare, the soliloquy has rightly received much attention.[12] Macbeth begins by attempting to evaluate his proposed action as coolly as Hamlet considers suicide in his 'To be or not to be' soliloquy. But here the private man's dilemma, which Hamlet strove to separate from his public situation, is inextricably bound up with public conduct. From the first, however, Macbeth's conscience denies to him the morality of the deed he would so love to encompass for its political spoils. Traversi[13] draws attention to the succession of uneasy suppositions with which his reflections open, and the avoidance, through the repeated use of 'it', of direct reference to the deed he fears to name:

> If it were done, when 'tis done, then 'twere well
> It were done quickly: if th' assassination
> Could trammel up the consequence, and catch
> With his surcease success; that but this blow
> Might be the be-all and the end-all — here,
> But here, upon this bank and shoal of time,
> We'd jump the life to come.

The latter part of the speech is one of the supreme expressions of Macbeth's visual imagination, a moment when the attempts of some critics to divorce the character from the distinctive poetry he speaks seem especially ridiculous:

> Besides, this Duncan
> Hath borne his faculties so meek, hath been
> So clear in his great office, that his virtues
> Will plead like angels, trumpet-tongu'd, against
> The deep damnation of his taking-off;
> And Pity, like a naked new-born babe,
> Striding the blast, or heaven's Cherubins, hors'd
> Upon the sightless couriers of the air,
> Shall blow the horrid deed in every eye,
> That tears shall drown the wind.

Macbeth's emotion grows as he considers the terror of the deed, so that he perceives the victim and the murder in full horror in a series of vivid pictures, his mind racing from metaphor to metaphor as his fear and excitement rise.

Macbeth's conscience has set before him in lurid detail the public, sacrilegious aspects of the murder he proposed. Lady Macbeth now uses their private, intimate links to force the great act of public evil. After her playing upon the warrior's sensitive manhood, she produces her most startling and uncompromising figure of all:

> I have given suck, and know
> How tender 'tis to love the babe that milks me:
> I would, while it was smiling in my face,
> Have pluck'd my nipple from his boneless gums,
> And dash'd the brains out, had I so sworn
> As you have done to this.

Predictably, this vivid demonstration of her strength of will, followed immediately by her detailed murder plan, has its effect upon her husband, who reels before her resolution and the specific account of a deed that has been but a monstrous vagueness to him. 'Bring forth men-children only!' he exclaims, forgetting for a brief moment in the excitement of their private bond the hideous public act they plan: they are never again to be so close.

As Macbeth waits alone in the courtyard for the bell which will send him to murder his king, his imagination produces for him his final warning, a hallucination of the dagger. When he thrusts the warning aside, Shakespeare in a dozen lines secures three effects. He heightens the atmosphere of unnatural evil, identifies Macbeth with the witches, and shows his mind reeling, inebriated by the force of his imagination instead of the drink his more mundane spouse has used:

> Now o'er the one half-world
> Nature seems dead, and wicked dreams abuse
> The curtain'd sleep. Witchcraft celebrates
> Pale Hecate's off'rings; and wither'd Murther,
> Alarum'd by his sentinel, the wolf,
> Whose howl's his watch, thus with his stealthy pace,
> With Tarquin's ravishing strides, towards his design
> Moves like a ghost. — Thou sure and firm-set earth,
> Hear not my steps, which way they walk, for fear
> Thy very stones prate of my where-about,
> And take the present horror from the time,
> Which now suits with it.

The contrast between Macbeth and his wife is nowhere more marked than in the scene following the murder. Macbeth's breadth of vision tells him he will never sleep peacefully again. At this moment of greatest stress and danger, his mind cannot thrust aside the superb personification of the thought:

> Methought, I heard a voice cry, 'Sleep no more!
> Macbeth does murther sleep,' — the innocent Sleep;
> Sleep, that knits up the ravell'd sleave of care,
> The death of each day's life, sore labour's bath,
> Balm of hurt minds, great Nature's second course,
> Chief nourisher in life's feast.

'What do you mean?' his wife interrupts in bewilderment, at the opposite pole of imaginative arousal. In a moment she assures him, with another sentiment which will echo chillingly through her sleep-walking scene, that

> The sleeping, and the dead,
> Are but as pictures; 'tis the eye of childhood
> That fears a painted devil.

Macbeth's imagination is a more accurate prophet of what is to come. Looking in horror at his bloodstained hands, he produces perhaps the most remarkable of the play's many nightmare images:

> Will all great Neptune's ocean wash this blood
> Clean from my hand? No, this my hand will rather
> The multitudinous seas incarnadine,
> Making the green one red.

It is left to Lady Macbeth to save the immediate situation, as Macbeth reels about the stage, staring at his hands and unaware of the source of the hideous knocking which threatens his discovery. She identifies the knocking as emanating from the south entry and ushers her helpless husband briskly away with the assurance that 'A little water clears us of this deed.' The consequences she has so scorned and Macbeth so feared are the material of the rest of the play. 'Wake Duncan with thy knocking!' says the murderer as he is hurried away, denied even the transient exultation of most usurpers.

Shakespeare plunges us straight into the relief of the drunken porter, though even this broad stuff has its irony: the inventive rascal is indeed the 'Porter of Hell-Gate' he simulates for his own and the audience's amusement. G. Wickham points out interesting correspondences between the scene and a playlet within the English Miracle Cycles, *The Harrowing of Hell*.[14] But to argue as some commentators have done for a larger Christian symbolism from the starting-point of this scene, seems to seek too much weight in a passage that has obvious effects as a daring and ingenious piece of stagecraft.

Shakespeare, with immense insight and subtlety of language, contrives that Macbeth shall be the private man we have just seen with bloodstained hands even as he acts out the discovery of the murder for the court. For, as he attempts to simulate an appropriate grief, the words he speaks are not only too elaborate for spontaneous distress but express a real apprehension of his own situation:

> Had I but died an hour before this chance,
> I had liv'd a blessed time; for, from this instant,
> There's nothing serious in mortality;
> All is but toys: renown, and grace, is dead;
> The wine of life is drawn, and the mere lees
> Is left this vault to brag of.

Called upon to explain his peremptory killing of the grooms, Macbeth is again himself, the man of intense visual imagination, but the conceit he indulges is too forced for genuine grief: it is that of a poet excited by words and their possibilities when terse understatement would be more suitable:

> Here lay Duncan,
> His silver skin lac'd with his golden blood;
> And his gash'd stabs look'd like a breach in nature
> For ruin's wasteful entrance: there, the murtherers,
> Steep'd in the colours of their trade, their daggers
> Unmannerly breech'd with gore.

He is silent for the rest of the scene as Banquo takes over and makes the claim he cannot: 'In the great hand of God I stand.'

Banquo is an ambivalent presence in the play, though not less effective on stage for that. His soliloquy at the beginning of Act III touches enigmatically on the tensions of reconciling private morality with political progress: he seems to be tempted to keep silent by the prospect the witches held out for him. In that expressive modern cliché, he maintains a low profile whilst it seems to be in his interest to do so:

> Thou hast it now, King, Cawdor, Glamis, all,
> As the Weird Women promis'd; and, I fear,
> Thou play'dst most foully for't; yet it was said,
> It should not stand in thy posterity;
> But that myself should be the root and father
> Of many kings. If there come truth from them
> (As upon thee, Macbeth, their speeches shine),
> Why, by the verities on thee made good,
> May they not be my oracles as well,
> And set me up in hope?

There is more than a hint of political opportunism here, but that is not the author's main preoccupation, and Banquo is swiftly dismissed from the play. Perhaps Shakespeare could not show an ancestor of James I in an unfavourable light; perhaps a scene or two have been lost from this shortest of major plays, as many have conjectured. What is certain is that Macbeth plots the detail of Banquo's death in a way that would have been impossible for him before Duncan's murder coarsened his sensibilities. His questions to Banquo ('Ride you this afternoon? . . .

Is't far you ride?. . .Goes Fleance with you?') are inserted into the conversation whilst Lady Macbeth, the stage-manager of Duncan's death,
stands uncomprehending and silent. They are interrupted only by the
glorious double irony of Macbeth's 'Fail not our feast' and Banquo's
reply 'My Lord, I will not,' a stage effect which should never fail, though
it is nowadays not often remarked by those intent on interpreting the
play as a theological tract or an extended dramatic poem.

When we see the play's two principals alone again, Shakespeare gives
us a terrible picture of ambition gone sour, of the private face of political disillusionment. The greatest change is in Lady Macbeth, whose
bright dreams and fierce energy of Act I are reduced now to exhausted
disillusion, in limp despairing couplets:

> Nought's had, all's spent,
> Where our desire is got without content:
> 'Tis safer to be that which we destroy,
> Than by destruction dwell in doubtful joy.

Macbeth's malaise is more expected: he foresaw it himself. But the
lethargy is more poignant in a man who made his earlier reputation as a
vigorous warrior:

> Duncan is in his grave;
> After life's fitful fever he sleeps well;
> Treason has done his worse: nor steel, nor poison,
> Malice domestic, foreign levy, nothing
> Can touch him further!

With a remarkable psychological insight, Shakespeare shows Macbeth
breaking from his wretchedness into bouts of desperate action, which
become more furious as they become ever more futile. There is a terrible
contrast between his agonised soliloquy before the murder of Duncan
and his preparation for the murder of Banquo. The imagery marks a
further move towards the witches; the blunted morality is marked
by an opening sentiment which would sit easily amidst Chicago film
gangsters:

> There's comfort yet; they are assailable:
> Then be thou jocund. Ere the bat hath flown
> His cloister'd flight; ere to black Hecate's summons
> The shard-born beetle, with his drowsy hums,

Hath rung Night's yawning peal, there shall be done
A deed of dreadful note.

In his invocation of night, we see the breadth of imagination which is his
hallmark, but the moral standpoint has become that of Lady Macbeth
in her first speeches: there is no hesitation of conscience now in a man
committed to evil:

> Come, seeling Night,
> Scarf up the tender eye of pitiful Day,
> And, with thy bloody and invisible hand,
> Cancel, and tear to pieces, that great bond
> Which keeps me pale!

The interest of the play is sustained around Macbeth's language: as
his fortunes decline and his spirit descends to the depths, his awareness
of each stage of his decline is captured in verse which is without parallel.
There is no better delineation of the diseased mind which is denied consolation than Macbeth's reception of the news of Fleance's escape at
the beginning of the banquet scene:

> Then comes my fit again: I had else been perfect;
> Whole as the marble, founded as the rock,
> As broad and general as the casing air:
> But now, I am cabin'd, cribb'd, confin'd, bound in
> To saucy doubts and fears.

Macbeth in his misery and moral squalor retains the breadth of vision
and powers of expression of his better days. When the banquet, the
symbol of order in the state and its government, has been rudely shattered, and Macbeth commits himself openly to the counsel of the
witches, he produces an awful image to mirror the extent of his degradation:

> For mine own good,
> All causes shall give way: I am in blood
> Stepp'd in so far, that, should I wade no more,
> Returning were as tedious as go o'er.

The banquet scene gives us a last glimpse of the doomed pair as they
were at the beginning of the play. Lady Macbeth shows the qualities

needed to survive and prosper in an everyday political world as she desperately attempts the impossible task of retrieving Macbeth's behaviour. Macbeth, in his horrified apprehension of the bloodsoaked world he has created, has a breadth of vision and imagination which, properly applied, would have been the equipment of a great man: a potential horribly perverted by his crimes.

Even when he confronts the witches, and we see the macrocosm of the state falling as he overturns his world with himself, Macbeth's breadth of imagery is a contrast to the witches' narrower view of evil:

> Though you untie the winds, and let them fight
> Against the churches; though the yesty waves
> Confound and swallow navigation up;
> Though bladed corn be lodg'd, and trees blown down;
> Though castles topple on their warders' heads;
> Though palaces, and pyramids, do slope
> Their heads to their foundations; though the treasure
> Of Nature's germens tumble all together,
> Even till destruction sicken, answer me
> To what I ask you.

The long scene in England between Malcolm and Macduff has recently received much attention from commentators. Those who search for a complex symbolism in the play often now regard this as a key passage, and the Arden editor thinks 'It does not seem tedious today.' He should consult any director of the play! Although Knights rightly emphasises the function of the scene as choric commentary[15] on Macbeth's Scotland, Shakespeare achieves similar effects much more briefly elsewhere. This is the one section of the play where economy of effect is absent.

Lady Macbeth's sleep-walking scene which immediately follows it neatly illustrates the point: it is economical to the point of frugality, and immensely effective for it. The scene is cleverly constructed so that all Lady Macbeth's actions and words are ironic echoes of her earlier thoughts as she sought power, heedless of the consequences. If the previous scene makes lengthy commentary on the effects upon the state of regicide, this brief, horrific scene, with its blood-chilling echoes of earlier words, is immensely more effective commentary upon the shattering of the individual minds concerned. Lady Macbeth's 'Yet who would have thought the old man to have had so much blood in him?' is a more thrilling stage moment than any which Malcolm's lengthy posturings could contrive.

The chorus commentary on Macbeth's Scotland is more effectively achieved by Angus's vivid passage in the characteristic clothes-imagery of the play in V ii:

> Now does he feel
> His secret murthers sticking on his hands;
> Now minutely revolts unbraid his faith-breach:
> Those he commands move only in command,
> Nothing in love: now does he feel his title
> Hang loose about him, like a giant's robe
> Upon a dwarfish thief.

Moments later, we see Macbeth superbly evoking the personal effects upon him of the state he has created:

> I have liv'd long enough: my way of life
> Is fall'n into the sere, the yellow leaf;
> And that which should accompany old age,
> As honour, love, obedience, troops of friends,
> I must not look to have; but in their stead,
> Curses, not loud, but deep, mouth-honour, breath,
> Which the poor heart would fain deny, and dare not.

There remains only the dismissal of the strong bond of love between Macbeth and his wife which was so powerful a factor in the original murder decision. We have seen the advancing army of Malcolm bringing order back to Scotland, heard the order to hew down leafy boughs which Macbeth will see as bringing Birnam wood to Dunsinane. Now Macbeth receives the news of the stilling of that 'undaunted mettle' which steeled his resolution to the murder of Duncan with dull resignation; it is but one more effect of a world that has become meaningless:

> She should have died hereafter:
> There would have been a time for such a word.
> To-morrow, and to-morrow, and to-morrow,
> Creeps in this petty pace from day to day,
> To the last syllable of recorded time;
> And all our yesterdays have lighted fools
> The way to dusty death. Out, out, brief candle!
> Life's but a walking shadow; a poor player,
> That struts and frets his hour upon the stage,

And then is heard no more: it is a tale
Told by an idiot, full of sound and fury,
Signifying nothing.

Macbeth's clear-sighted recognition of the stages of his moral decline, his capacity to convey his situation with pitiless vigour and vividness are what have sustained the play. They remain with him through to the final degradation, when he and his wife become 'this dead butcher and his fiend-like Queen' of Malcolm's last speech. They are the glory of the play, the effects by which Shakespeare transforms melodrama into tragedy.

## Notes

1. Introduction to Arden edition (1951), pp. 1vii–1ix.
2. Reprinted in K. Muir and P. Edwards (eds.), *Aspects of Macbeth*, pp. 76–86.
3. *Patterns in Shakespearean Tragedy*, p. 3.
4. *Aspects of Macbeth*, p. 78.
5. *Mighty Opposites: Shakespeare and Renaissance Contrariety*, pp. 153–65.
6. *Some Shakespearean Themes*, p. 120.
7. *An Approach to Shakespeare*, p. 150.
8. *Some Shakespearean Themes*, p. 122.
9. Ibid., pp. 120–2.
10. *The Wheel of Fire*, p. 153.
11. *Killing the King*, p. 141.
12. E.g. by F. R. Leavis in *Scrutiny* vol. 9 (March 1941), pp. 316–19.
13. *An Approach to Shakespeare*, p. 162.
14. See 'Hell-Castle and its Doorkeeper', reprinted in *Aspects of Macbeth*, pp. 39–45.
15. *Some Shakespearean Themes*.

The three plays usually grouped together as 'Roman' are characterised by a concern with great political events; in particular, each centres around the fall of a great and powerful man. Rossiter's remarks about *Coriolanus* might equally be applied to *Julius Caesar* or *Antony and Cleopatra*:

> *Coriolanus* is about power: about State or *the* State. . .if you cannot be excited about what happens to the Roman State (a branch or exemplum of what happens in States) then you cannot feel the play. For it is a kind of excitement very different from that generated by 'What happens to George?'[1]

Even though *Antony and Cleopatra* concerns itself with a man's rejection of Roman values, the steely presence of the Roman state is the key to the action and his fall.

This is not to say that Shakespeare does not concern himself with private man: although his starting-point is a series of great events familiar to many in his audience, he concerns himself continually with the aspects of individual character which make men react to political crisis in different ways. The Roman plays are constructed as clearly as any in the canon around the tensions arising between individual feelings and public actions. Shakespeare takes known great political events, fills in the private men we do not know, and builds his plays around the stresses arising between the two. *Julius Caesar* may be nearer to the spirit of the histories and the two later plays to that of the tragedies, but the basis of construction remains the same.

## Julius Caesar

That construction is nowhere more apparent than in the first of the Roman plays. Caesar is shown to us briefly at the height of his powers; but Shakespeare chooses not to show us the unrelenting and irresistible military force which is Marlow's Tamburlaine. Instead, he dwells rather on the individual defects which are the seeds of his downfall, some of them inherent features of the private man, some of them, he suggests, the results of the reactions of that individual to the access of supreme power.

And· as the centre of power passes from Caesar to other men, we see in turn the effects of the most extreme of all political acts, assassination, upon the principals involved on either side. Shakespeare investigates the qualities necessary for success upon a great political stage. Among them are courage, realism, judgement of men, an ability to persuade others, and a capacity to deceive when necessary. Caesar, Brutus and Cassius are all found wanting in one or more of these. Only Antony in this play dovetails private feelings and public actions successfully. Behind the treatment of the four men who dominate the play are the usual Shakespearian questionings about the relationship of private morality to public affairs. Every age discerns the politics of its own era in *Julius Caesar*.

In this most political of plays, the author suits the style to his material. Bradley wrote that Shakespeare seemed to be aiming at 'a dignified and unadorned simplicity – a Roman simplicity perhaps. . . Shakespeare's style is perhaps nowhere else so free from defects, and yet almost every one of his subsequent plays contains writing which is greater.'[2] Only two short early plays, *The Comedy of Errors* and *Two Gentlemen of Verona*, use a smaller stock of words than *Julius Caesar*. M. Charney[3] points out that although this play was probably written just after *Henry V* and shortly before *Hamlet*, its language is strikingly different, especially from that of *Hamlet*, which he thinks 'contains the largest and most expressive vocabulary' in the whole canon. This deliberately limited perfection is used to characterise the Roman world and its values, for it is apparent also in the two later Roman plays. Despite the strain of hyperbole which characterises the Egyptian scenes of *Antony and Cleopatra*, Charney is right to draw attention to the fact that in that play

> The Roman world is set forth in an austere imagery of hard, cold material objects and the practical business of state; it is only the imagery of Egypt that is luxuriant. The 'Roman' style is the natural speaking voice of Octavius Caesar as it is of Coriolanus.[4]

In *Julius Caesar* the only man who strains against the fetters of imagery and sometimes suggests a wider imaginative world is Antony; Shakespeare will build the whole of his later play around this conflict, but here it is suggested only.

Shakespeare plunges us straight into the perennial political issue which dominates the play, that of the great man growing too great. After the tribunes have set the scene, the Opposition leaders are set before us. Shakespeare presents Brutus, revered by Renaissance lore as the great liberator and patriot, with an immediate ambivalence which is dramatically highly effective. He suggests from the outset that 'the noblest Roman of them all' has the seeds of political failure within him. The audience may nod approval to the sentiments Brutus, the conscious public man, voices in his first reactions to Cassius:

What is it that you would impart to me?
If it be aught toward the general good,
Set honour in one eye, and death i' th' other,
And I will look on both indifferently;
For let the gods so speed me as I love
The name of honour more than I fear death.

But Shakespeare has already shown in the history plays what inadequate equipment a vague notion of honour is for political progress.

In contrast, Cassius is highly specific, but his tales of Caesar's physical weaknesses tell us more of the speaker than their subject. For these bitter tales of personal defects in Caesar totally ignore his public capacity. Shakespeare, taking Plutarch's phrase describing Cassius as 'hating Caesar privately more than he did the tyranny openly',[5] builds upon it his prototype of the arch-conspirator, more clear-sighted about his aims and the effects of particular actions than ever Brutus will be, yet limited in his public capacity by the strength of his private jealousies. Cassius is amazed at Caesar's success precisely because he fails to take account of the man's public, political qualities:

Ye gods, it doth amaze me
A man of such a feeble temper should
So get the start of the majestic world,
And bear the palm alone.

Brutus' response to this blazing personal resentment is cold, stoic, as carefully measured in its syntax as its tone:

What you would work me to, I have some aim:
How I have thought of this, and of these times,
I shall recount hereafter. For this present,

I would not (so with love I might entreat you)
Be any further mov'd. What you have said
I will consider; what you have to say
I will with patience hear, and find a time
Both meet to hear and answer such high things.

Brutus is already revolving Cassius' ideas, oblivious of the personality that is presenting them. It is Caesar a moment later who shows that most necessary part of the politician's equipment, a shrewd estimation of other men's capacities, divining in Cassius that extreme strain of envy which so often fuels the fanatic:

> He reads much,
> He is a great observer, and he looks
> Quite through the deeds of men. He loves no plays,
> As thou dost, Antony: he hears no music.
> Seldom he smiles, and smiles in such a sort
> As if he mock'd himself, and scorn'd his spirit
> That could be mov'd to smile at any thing.
> Such men as he be never at heart's ease
> Whiles they behold a greater than themselves,
> And therefore are they very dangerous.

Shakespeare follows this sharp insight immediately with one of those ironic contrasts at which he is by now adept: he shows us the overweening pride which clouds judgement. Moreover, he follows two lines in which Caesar speaks of himself as almost divine with the bathos of his deafness, the touch of fallibility which is one of the author's own additions to Plutarch's portrait of Caesar:

> I rather tell thee what is to be fear'd
> Than what I fear; for always I am Caesar.
> Come on my right hand, for this ear is deaf,
> And tell me truly what thou think'st of him.

As Charney writes:

> The official Caesar of Shakespeare's play is presented with all the pomp and ceremony of a great public person. Yet he is curiously undercut by our image of Caesar the private man, full of physical infirmities and an irritating insistence on his own dignity.[6]

This is the key to Shakespeare's portrait of Caesar. He is neither Hudson's 'grand strutting piece of puff-paste. . .full of lofty airs and mock-thunder'[7] nor Dover Wilson's 'Roman Tamburlaine of illimitable ambition and ruthless, irresistible genius'.[8] He is another exploration of that inexhaustible Shakespearian seam of human material, the man whose public and private images have moved out of phase with each other.

Cassius's soliloquy at the end of the scene shows how accurate is Caesar's estimate of the type; it is full of the political intriguer's narrow, amoral vision:

> Well, Brutus, thou art noble: yet I see
> Thy honourable mettle may be wrought
> From that it is dispos'd: therefore 'tis meet
> That noble minds keep ever with their likes;
> For who so firm that cannot be seduc'd?
> Caesar doth bear me hard; but he loves Brutus.
> If I were Brutus now, and he were Cassius,
> He should not humour me.

Brutus is too full of himself and his own moral stance to discern this strain in Cassius. When we next see him, he is carefully distinguishing personal commitment from a more general morality:

> It must be by his death: and for my part,
> I know no personal cause to spurn at him,
> But for the general.

The reaction which drives Antony to scale notable heights of emotional rhetoric will be exactly the reverse of this; his outraged personal friendship will find in him unsuspected reserves of courage and commitment.

It is the failure of Brutus to appreciate the strength of Antony's reaction to the murder which leads him to the first of his three great errors, the sparing of Mark Antony. Brutus' political judgement is affected because he cannot accept assassination as the squalid business it is. As at each of these moments of bad decision, he turns away from reality; in this case, his refusal to contemplate the killing for what it is leads him to disguise assassination as religious sacrifice:

> Let's be sacrificers, but not butchers, Caius.
> We all stand up against the spirit of Caesar,

And in the spirit of men there is no blood. . .
Let's carve him as a dish fit for the gods,
Not hew him as a carcass fit for hounds.

Brutus strives to ignore personal reactions as he resolves to kill his friend, and his judgement is impaired as a result. In Caesar, we see the full and confusing impact of near-supreme power upon the private man and his judgements. When he allows the closest of private relationships, that of husband and wife, to sway him, Calpurnia's fears persuade him to the right decision. He is undone by his sense of his public image: when Decius recalls this to him, his thrasonical strain bursts forth, as he drops again into the third person with 'Shall Caesar send a lie?' Caesar's last private moments are spent in drinking wine with the men who will strike him down in public: the confusion of his two worlds is complete. The reason for his downfall is etched sharply for us in this last scene. As Edward Dowden wrote: 'The real man Caesar disappears for himself under the greatness of the Caesar myth. He forgets himself as he is and knows only the vast legendary power named Caesar.'[9]

In his final moments, that power is prevalent as he struts the public stage. He turns aside his final hope of escape with an anticipatory lapse into the royal plural. 'What touches us ourself shall be last serv'd' he tells Artemidorus as he waves his warning aside. Shakespeare shows him at his least attractive as the conspirators unsheath their daggers behind him. The overweening pride, the sense that he is set above and apart from other men, are the sure predecessors to a fall, for under them the essential, alert, private man is submerged:

I could be well mov'd, if I were as you;
If I could pray to move, prayers would move me;
But I am constant as the northern star,
Of whose true-fix'd and resting quality
There is no fellow in the firmament.
The skies are painted with unnumber'd sparks,
They are all fire, and every one doth shine;
But there's but one in all doth hold his place.
So in the world: 'tis furnished well with men,
And men are flesh and blood, and apprehensive;
Yet in the number I do know but one
That unassailable holds on his rank,
Unshak'd of motion; and that I am he.

Brutus, like most men who try to subjugate personal responses to a philosophy, proves, when moved to reluctant action, the bloodiest of assassins. His earlier desire to see the murder as sacrifice is overlaid by the hysteria of violent action as he kneels to perform a blood rite:

> Stoop, Romans, stoop,
> And let us bathe our hands in Caesar's blood
> Up to the elbows, and besmear our swords:
> Then walk we forth, even to the market-place,
> And waving our red weapons o'er our heads,
> Let's all cry, 'Peace, freedom, and liberty!'

It is not until the arrival of Mark Antony that we have a personal reaction to the death and the assassins addressed in their true colours:

> I know not, gentlemen, what you intend,
> Who else must be let blood, who else is rank:
> If I myself, there is no hour so fit
> As Caesar's death's hour; nor no instrument
> Of half that worth as those your swords, made rich
> With the most noble blood of all this world.
> I do beseech ye, if you bear me hard,
> Now, whilst your purpled hands do reek and smoke,
> Fulfil your pleasure.

This is a speech full of courage and feeling; it hardly sorts with Brutus' dismissal of Antony as given over 'To sports, to wildness and much company' when he urged his sparing. Brutus offers this enigmatic figure 'kind love, good thoughts and reverence', abstractions which cannot carry much weight from assassins. Cassius, the realist untroubled by philosophic scruples, is decidedly more practical:

> Your voice shall be as strong as any man's
> In the disposing of new dignities.

Brutus now compounds his first error, the sparing of Antony, by allowing him to speak in the forum. Again he carries a private response into a political situation. He trusts Antony not to abuse the privilege allowed him, and expects the crowd to respect this chivalrous gesture to the fallen tyrant. As Palmer says: 'The republican philosopher persists in believing that, not only Antony himself, but the people to whom an account is to be rendered, will be decisively influenced by rational argument.'[10] The speech in which he overrules Cassius is full of an ingenuous moral smugness:

> I will myself into the pulpit first,
> And show the reason of our Caesar's death.
> What Antony shall speak, I will protest
> He speaks by leave and by permission:
> And that we are contented Caesar shall
> Have all true rites and lawful ceremonies,
> It shall advantage more than do us wrong.

Antony is the only man in this play who successfully unites private feeling with public action: he is entirely clear-sighted about both the conspirators and his own position. He has feigned reconciliation with the conspirators as his quick mind framed a political plan. When they leave him alone with Caesar's body upon a stage which has been crowded for so long, he combines an intense private reaction with a vision of public action which underlines the naivety of Brutus.

> O, pardon me, thou bleeding piece of earth,
> That I am meek and gentle with these butchers.
> Thou art the ruins of the noblest man
> That ever lived in the tide of times.
> Woe to the hand that shed this costly blood!
> Over thy wounds now do I prophesy
> (Which like dumb mouths do ope their ruby lips,
> To beg the voice and utterance of my tongue),
> A curse shall light upon the limbs of men;
> Domestic fury and fierce civil strife
> Shall cumber all the parts of Italy.

Brutus' oration in the forum is usually seen as a direct contrast to that of Antony which follows, full of cool logic and academic economy. Palmer, for instance, writes: 'Brutus might be addressing an academy of science, a congress of philosophers, an audience of literary equisites, capable of appreciating the exposition in which every sentence contributes to the formal symmetry of the rhetorical design.'[11] This is less than fair to Shakespeare's powers or his confidence in them. For in fact Brutus' speech is an effective and obviously public political oration, which succeeds in winning over an initially hostile crowd. He uses that most common construction of the hustings, the rhetorical question, as many times — five — as Antony does in a much longer address. He departs with the assurance that the dagger which slew Caesar will be turned upon himself if the interests of his country demand it: a familiar and empty political sentiment. His mistake is not in the form of the address, but in his assumption that its logic, rather than its rhetorical, emotional appeal, has succeeded. The shallowness of his rational penetration is cruelly revealed by the man who shouts 'Let him be Caesar!' as he concludes. Brutus follows this by his artless appeal for silence for Antony, entreating the crowd not to depart since he speaks by 'our permission'.

Antony's speech is not a direct contrast with that of Brutus: he uses the same devices with more skill and force, and adds other tricks of his own. He is himself a different man from the stoic Brutus, and he uses his personal grief to drive him forward with an intensity more direct and telling than Brutus' republican ideal. His skill comes in blending his own sincere emotion with a calculated appeal to audience emotion, maintaining his own control of himself and his listeners even as he drives them eventually into mass hysteria. Shakespeare embodies the heightening of intensity which Antony brings with him by a switch from prose to verse, which allows Antony to couch even his more dubious logic in a framework which emphasises its apparent good sense. Certainly he does not come to bury rather than praise Caesar; it is doubtful whether the evil that men do lives on whilst their good qualities are forgotten, as a glance at any modern political obituary will show. In any case, a man openly delivering a funeral oration will certainly not denigrate his subject. But Antony's verse-structure seems to assure a hostile audience that it will be so. More subtly, it enables him to use the word 'honourable' in a way that could never be so effective in prose, so that it gradually acquires an ironic ring through its repetition beside the account of Caesar's virtues.

It is usually said that Antony's appeal is an emotional one, and it is true that his feel for his audience and his lack of scruple allows him eventually to play upon emotion rather than reason. But his speech moves through a series of stages, at the end of each of which he pauses to probe the reactions of his listeners. His initial stage, in which he refutes the charge of Caesar's ambition and casts doubt upon the honour of the conspirators, is tightly reasoned. He asks initially only for the decency of mourning for his friend:

I speak not to disprove what Brutus spoke,
But here I am to speak what I do know.

You all did love him once, not without cause;
What cause withholds you then to mourn for him?

But Antony has brought with him an appalling visual aid, the body
of Caesar. This he uses with consummate skill as the emotional pulse of
his speech quickens: his heart, he protests, 'is in the coffin there with
Caesar' and he pauses to assess the effectiveness of the first section of
his speech. He mentions the will for the first time, then with an actor's
sense of timing denies the audience the contents until he chooses to
reveal them. Cool and secure amidst the tumult all around him, he uses
the moment to discredit finally Caesar's assassins:

Have patience, gentle friends; I must not read it.
It is not meet you know how Caesar lov'd you.
You are not wood, you are not stones, but men;
And being men, hearing the will of Caesar,
It will inflame you, it will make you mad. . .
I have o'ershot myself to tell you of it.
I fear I wrong the honourable men
Whose daggers have stabb'd Caesar; I do fear it.

Antony makes his most naked appeal for an emotional response
through the corpse. Gathering his audience close about the body, he
first reconstructs the murder at which he was not present, imagining
which of the conspirators' daggers made each blood-soaked rent, indulging in a grim conceit when he comes to the most dangerous of his
enemies:

Through this the well-beloved Brutus stabb'd;
And as he pluck'd his cursed steel away,
Mark how the blood of Caesar follow'd it,
As rushing out of doors, to be resolv'd
If Brutus so unkindly knock'd or no;
For Brutus, as you know, was Caesar's angel.

Then Antony snatches away the vesture to show the corpse of the
fallen demigod in all its piteous gore. Reason is now suspended; emotion
is rampant and searching feverishly for a violent outlet. Antony, still
with the will to deliver as his final stroke, perpetrates the most outrageous of his orator's effects. He assures his audience he is merely the voice

of the common sense that is within them all: logic and experience may
now be stood upon their heads if he wishes:

> I am no orator, as Brutus is,
> But (as you know me all) a plain blunt man,
> That love my friend; and that they know full well
> That give me public leave to speak of him.
> For I have neither wit, nor words, nor worth,
> Action, nor utterance, nor the power of speech
> To stir men's blood; I only speak right on.
> I tell you that which you yourselves do know,
> Show you sweet Caesar's wounds, poor poor dumb mouths,
> And bid them speak for me.

There remains the will. In place of Brutus' vague offer of 'a place in
the commonwealth' and the great abstractions of freedom, Antony
offers new-planted orchards and seventy-five drachmas, and sends the
mob away to fire the traitors' houses. Private grief never had a more
devastating public spokesman.

Antony's performance in the forum has the exultance that goes
with its success: Antony can move men's hearts as triumphantly in
stirring public speeches as Henry V, whose great deeds in France were
celebrated immediately before the author turned to his Roman material. Lest we too be beguiled by the heady presence of political
power, Shakespeare shows us immediately its other side. The ludicrous
victim of the mob's bloodlust is the pathetic poet Cinna. And when
we see Antony again, thirty-seven lines after his forum triumph, there
is another aspect of the effective man of power. His appraisal of the
men around him is cool and accurate, his dismissal of those with nothing to offer ruthless. His account of Lepidus shows an awareness of
the squalid realities of power: unlike Brutus, he does not shrink from
them:

> Octavius, I have seen more days than you;
> And though we lay these honours on this man,
> To ease ourselves of divers sland'rous loads,
> He shall but bear them as the ass bears gold,
> To groan and sweat under the business,
> Either led or driven, as we point the way;
> And having brought our treasure where we will,
> Then take we down his load, and turn him off,

Like to the empty ass, to shake his ears,
And graze in commons.

Had Brutus evaluated the character and motives of Cassius as coolly,
the conspiracy would have taken a different course. In quarrelling with
Cassius he shows a reluctance to confront sordid necessities which is ill
equipment for civil war, an estimation of the common people he needs
which is dangerously near to that of Coriolanus:

For I can raise no money by vile means:
By heaven, I had rather coin my heart,
And drop my blood for drachmas, than to wring
From the hard hands of peasants their vile trash
By any indirection.

When he over-rules Cassius and makes the third of his great errors in
determining to fight at Philippi, he dismisses military tactics in a cloud
of lofty metaphor:

There is a tide in the affairs of men,
Which, taken at the flood, leads on to fortune;
Omitted, all the voyage of their life
Is bound in shallows and in miseries.
On such a full sea are we now afloat,
And we must take the current when it serves,
Or lose our ventures.

The particular decision disappears beneath the figurative generalisation
as Brutus convinces himself: when we see his enemies, Octavius declares
their 'hopes are answered' by the decision.

Antony, for all his political qualities, retains the individual responses
of a man who has more in his life than politics. His epitaph on Brutus is
the genuine response of a large spirit combined with the statesman's instinct to heal breaches by generosity in victory:

This was the noblest Roman of them all.
All the conspirators save only he
Did that they did in envy of great Caesar;
He only, in a general honest thought
And common good to all, made one of them.
His life was gentle, and the elements

So mix'd in him, that Nature might stand up
And say to all the world, 'This was a man!'

For the moment, public capacity and generous private man are in harmony in Antony. But in the Roman world, they are perilous companions. In a few years, Shakespeare will build a great play around their conflict in Antony.

### Antony and Cleopatra

Shakespeare could have planned and executed *Antony and Cleopatra* only at the height of his powers. The plot he took from history seems to emphasise the virtues of reason and calculation. Yet he indicates throughout the play the limitations of these qualities and suggests, particularly in the later stages, the attractiveness of a reckless disregard of them.

He makes the play hinge not upon the facts of history but upon our reactions to Antony, Cleopatra and Caesar. Antony casts away the world with his eyes open: his constant awareness of his public omissions as he indulges private passion is one of the ways in which Shakespeare infuses tension into seemingly unpromising dramatic material. That other contemporary study of hedonism, Marlow's *Dr. Faustus*, presents an interesting contrast. Even when Faustus is seen as Everyman, the dramatic tension drops startlingly between a few great scenes. Shakespeare's use of his public-private theme, through the constant and ominous presence of Rome alongside the exotic world of Egypt, gives his tragedy a breadth which Marlowe's cannot match. Philo's opening commentary on Antony's fall, 'The triple pillar of the world transform'd / Into a strumpet's fool' has no counterpart in Marlowe, because it is a comment on Antony's decline as a public figure of power and authority. There is a wider interest in 'the triple pillar of the world' in Cleopatra's arms than Faustus in Helen's because of our apprehension of Antony's public role. To develop this dramatic tension, Shakespeare creates a Cleopatra that Marlowe could not even have attempted; and above all, he sets his hedonist against his linear opposites in Octavius Caesar.

To grasp how deliberately Shakespeare planned his play, we have to remember the reputation of Octavius amongst the author's contemporaries. In Elizabethan histories, he was seen as the ideal Roman emperor, who restored peace and presided over the fourth earthly monarchy.[12] Shakespeare's Octavius

> remains a formidable figure, implacable, menacing, cold as the historical Octavius doubtless was; but a power rather than a person, a function of the developing action, the nemesis of Antony and Cleopatra, the tragic measure of their human limitation

according to H. S. Wilson.[13] This goes a little too far: Octavius remains a real rather than a symbolic figure, in the way that Henry IV does. He is the cold man of power who has subdued personal responses to other considerations until the process has destroyed most of his spontaneous private feeling. He is the representative of Rome, the personification of its efficiency and coldness. M. R. Ridley summarises it thus:

> Octavius remains an unattractive figure, but one worth study, not so much for himself as because he draws our wondering attention to a noticeable feature of the play. In the first three acts, by touch on subtle touch, the relentless power of Rome is forced on our subconscious notice. We are made to feel that it is something against whose ineluctable march no individuals, however great, can for one moment stand. Octavius. . .is the typical Roman; and at the end he, the 'cold Caesar', is more than himself: he is Rome, looking down, with a just and not unsympathetic estimation, on the 'pair so famous' over whom her chariot wheels have rolled.[14]

This contrast between Egypt and Rome is what preserves order in the play's construction, giving a coherence to the dizzying multiplication of short scenes as the action leaps from Egypt to Rome, Sicily and Syria. Shakespeare, in transforming history into drama, provides a convincing and moving explanation of events in terms of his favourite theme of power and the individual. In the words of J. Markels:

> The play is built upon the opposition of public and private values. However we name them — love or honour, lust or empire — we know from the moment of Philo's opening speech that the issue before us is the form in which this opposition is to be resolved.[15]

Representing the public virtues of prudence, discipline and conquest is Rome, what Northrop Frye called the 'day-world of history';[16] against it is set 'the night-world of passion', Egypt, with its associations of fertility, pleasure and love.

Antony, who bestrides these worlds, is undone by his very capacity: he is larger than Roman life, as it is represented in the play. His vitality overflows as easily into his sensuous individual life with Cleopatra as it did into his political drive and his soldiering in *Julius Caesar*. Antony never rejects the part of his nature which Henry V set aside as he assumed great public office. And through his attitude, Shakespeare suggests some of the tawdriness and the transience of power. Antony reminds us of the great batsman who throws his wicket away once he has proved his mastery in the game. If this old-fashioned comparison provokes the response that life is not a game, Shakespeare suggests at times that perhaps only the very great of spirit can afford to treat it as one.

The play is an interesting example of how the great artist uses various sources of material and stamps them with his individual seal. Shakespeare grafts Renaissance ideas and experiences on to his Roman material. R. A. Brower argues that the play is a blend of the Virgilian heroic and the Ovidian erotic strains:[17] Shakespeare shows what might have happened if Aeneas had stayed with Dido. He was no doubt well acquainted with Marlowe's *Dido, Queen of Carthage*, in which Dido urges Aeneas:

Stout love, in mine arms make thy Italy
Whose crown and kingdom rest at thy command.
                                                (III, 4, 56–7)

Antony, as he prepares to join his Cleopatra in death, imagines an underworld in which

Dido, and her Aeneas, shall want troops,
And all the haunt be ours.

M. Rose points out[18] that whilst Plutarch provided the play's source material, an important influence upon Shakespeare's treatment of it is the tradition of the Renaissance epic poem (Ariosto's *Orlando Furioso*, Spenser's *Faerie Queene*) with its dual focus and its recurring figure of the great hero torn between his love for a beautiful enchantress and the claims of glory, duty and the battlefield. Antony never does break his fetters as Aeneas does: this is how Shakespeare transforms an epic formula into tragedy. It also allows him the same kind of approach to the ambivalence of power as is evident throughout his work.

Despite these influences, there is no more original work of art in literature than *Antony and Cleopatra*. Shakespeare sets about transforming apparently static and unpromising material into dramatic terms with the incidental handicap of a boy to play history's most fascinating amorist. The language and stagecraft of his full maturity combine in a triumphant *tour de force*. He unites in the play three themes from his previous work. The first, the celebration of sexual love and the urge to see it as a manifestation of spiritual values, derives from the sonnets: whilst it has appeared before in his work, notably in *Romeo and Juliet* and the middle comedies, *Antony and Cleopatra* is his most confident and remarkable exposition of it. The second theme is what is usually regarded as the basis of Shakesperian tragedy: the exploration of a tragic weakness which brings an otherwise great man to ruin. It is present most strongly in the great works of the first years of the new century which immediately precede this play. The third theme is that of the political study starting from known facts of history, in which Shakespeare conjectures in dramatic terms about the private personalities of great public figures and the part played by these in great historical events.

The achievement of *Antony and Cleopatra* is to unite these three strains in a work which enables each of them to illuminate the other two. Opinion has swung through the centuries between a view of the play as a tragedy which leaves us exalted by its presentation of love triumphant over death and the view which sees it as a relentless exposure of the disastrous results of undisciplined surrender to passion. The truth is surely that Shakespeare has presented both of these, and moved us with the pity of both, using them as complementary rather than contradictory aspects of life and an artist's interpretation of life.

It is a construction which requires the full resources of his language to hold the two aspects in balance. In the hands of other writers Antony would be no more than an aging roué, pathetic, even ridiculous, as events move inexorably to their conclusion, but certainly not tragic. Shakespeare, in concentrating upon his pair of lovers, maintains the epic structure of his tale whilst turning away from military glory. He does so by stretching his poetic powers to the full, and enhancing poetry by setting key passages with all his dramatic craft. Antony's stature is maintained by the scale of metaphor employed; when Cleopatra has to rise to similar heights in the play's last section, the author's language is equal to the task, and the dramatic context which shows her moving falteringly towards greatness only enhances the grandeur of that language.

The play's characteristic figure is the hyperbole. Coleridge called it 'feliciter audax', which he defined as 'a happy valiancy of style'. It is the Marlovian over-reacher's strain brought to maturity and control. When Charmian looks down on Cleopatra's body and says,

> Now boast thee, death, in thy posession lies
> A lass unparallel'd

we believe her, not just because of the force of the words themselves, but because they are the climax of a superb linguistic fugue, with every note of language leading to this masterly conclusion.

Shakespeare's tremendous confidence in the task he has set himself is shown in the opening lines of the play. In them the practical soldier denounces the play's central figure in the most rigorous and uncompromising terms:

> Nay, but this dotage of our general's
> O'erflows the measure: those his goodly eyes,
> That o'er the files and musters of the war
> Have glow'd like plated Mars, now bend, now turn
> The office and devotion of their view
> Upon a tawny front: his captain's heart,
> Which in the scuffles of great fights hath burst
> The buckles on his breast, reneges all temper,
> And it become the bellows and the fan
> To cool a gypsy's lust. Look, where they come:
> Take but good note, and you shall see in him
> The triple pillar of the world transform'd
> Into a strumpet's fool: behold and see.

It is the Roman view. As the play proceeds, only the Romans, of whom Antony in his Roman moods is one, disdain love as dotage. This first scene is only sixty lines long, yet it establishes the play's construction, and 'sets up the swinging ambivalence. . .which will control our whole reaction to the play'.[19] For, a few lines after Philo's devastating opening, Antony is providing a different perspective on the play's central relationship with the poetic exaltation of his declaration of it:

> Let Rome in Tiber melt, and the wide arch
> Of the rang'd empire fall! Here is my space,
> Kingdoms are clay: our dungy earth alike
> Feeds beast as man; the nobleness of life
> Is to do thus.

This middle section of the short scene is framed by a final part which reiterates the Roman reaction to the affair as Caesar's messenger is ignored. Against the calculating sureness of the public man Caesar, and his Roman world, we watch the impulsive energies of individual man in Antony and Cleopatra, unpredictable but vital. The copious employment of messengers in the play is an effective dramatic ploy, isolating the reactions of each of the principals in turn and giving them full attention, but reserving a fresh surge of excitement for the moments when we see these principals together and reacting directly to each other.

When Antony consents to hear the messenger's grim news, we see him not as the blind victim of infatuation, but with his eyes fully open to the implications of his conduct:

> Speak to me home, mince not the general tongue:
> Name Cleopatra as she is call'd in Rome;
> Rail thou in Fulvia's phrase, and taunt my faults
> With such full licence, as both truth and malice
> Have power to utter.

The news of Fulvia's death provokes a reaction that shows his old awareness of political reality:

> I must from this enchanting queen break off,
> Ten thousand harms, more than the ills I know,
> My idleness doth hatch.

Cleopatra's reaction to this resolution puts their affair again in cosmic terms:

> Eternity was in our lips, and eyes,
> Bliss in our brows' bent: none our parts so poor,
> But was a race of heaven.

There could be no greater contrast to such verse than Caesar's bare, functional language in our first view of him: Antony, he says, is 'the abstract of all faults' and there is the distaste of the ascetic in his account of him to Lepidus:

> You are too indulgent. Let's grant it is not
> Amiss to tumble on the bed of Ptolemy,
> To give a kingdom for a mirth, to sit

And keep the turn of tippling with a slave,
To reel the streets at noon, and stand the buffet
With knaves that smell of sweat: say this becomes him.

Rose[20] describes the Roman style as emphatic, relatively free from
metaphor, and designed to hide rather than reveal emotion. Shakespeare
follows it with Cleopatra at her most attractive:

O happy horse to bear the weight of Antony!
Do bravely, horse, for wot'st thou whom thou mov'st,
The demi-Atlas of this earth, the arm
And burgonet of men. He's speaking now,
Or murmuring, 'Where's my serpent of old Nile?'
For so he calls me.

Shakespeare, reluctant as always to place many great lines in the mouth
of a boy actor, does not give Cleopatra many passages like this in the
first three acts of his play. He shows her tantrums and her fiery switches
of mood rather than the wonders of love, developing by his own additions to his source material, such as the scenes of the beating and in-
terrogation of the messenger, the character who will rise in the fifth act
to sublime heights. The impression of Cleopatra the enchantress is built
up largely through the descriptions of others, notably the shrewd and
disillusioned Enobarbus. That doughty soldier concludes his famous
description of Cleopatra's arrival in her barge with a most uncharacteristic poetic conceit, which emphasises the cosmic breadth of the Queen's
spell:

                    The city cast
Her people out upon her; and Antony,
Enthron'd i' the market-place, did sit alone,
Whistling to the air; which, but for vacancy,
Had gone to gaze on Cleopatra too,
And made a gap in nature.

It is Enobarbus again who emphasises Cleopatra's unique, supra-mortal
quality as he denies that Antony will leave her:

Age cannot wither her, nor custom stale
Her infinite variety: other women cloy
The appetites they feed, but she makes hungry,

Where most she satisfies. For vilest things
Become themselves in her, that the holy priests
Bless her, when she is riggish.

Shakespeare shows in his treatment an awareness of both ancient
and Renaissance formulas: Cleopatra is here partly the dangerous enchantress of epics, partly the magical embodiment of things above the
world, who was familiar in the moralities of his own time. But he makes
Cleopatra also the focus of the conflict between public and private
drives in Antony, and so gives dramatic impetus to his material. For this
scene full of marvellous descriptions of Cleopatra is followed immediately by nine lines of muted exchanges between Antony and the coldly
virtuous Octavia; whatever our moral feelings, our dramatic interest
quickens when Antony determines at the end of the scene:

I will to Egypt:
And though I make this marriage for my peace,
I' the east my pleasure lies.

There follows the splendid scene of Cleopatra and the messenger. After
this vivid and spirited low comedy, we have the Roman world before
us again at Misenum; hot Cleopatra we still have in our minds when
Enobarbus says that Antony 'will to his Egyptian dish again' and sums
up Antony's political bride: 'Octavia is of a holy, cold and still conversation.' Heat is used throughout as a sign of passion: Antony at the outset was seen as 'the bellows and the fan to cool a gypsy's lust' and
Octavia's coldness personifies the contrary Roman factor of temper-
ance. Similarly, the brisk despatch of business in Rome is contrasted
with the languor of Egypt: 'the beds i' the east are soft,' confesses
Antony.

But Roman efficiency gets some hard knocks: the drunken carousing
in Pompey's galley is followed by the brief scene of Ventidius in triumph in Syria. The general's shrewd comment on loyalties in Roman
life shows an awareness of its squalid realities:

Better to leave undone, than by our deed
Acquire too high a fame, when him we serve's away.
Who does i' the wars more than his captain can,
Becomes his captain's captain: and ambition,
The soldier's virtue, rather makes choice of loss,
Than gain which darkens him.

Antony has thus far attempted to unite the contrary worlds of Rome and Egypt by maintaining his Roman position. But in the exact centre of the play in Act III, he abandons Rome and makes an unreserved avowal of his allegiance to Egyptian values. With the decision, his political and military insights seem to desert him, but in the second half of the play Shakespeare devotes his skills to defending the indulgence of the individual self. He succeeds so well that we have an unsurpassed sense of elevation, even exultation, in death.

Shakespeare is so confident of his ability to achieve these remarkable effects that he makes no attempt to disguise Antony's criminal disregard of strategy or Cleopatra's foolishness in battle. The soldier who is a veteran of Antony's better days begs him, 'Trust not to rotten planks' and the grizzled Enobarbus speaks for the General Staff:

> Most worthy sir, you therein throw away
> The absolute soldiership you have by land,
> Distract your army, which doth most consist
> Of war-mark'd footmen, leave unexecuted
> Your own renowned knowledge, quite forgo
> The way which promises assurance, and
> Give up yourself merely to chance and hazard,
> From firm security.

Antony defends his decision with no reasons, and when disaster happens Shakespeare spares neither of the famous pair in Scarus's account of it. The 'ribaudred nag of Egypt' flees 'like a cow in June' whilst

> The noble ruin of her magic, Antony,
> Claps on his sea-wing, and (like a doting mallard)
> Leaving the fight in heighth, flies after her:
> I never saw an action of such shame;
> Experience, manhood, honour, ne'er before
> Did violate so itself.

It is a Roman speaking, with the full Roman contempt for Antony's failure, but Shakespeare now begins the formidable task of raising the routed and ridiculous pair to sublimity in death. He does it by emphasising their greatness as individuals as their public roles shrivel and die. Antony begins the process when Cleopatra begs for pardon at his feet:

> Fall not a tear, I say, one of them rates
> All that is won and lost: give me a kiss,
> Even this repays me.

From this moment, the intensity of their relationship rises as the graph of their political fortunes declines. The Romans see only the baseness of Antony's dalliance: he is a-whoring to them, though Enobarbus appreciates Cleopatra's quality as a courtesan. Antony and Cleopatra alone see the elevated quality of their love, as lovers always will; Shakespeare's greatness enables them to transmit their sense of elevation to the audience. Whether they deceive themselves is eventually almost irrelevant: we are made to see this mysterious, disturbing and precious aspect of individual man. The pair rise to greatness as power passes from them: in this they are ranged with characters as different as Richard II and King Lear.

Alongside their increasing preoccupation with the quality of their love, Shakespeare sets a merciless commentary on Antony's political decline. When he challenges Caesar to settle their differences by individual combat, Enobarbus immediately underlines the braggadocio emptiness of the thought:

> Yes, like enough! High-battled Caesar will
> Unstate his happiness, and be stag'd to the show
> Against a sworder! I see men's judgements are
> A parcel of their fortunes, and things outward
> Do draw the inward quality after them,
> To suffer all alike, that he should dream,
> Knowing all measures, the full Caesar will
> Answer his emptiness; Caesar, thou hast subdued
> His judgment too.

Enobarbus prepares to leave, and Antony himself is, as always, aware of his political decline. 'Authority melts from me' he says when next we see him. Charney points out how 'Antony's fallen state is represented most brilliantly by the imagery of dissolution. The pattern in the play is one of melting, fading, dissolving, discandying, disponging, dislimning and losing of form that marks his downward course after Actium.'[21] Antony's decline from the breadth and confidence of

> Let Rome in Tiber melt, and the wide arch
> Of the rang'd empire fall!

at the opening of the play is marked by his whipping of Thidias. It is a pointless gesture to Caesar's emissary, indulging the private man's pique, storing up trouble for the public man for no tangible return. It is a moment which allies him with Cleopatra, through her earlier treatment of the messenger who brought the news of Antony's marriage. His message to Caesar shows him refusing to confront the new reality of power.

> Get thee back to Caesar,
> Tell him thy entertainment: look thou say
> He makes me angry with him. For he seems
> Proud and disdainful, harping on what I am
> Not what he knew I was.

The Antony of *Julius Caesar* would never have turned away from the present. The truth is that Antony, in exploring the emotions of his private self, has lost his touch for public affairs. His preoccupation at this moment is with Cleopatra's seeming treachery to him. 'You have been a boggler ever,' he says bitterly to her; the last section of the play is built upon Cleopatra's rising above her past. When she convinces him here of her loyalty, his energy returns, though its outlet is a desperate carousing which has all the marks of escapism from a dark public situation. 'Let's have one other gaudy night' he calls desperately, 'Let's mock the midnight bell.' Maynard Mack[22] shows how the persistent use of the optative mood in the play, allied to the more obvious device of the copious use of messengers, gives the impression of a world in constant motion. Lest we be too beguiled by Antony's desperate revelry, Shakespeare makes it the occasion for the poignant moment of Enobarbus's desertion, underlining the political reality of the moment:

> Now he'll outstare the lightning; to be furious
> Is to be frighted out of fear, and in that mood
> The dove will peck the estridge; and I see still,
> A diminution in our captain's brain
> Restores his heart; when valour prays on reason,

It eats the sword it fights with: I will seek
Some way to leave him.

Caesar's contemptuous comment on Antony's challenge to personal
combat underlines its futile bravado:

> Let the old ruffian know,
> I have many other ways to die; meantime
> Laugh at his challenge.

Whilst Caesar coolly closes the net, Antony wrings an emotional personal
response from his household servants and prepares to 'drown consideration' in feasting.

Antony, deserted by most of his troops, is at his most attractive on
the morning of his final battle; indeed the fourth act of the play is full
of evidence of his greatness of spirit as an individual. The most moving
instance is his reaction to the desertion of Enobarbus:

> Go, Eros, send his treasure after, do it,
> Detain no jot, I charge thee: write to him —
> I will subscribe — gentle adieus, and greetings;
> Say, that I wish he never find more cause
> To change a master. O, my fortunes have
> Corrupted honest men.

Scepticism, and the Roman virtue of calculation, are treated harshly in
the rest of the play. When Enobarbus, who has persistently questioned
the passions, follows his reason, his heart is broken by the news of
Antony's generosity:

> O Antony,
> Thou mine of bounty, how wouldst thou have paid
> My better service, when my turpitude
> Thou dost so crown with gold!

As the play moves towards the conclusion known to the audience in
advance, the language rises to secure the effects the author has designed.
'Shakespeare's highest level of pregnant metaphor and melodious phrase
swells into the organ-notes of a magnificent dirge'[23] in the last stages of
the play.

Antony in defeat begins the dirge; the breadth of comparison is still there as he speaks of himself, but his chiefest hurt, his private man's resentment of personal disloyalty, runs through his lament for the public Antony:

> O sun, thy uprise shall I see no more,
> Fortune and Antony part here, even here
> Do we shake hands. All come to this? The hearts
> That spaniel'd me at heels, to whom I gave
> Their wishes, do discandy, melt their sweets
> On blossoming Caesar; and this pine is bark'd
> That overtopp'd them all.

Antony's relinquishing of his armour has a symbolic significance. Charney points out that 'Antony's public position of Roman soldier and triumvir has been expressed by sword and armour throughout the play, so that his unarming here marks a new and final movement in the action.'[24] It is the news of the supposed death of Cleopatra that marks the final ebbing of Antony's great energy:

> Unarm, Eros, the long day's task is done,
> And we must sleep.

Antony achieves in his last moments an effect best described by Traversi:

> Not for the first time in Shakespeare the tragic hero, as he approaches the moment of resolution, incorporates expressions that proceed from the weakness, the self-indulgence that is destroying him, into an effect that transcends them. Antony's suicide becomes thus an integral part of the final assertion of emotional *value* and therefore, up to a point, of life.[25]

It is the effect achieved at the beginning of his final exchange with Cleopatra:

> I am dying, Egypt, dying; only
> I here importune death awhile, until
> Of many thousand kisses, the poor last
> I lay upon thy lips.

Cleopatra's words at his death marvellously enhance the stature of both the lovers:

O, wither'd is the garland of the war,
The soldier's pole is fall'n: young boys and girls
Are level now with men: the odds is gone,
And there is nothing left remarkable
Beneath the visiting moon.

The wanton drops away from Cleopatra as she speaks these austere and monumental phrases. Desolation and triumph, emotions separately explored in the sonnets, are here secured as integral parts of a complete mood, which is echoed in the harmony of the lines' dying fall.

This is great poetry enhanced by its dramatic context, placed at the exact moment where stage action enhances its effect. Drama and poetry run now in perfect harness to the end of the play as the intensity of passion rises in death. John Holloway writes:

Both the lovers find, in their love, the manifestation and continuance of their own greatness, their glory as people made on a larger and grander scale than average life. . .This is what gives it its quality of dramatised exaltation, its eloquence, its superb if almost savage egotism.[26]

It is the triumph of the individual, asserting itself in the face of public disaster.

Shakespeare concentrates attention wholly on Cleopatra after Antony's death. She is anxious to be noble in her death, and the antithesis of noble and base is a constant one. The concluding scene of 350 lines is much the longest in the play: 'the rush of events ceases and the play builds to a full orchestral close'.[27] She will die royally, but with an elemental simplicity which will emphasise her womanhood. She strikes the note before the attention is turned to her own death, as Iras attempts to stir her from her grief over Antony with reminders of her public offices of Queen and Empress:

No more but e'en a woman, and commanded
By such poor passion as the maid that milks,
And does the meanest chares.

By the last scene, Iras has caught the note of cosmic grandeur which characterises the climax of the play:

Finish, good lady, the bright day is done,
And we are for the dark.

Cleopatra, robing for her last role, triumphantly secures the connection between the way the lovers die and the way they have lived:

Give me my robe, put on my crown, I have
Immortal longings in me. Now no more
The juice of Egypt's grape shall moist this lip.
Yare, yare, good Iras; quick: methinks I hear
Antony call. I see him rouse himself
To praise my noble act. I hear him mock
The luck of Caesar, which the gods give men
To excuse their after wrath. Husband, I come:
Now to that name, my courage prove my title!

Shakespeare uses at the climax of his play a device he has used often and effectively earlier in it, the yoking together of colloquial and Latinate words to secure an effect of searing and precise simplicity. Cleopatra's last mention of the Caesar who comes in public triumph is as an 'ass unpolicied', and the sound of the phrase as well as the linguistic device is echoed seven lines later in Charmian's epitaph for her mistress:

Now boast thee, death, in thy possession lies
A lass unparallel'd.

Caesar is baulked of his prey: whilst the public man has his material victory, private man in death raises Shakespeare's most persuasive cry for the individual spirit.


## Coriolanus

*Coriolanus* is and will remain a play which excites admiration rather than affection. It is clearly planned and flawlessly executed, but it moves us less than any of the great tragedies.

Yet the play revolves around the familiar divisions of public and private man. Coriolanus is ineffective politically because he cannot dissimulate his private feelings about the plebeians long enough to secure office, let alone exercise it effectively. And in the play's greatest scene, the third one of Act V, he turns aside from public triumph to his death precisely because he responds to the call of the ancient private bond between mother and son. There is the stuff of tragedy here, for Coriolanus goes to his fate like a martyr acknowledging the consequences of a creed he cannot reject.

Why then is the play a relative failure in the English-speaking world, though its similarities with Corneille seem to make it often Shakespeare's most popular work in France? It is not from any haziness in Shakespeare's depiction of the dramatic equation which has private man on one side and the public world on the other. Neither the character of the hero nor the political world in which he is set could be more unequivocally set before us. But here is the key to the problem. Neither the private man nor the public world around him excite in us the interest and sympathy which would make their conflict poignant. In a splendidly pithy review of a production of the play,[28] Eric Bentley wrote: 'Melodrama presents the struggle of right and wrong; tragedy — on one famous view of it — the struggle of right and right; Shakespeare's *Coriolanus* the struggle of wrong and wrong. That's what makes the play so hard to take.'

In *Antony and Cleopatra* we see the greatness as well as the coldness of the Roman state, and Antony has a cosmic stature and a radiance which grow greater as his political folly deepens. But in *Coriolanus* neither the eponymous hero nor the Rome he aspires to lead seem to us worth much expense of spirit: had Shakespeare been in the mood of *Troilus and Cressida*, they might have brought bitter satire from him rather than this austere tragedy.

There are critics, most of them from previous centuries, who have seen Coriolanus as a simple, romantic warrior struck down by the ungrateful people of a primitive state; they ignore the text. His obstinate pride and distaste for humanity in general are meant to be highly unsympathetic. The warrior-ethic was much more persuasive to the Elizabethans than to the war-scarred twentieth century. Cominius states the hero's claim in Act II:

> It is held
> That valour is the chiefest virtue and
> Most dignifies the haver: if it be,
> The man I speak of cannot in the world
> Be singly counterpoised.

Coriolanus' virtues are those of the warrior: heroism in battle and unwavering integrity. But Shakespeare shows the inflexibility and unrelenting egoism which are the defects of the military man who dwells only upon glory in war. The warrior ethic, shown more brightly in *Othello* and *Macbeth* because it was merely a starting-point for the events of those plays, is here examined ruthlessly and found wanting. At each key moment of his military progress, Coriolanus is reduced to a war-machine, fearsome but inhuman: 'he moves like an engine, and the ground shrinks before his treading' says Menenius as he moves upon Rome in Act V. Traversi notes:

> *Coriolanus*, in fact, is at once the complement of *Antony and Cleopatra* and its reversal. In the latter play defeat in war becomes, in some sense and for the duration of certain scenes, the prelude to a triumph in the vitality of love; in *Coriolanus* victory in war is accompanied by a callous hardening of feeling, which only reasserts itself to give an ironic note to the hero's fate.[29]

The private man in Coriolanus is as uninteresting as that in Antony is fascinating. His reaction to political failure is to ally with his former enemies to sack Rome; he wanted power only for self-aggrandisement and his reaction to rejection is couched purely in terms of personal revenge. When his private self provides the one flaw in the armour of the war-machine and his mother turns him aside from his purpose, our sympathy for him is more limited than that we feel for any other major Shakespearian hero. Granville-Barker thought that 'Shakespeare treats Caius Marcius himself detachedly, as a judge might, without creative warmth.'[30] The last phrase is the important one. There is no sense in *Coriolanus*, as there is in any of the other mature tragedies, of a great soul in torment. Coriolanus is as great in arms as Othello or Antony, as massive in pride as Lear, but because the inner man is uninteresting, his fate does not move us. Still less do we have that sense of an ennobling of the spirit we feel as inevitable physical retribution overtakes these other figures, that sense of individual greatness rising amidst public disaster.

If the central figure is both less elusive and less attractive than we have come to expect, the other side of the dramatic equation, the public world in which he acts out his tragedy, is also less interesting and appealing than elsewhere in the canon. For the body politic is here shown in all its shabby complexity. Neither the patricians who desire to be a ruling elite nor the plebeians groping towards democracy are shown to be worthy of government, though the plebeians, when they discuss matters individually rather than reacting *en masse*, strive harder to accommodate Caius Marcius than many critics have allowed. Between them the tribunes, far from catalysing these dangerous elements, are self-seeking and lacking in vision. In *Julius Caesar*, the early scenes revolved around the charge of tyranny and Brutus' inner conflict over this. Here another Brutus, Junius, uses the charge of tyranny as a political tactic only in Act III, with no evidence of real fears for the Roman state.

If by the highest standards of all, his own, Shakespeare is not totally successful in *Coriolanus*, we should not underestimate his achievement. As in all the Roman plays, he deals with a series of historical facts well known to his audience, and yet manages to make them dramatic.

> He has again performed that miracle, which is his own peculiar secret, of surprising us with an event which was, in fact, ordained. . .He moves to a point determined from the outset by the inexorable play of character and circumstance, and yet contrives to make every step towards his conclusion seem like the adventure of a free spirit.[31]

He does this by devising characters who behave in totally believable ways in the situations in which they are placed, and operating the familiar tensions between private personality and public context as the mainspring of his action. The effects he achieves seem more remote from us than his usual ones, because we have less sympathy than elsewhere with both the central character and his particular political context.

The tawdry quality of the Roman state is emphasised throughout the opening scenes. 'The opening statements in the play point to an ominous disorder in the body politic.'[32] Menenius is scarcely conciliatory in his opening statement to the citizens:

> For your wants,
> Your suffering in this dearth, you may as well
> Strike at the heaven with your staves as lift them
> Against the Roman state; whose course will on
> The way it takes, cracking ten thousand curbs
> Of more strong link asunder than can ever
> Appear in your impediment.

The citizens in turn have no illusions about the patricians: 'If the wars eat us not up, they will; and there's all the love they bear us.'

The patrician-plebeian conflict is then argued out in elaborate, deliberately unheroic, imagery of the belly and food. The entry of the play's hero might be expected to elevate the tone. Instead, Marcius' first words not only show his vigorous distaste for the citizenry, but are couched in the unpleasant imagery of disease:

> What's the matter, you dissentious rogues,
> That, rubbing the poor itch of your opinion,
> Make yourself scabs?

From what we have already seen in the opening exchanges between Menenius and the citizenry, there is room for leadership in Rome; a consul who could achieve conciliation would make a notable contribution to the development of the republic. Marcius, warming to his theme as he addresses his social inferiors, is plainly not such a man:

> What would you have, you curs,
> That like not peace nor war? the one affrights you,
> The other makes you proud. He that trusts to you,
> Where he should find you lions, finds you hares,
> Where foxes, geese; you are no surer, no,
> Than is the coal of fire upon the ice,
> Or hailstone in the sun. Your virtue is
> To make him worthy whose offence subdues him
> And curse that justice did it. Who deserves greatness
> Deserves your hate; and your affections are
> A sick man's appetite, who desires most that
> Which would increase his evil.

Faced with the argument that the city's grain should be more evenly distributed, he grows even more vehement. He is not prepared to argue the citizen's grievances: for him it is an outrage that such men should presume to have an opinion at all:

> Would the nobility lay aside their ruth,
> And let me use my sword, I'ld make a quarry
> With thousands of these quarter'd slaves, as high
> As I could pick my lance.

Here is a nature which, as Sicinius bitterly remarks, 'disdains the shadow / Which he treads on at noon'.

One of the flaws of the play's organisation is that Virgilia is bound to be insubstantial. She cannot appear more than pathetic, for none of Shakespeare's varied range of great heroines could love the monotonous war-machine which is all we see. Helena, it is true, sees qualities in Bertram which the rest of us find difficult to discern, but Bertram is not so formidably and unvaryingly violent as Marcius. Shakespeare has to set a key passage about Marcius' son in the mouth of Valeria rather than the gentle Virgilia:

> O' my word, the father's son: I'll swear, 'tis a very pretty boy. O' my troth, I looked upon him o'Wednesday half an hour together; has such a confirmed countenance. I saw him run after a gilded butterfly; and when he caught it, he let it go again; and after it again; and over and over he comes, and up again; catched it again: or whether his fall enraged him, or how 'twas, he did so set his teeth, and tear it; O, I warrant, how he mammocked it!

This passage, a clear Shakespearian addition to Plutarch in his distinctive prose, leaves no doubt that he is questioning the destructiveness of the military ethic. Volumnia says with satisfaction that the child shows one of his father's moods and Valeria's 'Indeed, la, 'tis a noble child' is clearly ironical on the author's, though not the speaker's, part.

Marcius in war deploys upon his troops an even more vigorious strain of the disease and animal imagery we have seen previously:

> All the contagion of the south light on you,
> You shames of Rome! you herd of — Boils and plagues
> Plaster you o'er; that you may be abhorr'd
> Farther than seen, and one infect another
> Against the wind a mile! You souls of geese,
> That bear the shapes of men, how have you run
> From slaves that apes would beat!

His vituperative approach is effective but unattractive; his choler contrasts markedly with the bright, positive note of Henry V's 'Once more into the breach' speech in similar circumstances at Harfleur. For the duration of the campaign at least, Henry's troops are his 'dear friends' and his positive approach moulds all levels of his army into a proud unity. Whilst Henry is on stage also, the audience catches the excitement, the heady stimulation of military glory; Marcius' formidable anger leaves us awed but detached. Henry can threaten violence just as formidably, as he does to compel the surrender of Harfleur,[33] but it is merely one note in his rhetorical equipment, and that not the most typical. It is also reserved for the enemy!

Marcius lacks both grace and balance. When he refuses the treasure offered him in recognition of his victory, what should be a becoming modesty emerges as an inverted pride:

> I thank you, general;
> But cannot make my heart consent to take
> A bribe to pay my sword: I do refuse it. . .
> You shout me forth
> In acclamations hyperbolical;
> As if I loved my little should be dieted
> In praises sauced with lies.

When he re-enters Rome in triumph, his mother, far from tenderly anticipating the resumption of intimate filial ties, gives us the most chilling portrait so far of her martial son:

> These are the ushers of Marcius: before him
> He carries noise, and behind him he leaves tears;
> Death, that dark spirit, in's nervy arm doth lie;
> Which being advanced, declines, and then men die.

Coriolanus is so much the public general, so little the private man, that his wife stands silent in her tears of joy. Shakespeare's sense of irony has never been sharper than when he makes the husband remind this gentle creature of the widows he has left in Corioli:

> My gracious silence, hail!
> Wouldst thou have laughed had I come coffin'd home,
> That weep'st to see me triumph? Ah, my dear,
> Such eyes the widows in Corioli wear,
> And mothers that lack sons.

The moment completes Shakespeare's dark portrait. The grim image which Coriolanus offers us is in marked contrast to Antony's pride in his military prowess as Cleopatra buckled on his armour:

> O, love,
> That thou coulds see my wars today, and knew'st

The royal occupation, thou shouldst see
A workman in it.

Antony uses his military prowess as a moment of intimate contact
with his love; Coriolanus in his egotism uses his public violence to
set aside the intimacy that should come in a long-delayed private
moment.

As he reluctantly parades himself in his gown of humility and seeks
plebeian support, his egomania becomes ever more dominant, and ever
more injurious to our sympathy. As Palmer emphasises:

> The contempt of Marcius for the people is rooted neither in concern
> for his country, which he betrays, nor in allegiance to an ordered
> system of government, which he is prepared to reject in any particu-
> lar if it does not happen to please him. He dislikes having to seek
> the suffrage of the commons. Let the suffrage be abolished. His elec-
> tion is opposed later on by the tribunes. Let the tribunes be re-
> moved.[34]

Brutus is perfectly correct when he tells Coriolanus eventually:

> You speak o' the people,
> As if you were a god to punish, not
> A man of their infirmity.

Shakespeare in the third act of his play shows a low opinion of public men of many ranks. Yet as always he does not shirk the issue that
government has to exist and power must reside somewhere. Disregard
of the law will lead to anarchy, the worst and most violent of all states
for a nation. When Coriolanus shows his contempt for the law and his
willingness to flout it, Sicinius descends to the lynch-law which emerges
from chaos in the state:

> He shall be thrown down the Tarpeian rock
> With rigorous hands: he hath resisted law,
> And therefore shall law scorn him further trial
> Than the severity of the public power,
> Which he so sets at nought.

Volumnia has more acumen than her son, but it is the cunning of Hotspur's 'vile politician':

I would have had you put your power well on,
Before you had worn it out. . .lesser had been
The thwartings of your dispositions, if
You had not show'd them how ye were disposed,
Ere they lack'd power to cross you.

The realities of political life for Volumnia go no further than the need to consolidate power before beginning to abuse it in safety. Her son takes from her only the need to dissimulate: acting a part is all he understands of politics. His imagery catches the shabbiness of his aspirations:

You have put me now to such a part, which never
I shall discharge to the life. . .
Away my disposition, and possess me
Some harlot's spirit!. . .
Mother, I am going to the market-place;
Chide me no more. I'll mountebank their loves,
Cog their hearts from them, and come home beloved
Of all the trades in Rome.

Coriolanus has no desire to achieve great things through power; his end is the aggrandisement of his own ego. Antony goes to the forum to play upon the mob with as little scruple, though infinitely more skill and imagination, but he is moved by genuine grief for 'the ruins of the noblest man / That ever lived in the tide of times'. Coriolanus' failure to move us stems from his limited imagination: for a tragic hero that is the most severe limitation of all.

When Coriolanus' pride bursts through at his banishment, it is in his characteristic violent choler; the unpleasant and by now familiar imagery reflects the narrowness of his personality:

You common cry of curs! whose breath I hate
As reek o' the rotten fens, whose loves I prize
As the dead carcasses of unburied men
That do corrupt my air, I banish you.

Coriolanus allies himself with his fierce enemy Aufidius without a qualm of conscience: his revenge on Rome is his only motivation. Yet it is not long before even that insensitive warrior is shocked by his new associate's arrogance:

> He bears himself more proudlier,
> Even to my person, than I thought he would
> When first I did embrace him: yet his nature
> In that's no changeling; and I must excuse
> What cannot be amended.

Suffering and privation usually elevate the individual soul in great Shakespearian tragedy; in Coriolanus they merely accentuate the implacable ruthlessness which has been characteristic from the first. Cominius tells of his attempt to appeal to the private man's ties of friendship:

> I offer'd to awaken his regard
> For's private friends: his answer to me was,
> He could not stay to pick them in a pile
> Of noisome musty chaff: he said, 'twas folly,
> For one poor grain or two, to leave unburnt,
> And still to nose the offence.

To Menenius, his staunchest friend and champion from the first, Coriolanus voices his subjugation of his private responses:

> Wife, mother, child, I know not. My affairs
> Are servanted to others: though I owe
> My revenge properly, my remission lies
> In Volscian breasts. That we have been familiar,
> Ingrate forgetfulness shall poison rather
> Than pity note how much. Therefore be gone.

The elaborate formality of the last two lines of this mark a deliberate attempt to subjugate the individual response under a marmoreal obduracy. When confronted by his family, Coriolanus voices the attempt openly:

> My wife comes foremost; then the honour'd mould
> Wherein this trunk was framed, and in her hand
> The grandchild to her blood. But out, affection!
> All bond and privilege of nature, break!
> Let it be virtuous to be obstinate...

> Let the Volsces
> Plough Rome and harrow Italy: I'll never
> Be such a gosling to obey instinct; but stand,
> As if a man were author of himself
> And knew no other kin.

This great scene is one between two characters who are equally wilful and resolute, for Shakespeare has taken pains from the first to show us not only that Coriolanus is a true son of his remarkable mother, but that she is the only character in the play who can influence him. Now, as earlier when he pursued the consulship, Coriolanus 'does not succumb to his mother's argument, but again to the rough edge of her tongue'.[35] Palmer, summarising Coriolanus' collapse before his mother, believes:

> This is a fundamental trait in the character of our hero. He is essentially the splendid oaf who has never come to maturity. His vanity in the field, his insolence to persons outside his own particular set, his intolerance of anything outside his special code of honour are more characteristic of an adolescent than a grown man.[36]

While Menenius makes the tribunes tremble with his picture of the war-machine with 'no more mercy in him than there is milk in a male tiger', we know that Coriolanus has capitulated to his mother. It is characteristic of Coriolanus to deride his few tender words to his wife after his exile ('Ye gods! I prate') and turn for the rest of the scene to the mother who controls him. The warrior-ethic receives its final, mortal blows from Shakespeare here. The implacable war-machine which is Coriolanus' public image disintegrates as his still-adolescent private self defers to his formidable mother.

If we doubt this, we should consider the near-anticlimax of Coriolanus' death. Flights of angels sung Hamlet to his rest, and the death of Antony left nothing remarkable beneath the visiting moon. Brutus died the noblest Roman of them all, because of the breadth of his vision of the common good. Coriolanus, struck down by his late ally in the city where he killed so many himself, has the muted, war-weary epitaph of the Second Lord:

> His own impatience
> Takes from Aufidius a great part of blame.
> Let's make the best of it.

*Coriolanus* shows much evidence of Shakespeare at the height of his powers: its sinuous and elliptical verse is full of those packed compressions of his greatest period. By the highest standards, it fails, because neither the central figure nor the political world in which he operates moves us. It is striking that this most austere of Shakespeare's tragedies should coincide with his turning away from realism to fantasy. The implication is that he is no longer able to undertake the strain of developing private individual man with that intensity which secures the sense of pain and waste in death, and thus establishes the distinctive greatness of Shakespearian tragedy.

## Notes

1. *Angel with Horns*, pp. 240, 295.
2. *Shakespearean Tragedy* (1905), pp. 85–6.
3. *Shakespeare's Roman Plays: the Function of Imagery in the Drama*, Chapter 1.
4. Ibid., pp. 16–17.
5. W. Keat (ed.), *Shakespeare's Plutarch* (1875), p. 111.
6. *Shakespeare's Roman Plays*, p. 67.
7. *Shakespeare: his Life, Art and Characters* (1872), LL, p. 224.
8. Introduction to New Cambridge edition, p. xxxv.
9. *Shakspere: a Critical Study of his Mind and Art* (1875), p. 285.
10. *Political Characters of Shakespeare*, p. 20.
11. Ibid., p. 23.
12. See J. L. Barroll, *Shakespeare and Roman History* (1959), pp. 327–43.
13. *On the Design of Shakespearean Tragedy* (Oxford University Press, Oxford, 1957), p. 161.
14. Introduction to Arden edition (1954), p. xlvii.
15. 'The Pillar of the World: *Antony and Cleopatra* in Shakespeare's Development', reprinted in Mark Rose (ed.), Twentieth Century Interpretations of *Antony and Cleopatra* (Prentice-Hall, Englewood Cliffs, New Jersey, 1977).
16. Quoted by Mark Rose in his introduction to Twentieth Century Interpretations of *Antony and Cleopatra*, pp. 1–13.
17. See *Hero and Saint: Shakespeare and the Graeco-Roman Tradition* (Oxford University Press Oxford, 1971), pp. 346–53.
18. Introduction to Rose (ed.), Twentieth Century Interpretations of *Antony and Cleopatra*.
19. '*Antony and Cleopatra*: a Shakespearean Adjustment' by J. F. Danby, ibid., p. 45.
20. Introduction, ibid.
21. *Shakespeare's Roman Plays*, p. 136.
22. 'The Stillness and the Dance' in Rose (ed.), Twentieth Century Interpretations of *Antony and Cleopatra*, pp. 89–95.
23. E. K. Chambers, *Shakespeare: a Survey*, p. 196.
24. *Shakespeare's Roman Plays*, p. 132.
25. *An Approach to Shakespeare*, p. 255.

26. Rose (ed.), Twentieth Century Interpretations of *Antony and Cleopatra*, p. 66.

27. Rose, introduction to Twentieth Century Interpretations of *Antony and Cleopatra*.

28. Reprinted in L. Lerner (ed.), *Shakespeare's Tragedies*, pp. 258-60.

29. *An Approach to Shakespeare*, p. 231.

30. *Preface to Shakespeare*, Vol. III, p. 113.

31. J. Palmer, *Political Characters of Shakespeare*, pp. 296-7.

32. M. Charney, *Shakespeare's Roman Plays*, p. 144.

33. See p. 88.

34. Palmer, *Political Characters of Shakespeare*, pp. 269-70.

35. Ibid., p. 297.

36. Ibid., p. 297.

# 9 THE LATE ROMANCES

I concluded my last Chapter with the suggestion that *Coriolanus* showed the increasing strain Shakespeare felt in depicting a great soul in torment as the centre of a drama. This is speculation. What is certain is that the four plays generally grouped as the Late Romances are less realistic, more generalised, and less concerned with studies of particular men and their personalities than all those which precede them.

In a typical reaction against Victorian bardology,[1] Lytton Strachey in 1904 saw these works as also characterised by a failure of concentrated artistic determination and purpose. Modern critics have generally been more generous in recognising the allegoric and symbolic strains in them. Undoubtedly the new indoor theatre at Blackfriars, in which Shakespeare's company began to play from about 1609, helped to shape the form of these later plays, though it is as well to remember that they were performed also at the Globe. How far the new possibilities of lighting and other effects affected the material of these plays rather than its treatment, we shall never know.

There are certain common elements in the plays which argue the author's preoccupation with particular themes. Frank Kermode summarises these elements:

> All the Romances treat of the recovery of lost royal children, usually princesses of great, indeed semi-divine virtue and beauty; they all bring important characters near to death, and sometimes feature almost miraculous resurrections; they all end with the healing, after many years of repentance and suffering, of some disastrous breach in the lives and happiness of princes, and this final reconciliation is usually brought about by the agency of beautiful young people; they all contain material of a pastoral quality or otherwise celebrate natural beauty and its renewal.[2]

The plays do not mark a retreat from contemporary political events. Frances Yates makes out a convincing case for direct parallels between the theme of *Cymbeline* and the hoped-for revival of chivalry through the young Henry, Prince of Wales, who died on 17 November 1612, at the age of 19.[3] Certainly one can detect in all these plays the hopes held of Henry and the young Princess Elizabeth, who disappeared from the

English scene a month after her brother's death, carried as the bride of the Elector Palatine into the protracted trauma of the Thirty Years War. The continual theme of resuscitation through youth runs through these dramas, and youth is often more important for its life-force than because of anything remarkable or particular in individual characters. Wilson Knight, for instance, sees Imogen as representing something as vague as 'Britain's soul integrity' in *Cymbeline*.[4]

All this implies that these late plays are deliberately less realistic in their treatment of character and plot than almost all the previous works in the canon. Most critics and directors would agree with Kermode in detecting within them 'a new disregard of psychological and narrative plausibility'.[5] There are exceptions to this: Hermione in *The Winter's Tale* is as resolute as Cordelia, as touching as Desdemona, and she is given better speeches than either of them. The portraiture of Leontes' jealous insanity in the early part of the play is disturbingly intense, so that his 'There is no truth in the oracle' which marks its climax is a terrifying dramatic moment. But the radiant Perdita of the second half of the play is important less as a forceful and determined character — as for instance Viola is — than as a representative of the forces of rebirth and fertility which dominate the fourth act of the play. Behind her stands not a dramatic development but the lost princesses of medieval romance, and especially the Pastorella of *The Faerie Queene*, then at the height of its fame.

Shakespeare does not discard plausibility of character in these plays: no dramatist could afford to dispense completely with such considerations. What happens is that realism of character, and even more credibility of plot, become secondary to other effects, to the over-all themes of destruction, rebirth and reconciliation which character-ise the Late Romances. Whilst there is still evidence of Shakespeare's concern with the public and private faces of man, and particularly with the effect of power upon individuals, the public-private tension ceases now to be the mainspring of dramatic action. In that respect, there is no case for a detailed analysis of the construction of these final plays.

Yet amidst this new material, planned for a new theatre and perhaps a new audience, Shakespeare's development of his ideas about power is consistent. Disaster in each play stems from an abuse of power as harsh as anything in the earlier works. But here the clash between power and individual morality is worked out not within particular individuals, but through an importing of a youth and freshness untainted by the original abuse. It is notable that in these plays Shakespeare divorces power from virtue. The instruments of regeneration and beauty are always here young, innocent, inexperienced and powerless.

In *Pericles*, only the scenes of Marina in the brothel have a background which is sketched in realistic detail. Shakespeare is almost certainly not the sole author of the play, which may account for the lack of light and shade in the development of the eponymous central character. Pericles' main quality is the passive endurance of an Old Testament figure, and this is hardly an instrument of dramatic energy. At the nadir of his tribulations, Marina is the means of curing his spiritual darkness, but she needs the grace of Diana, the play's presiding goddess, to help her. The double plot-structure, involving parents and children, will be characteristic of these Romances. Most people would agree with F. D. Hoeniger that: 'The dramatist is deliberately aiming at an effect that is something else than dramatic. It is more like that of *The Magic Flute* than that of *Macbeth* or *As You Like It*.'[6] The appeal is to our sense of wonder and the climax is in the scenes of recognition. But both father and daughter are divorced from power. Antiochus in the early section of the play misuses power so harshly that one suspects the author distrusts all authority, an impression reinforced by his use now of divine rather than human intervention to restore a proper moral order.

*Cymbeline* is no more realistic: the Arden editor defends it as 'a comprehensive piece of impressionism'.[7] Of the villain of the piece, who has sometimes been seen to give some conventional dramatic impetus to the play, he thinks:

> Iachimo is less a symbol than a stock figure, a reduced pattern of the Italian villain. . .He lacks the personality, the insistent malice, the cue to revenge, the long-term policy of evil which the tragic villains undoubtedly possess. . .It is not possible to accept this self-deluding, self-excusing libertine, with his small repertoire of tricks, as the thoroughbred Machiavellian villian of tragic tradition.[8]

The treatment of power and the men who exercise it is again almost entirely pessimistic, and there is an assumption in the famous dirge for Imogen in Act IV that authority will be abused:

> Fear no more the frown o' the' great
> Thou art past the tyrant's stoke.

In *The Winter's Tale*, there is more material which could come from earlier plays. The depiction of Leontes' jealousy, of the noble resistance of Hermione, and the sturdy common sense of Paulina are all psychologically convincing and often moving. The first three acts are different enough in tone from the rest of the play to be treated as a self-contained tragedy. Leontes' insane jealousy is as convincing as that of Othello, though we have to take it as a fact from the beginning of the play: there is not the dramatic interest here of a man's gradual descent into the darkness.

The all-powerful Leontes is the only holder of office who wields real power in this section of the play. And he abuses it consistently and terribly, so that it becomes an instrument in the consolidation of his madness. When challenged by the faithful Camillo in the play's second scene, Leontes' logic sinks to that of the spoilt child, but his tone is that of the megalomaniac:

> It is; you lie, you lie:
> I say thou liest, Camillo, and I hate thee,
> Pronounce thee a gross lout, a mindless slave,
> Or else a hovering temporizer, that
> Canst with thine eyes at once see good and evil,
> Inclining to them both.

When he incarcerates the unfortunate Hermione, the strain is heard again:

> Away with her, to prison!
> He who shall speak for her is afar off guilty
> But that he speaks.

In the trial scene Hermione, haled forth from her child-bed in prison to answer the tyrant's vicious charges, sounds the noblest moral note in all these plays as she is threatened with death:

> Sir, spare your threats:
> The bug which you would fright me with I seek.
> To me can life be no commodity:
> The crown and comfort of my life, your favour,
> I do give lost; for I do feel it gone,
> But know not how it went. My second joy
> And first-fruits of my body, from his presence
> I am barr'd, like one infectious. My third comfort,
> Starr'd most unluckily, is from my breast,

The innocent milk in its most innocent mouth,
Healed out to murder: myself on every post
Proclaim'd a strumpet: with immodest hatred
The child-bed privilege denied, which 'longs
To women of all fashion; lastly, hurried
Here to this place, i' the open air, before
I have got strength of limit. Now, my liege,
Tell me what blessings I have here alive,
That I should fear to die?

This measured, exalted logic comes from one stripped of all power; in the next moment the supremely powerful Leontes is rejecting the divine pronouncement of the oracle and bringing about the deaths which end the first section of the play.

In the second section, which comprises the fourth act of the play, we see nature working its accelerating act of regeneration, with Perdita's great speech about the flowers as its centre and Perdita and Florizel the human symbols of hope and rebirth. The one harsh note is struck by the only wielder of political power who intrudes upon the rural celebrations. Polixenes, intervening to fracture the bond between the young people, addresses Perdita and Florizel in these terms:

I'll have thy beauty scratch'd with briers, and made
More homely than thy state. For thee, fond boy,
If I may ever know thou dost but sigh
That thou no more shalt see this knack, as never
I mean thou shalt, we'll bar thee from succession;
Not hold thee of our blood, no, not our kin,
Far than Deucalion off: mark thou my words:
Follow us to court.

In the quasi-divine resolution and reconciliations of the final act, any consideration of temporal power is avoided. The play closes amidst the quiet notes of individual healing and the pairing off of lovers young and old.

In *The Tempest* Ferdinand and Miranda emerge with simple and untainted virtue to resolve a situation which they do not understand. Prospero, who has held temporal authority and now controls his island with supra-mortal power, shows vestiges of harshness in his treatment at certain moments of Ariel, Caliban and Ferdinand. At the end of what we presume to be his last play, Shakespeare shows Prospero not resuming office but retiring to peaceful and uncomplicated old age. Significantly, he does this by breaking his staff and formally resigning all power and public actions. This final work ends like all the Late Romances with a moral atmosphere which rises beyond temporal considerations to a divine resignation:

> And my ending is despair,
> Unless I be relieved by prayer,
> Which pierces so, that it assaults
> Mercy itself, and frees all faults.
> As you from crimes would pardon'd be,
> Let your indulgence set me free.

Shakespeare, in retaining his old scepticism about power and its effects upon those who exercise it, has made it in these last plays not the cardinal point of his construction, but a starting-point for effects which look beyond particular, realistic situations to a more eternal truth. He has no longer the energy to work out the triumph of the human spirit through particular characters, as in the great tragedies, but he attempts the same sense of elevation through a variety of visual and aural effects. We are rightly less moved, because we are aware of artifice deliberately applied, and we are denied the elemental force and simplicity of the greatest plays. But the Romances are a fitting epilogue to Shakespeare's examination of power and its effects upon men.

## Notes

1. Reprinted in *Literary Essays* (Chatto and Windus, London, 1948).
2. *Shakespeare: the Final Plays*, pp. 5–6.
3. See *Shakespeare's Last Plays: a New Approach*, pp. 41–59.
4. *The Crown of Life*, p. 148.
5. *Shakespeare: the Final Plays*, p. 5.
6. Arden edition of *Pericles*, pp. lxxvii–lxxviii.
7. J. M. Nosworthy, Arden edition, p. lxxx.
8. Ibid., pp. lviii–lix.

# SELECT BIBLIOGRAPHY

Two very useful series which bring together criticism of individual plays are the Casebook (Macmillan) and Twentieth Century Interpretations (Prentice-Hall). Most of the major plays are now covered, though the dates, and thus the critical selections, vary. The Granville-Barker prefaces to various plays still have much that is useful and salutary, since they concentrate always on the problems of production and treat the works resolutely as material for the playhouse.

Barber, C. L. *Shakespeare's Festive Comedy: a Study of Dramatic Form in Relation to Social Comedy* (Princeton University Press (paperback), Princeton, New Jersey, 1972)

Baxter, J. *Shakespeare's Poetic Styles: Verse into Drama* (Routledge, London, 1980)

Bergeron, D. M. *Shakespeare: a Study and Research Guide* (Macmillan, London, 1976)

Birney, A. L. *Satiric Catharsis in Shakespeare* (University of California Press, Berkeley, 1973)

Bradbrook, M. C. *The Living Monument: Shakespeare and the Theatre of his Time* (Cambridge University Press, Cambridge, 1976)

—— *Shakespeare: the Poet in his World* (Weidenfeld and Nicolson, London, 1978)

Brooke, N. *Shakespeare's Early Tragedies* (Methuen, London, 1973)

Brown, J. R. *Shakespeare in Performance: an Introduction through Six Major Plays* (Harcourt, Brace and World, New York, 1976)

—— and Harris, B. (eds.) *The Later Shakespeare* (Edward Arnold, London, 1973)

Chambers, E. K. *Shakespeare: a Survey* (Pelican, Harmondsworth, 1964)

Charney, M. *Shakespeare's Roman Plays: the Function of Imagery in the Drama* (Oxford University Press, Oxford, 1971)

Clemen, W. H. *Shakespeare's Dramatic Art* (Methuen, London, 1972)

—— *The Development of Shakespeare's Imagery* (Methuen, London, 1977)

Coghill, N. *Shakespeare's Professional Skills* (Cambridge University Press, Cambridge, 1964)

Danby, J. F. *Shakespeare's Doctrine of Nature* (Faber, London, 1949)

Dillon, J. *Shakespeare and the Solitary Man* (Macmillan, London, 1981)

Edwards, P., Ewbank, I. and Hunter, G. K. (eds.) *Shakespeare's Styles: Essays in Honour of Kenneth Muir* (Cambridge University Press, Cambridge, 1980)

Ellis-Fermor, U. *The Jacobean Drama* (Methuen, London, 1958)

Evans, B. *Shakespeare's Comedies* (Oxford University Press, Oxford, 1960)

— *Shakespeare's Tragic Practice* (Oxford University Press, Oxford, 1979)

Garber, M. B. *Dream in Shakespeare* (Yale University Press, New Haven, Conn., 1974)

Grudin, R. *Mighty Opposites: Shakespeare and Renaissance Contrariety* (University of California Press, Berkeley, 1979)

Hunter, G. K. *Shakespeare and his Contemporaries* (Liverpool University Press, Liverpool, 1978)

Kermode, F. *Shakespeare: the Final Plays* (Longman, London, 1973)

Knight, W. *The Wheel of Fire*, 4th edn (Methuen, London, 1949)

— *The Crown of Life* (Methuen (paperback), London, 1965)

Knights, L. C. *Some Shakespearean Themes* (Chatto and Windus, London, 1959)

Lawrence, W. W. *Shakespeare's Problem Comedies*, new edn (Penguin, Harmondsworth, 1964)

Lerner, L. (ed.) *Shakespeare's Tragedies: an Anthology of Modern Criticism* (Penguin, Harmondsworth, 1970)

Long, M. *The Unnatural Scene: a Study in Shakespearean Tragedy* (Methuen, London, 1978)

Lyman, S. M. and Scott, M. B. *The Drama of Social Reality* (Oxford University Press, New York, 1975)

McAlindon, T. *Shakespeare and Decorum* (Macmillan, London, 1973)

Mack, M. *Killing the King* (Yale University Press, New Haven, Conn., 1973)

Manheim, M. *The Weak King Dilemma in the Shakespearean History Play* (Syracuse University Press, New York, 1973)

Miles, R. *The Problem of Measure for Measure* (Vision Press, London, 1976)

Muir, K. *Shakespeare the Professional* (Heinemann, London, 1973)

— and Edwards, P. (eds.) *Aspects of Macbeth* Cambridge University Press, 1977)

—, — (eds.) *Aspects of Othello* (Cambridge University Press, Cambridge, 1977)

— and Schoenbawm, S. *A New Companion to Shakespeare Studies* (Cambridge University Press, Cambridge, 1971)

Palmer, J. *Political Characters of Shakespeare* (Macmillan, London, 1945)

Parker, M. D. H. *The Slave of Life: a Study of Shakespeare and the Idea of Justice* (Chatto and Windus, London, 1955)

Prior, M. E. *The Drama of Power: Studies in Shakespeare's History Plays* (Northwestern University Press, Illinois, 1973)

Prosser, E. *Hamlet and Revenge*, 2nd edn (Stanford University Press, Stanford, 1971)

Reese, M. M. *The Cease of Majesty: a Study of Shakespeare's History Plays* (Edward Arnold, London, 1961)

— *Shakespeare: his World and his Work* (Edward Arnold, London, 1980)

Reibetanz, J. *The Lear World: a Study of King Lear in its Dramatic Context* (Heinemann, London, 1977)

Ribner, I. *Patterns in Shakespearean Tragedy*, rev. edn (Methuen, London, 1979)

Richmond, H. M. *Shakespeare's Political Plays* (Smith, Gloucester, Mass., 1977)

Riemer, A. P. *A Reading of Shakespeare's Antony and Cleopatra* (Sydney University Press, Sydney, 1968)

Rossiter, A. P. *Angel with Horns: Fifteen Lectures on Shakespeare* (Longman, London, 1970)

Smith, H. *Shakespeare's Romances* (Huntingdon Library, California, 1972)

Speaight, R. *Shakespeare: the Man and his Achievement* (Dent, London, 1977)

Spivack, C. *The Comedy of Evil on Shakespeare's Stage* (Fairleigh Dickinson University Press, Rutherford, New Jersey, 1979)

Spurgeon, C. *Shakespeare's Imagery* (Cambridge University Press, Cambridge, 1965)

Styan, J. L. *The Shakespeare Revolution* (Cambridge University Press, Cambridge, 1977)

Tillyard, E. M. W. *Shakespeare's History Plays* (Chatto and Windus, London, 1948)

— *Shakespeare's Last Plays* (Chatto and Windus, London, 1958)

— *Shakespeare's Problem Plays* (Chatto and Windus, London, 1961)

Traversi, D. *An Approach to Shakespeare* (Hollis and Carter, London, 1968 (vol. 1) and 1969 (vol. 2))

— *Shakespeare: the Roman Plays* (Hollis and Carter, London, 1963)

— *Shakespeare: the Last Phase* (Hollis and Carter, London, 1965)

Ure, P. *Shakespeare: the Problem Plays* (Longman, London, 1961)

Weiss, T. *The Breath of Clowns and Kings: Shakespeare's Early Histories and Comedies* (Chatto and Windus, London, 1971)

Wilders, J. *The Lost Garden: a View of Shakespeare's English and Roman History Plays* (Macmillan, London, 1978)

Wilson, J. D. *What Happens in Hamlet?* (Cambridge University Press, Cambridge, 1951)

Winney, J. *The Player King: a Theme of Shakespeare's Histories* (Chatto and Windus, London, 1968)

Yates, F. *Shakespeare's Last Plays: a New Approach* (Routledge and Kegan Paul, London, 1973)

# INDEX